FILM AND COMMUNITY: BRITAIN AND FRANCE

From *La Règle du jeu* to *Room at the Top*

Margaret Butler

I.B. TAURIS

LONDON · NEW YORK

Published in 2004 by I.B. Tauris & Co Ltd
6 Salem Road, London W2 4BU
175 Fifth Avenue, New York NY 10010
Website: http://www.ibtauris.com

In the United States and Canada distributed by Palgrave Macmillan,
a division of St. Martin's Press, 175 Fifth Avenue, New York NY 10010

ISBN hardback 1 86064 954 8
      paperback 1 86064 955 6
EAN   hardback 978 1 86064 954 7
      paperback 978 1 86064 955 4

A full CIP record for this book is available from the British Library
A full CIP record for this book is available from the Library of Congress
Library of Congress catalog card: available

Typeset in Garamond by Dexter Haven Associates Ltd, London
Printed and bound in Great Britain by TJ International Ltd, Padstow, Cornwall

Film and Community: Britain and France

For my parents
John and Anne Butler

Contents

Illustrations

General Editor's Introduction

Relations between France and Britain have always been uneasy and ambivalent. Tabloid headlines such as 'Hop off, you frogs' and 'Up yours, Delors' encapsulate a longstanding popular suspicion and dislike of 'Johnny Frenchman'. Alongside this feeling, however, there has also been continuing admiration among intellectuals for French culture, French thought and French cuisine.

One high point of sympathy for France was the Second World War. The British cinema paid many tributes to the spirit of the fighting French. Ealing Studios were particularly Francophile, to the extent of commissioning scores from Georges Auric and creating vehicles for the veteran actress Françoise Rosay. This continued in such post-war productions as *Passport to Pimlico*, in which the inhabitants of Miramont Place, Pimlico, proudly declare themselves to be Burgundians. During the war itself, the Ministry of Information vetoed plans to film Shaw's *Saint Joan*, deeming it impossible to show the English burning France's national saint.

But the wartime fortunes of the two countries were very different, with France experiencing German occupation, collaboration and resistance, things that mainland Britain never had to face. After the war, both countries had to deal with the problem of reintegrating returning servicemen and prisoners of war and with accommodating the changed expectations and aspirations of women. These are just some of the subjects explored by Margaret Butler in her fascinating comparative study of the cinemas of Britain and France during and after the war.

By focussing on the concept of community, she is able to chart the various ways in which cinema dealt with the ideas of belonging and alienation, inclusion and exclusion, unity and division. Drawing on debates in the contemporary sources and on a careful reading of key films, she is able to bring fresh insight and understanding to the meaning and appeal of such French classics as *Farrebique*, *Le Corbeau* and *Les Enfants du paradis*, as well as such notable British productions as *Waterloo Road*, *Blanche Fury* and *No Room at the Inn*.

Jeffrey Richards

Acknowledgements

My greatest professional debt is to Professor Geoff Crossick, who encouraged me to undertake the PhD research at the University of Essex on which this book is based. As my supervisor, I was very fortunate indeed to have benefited from his experience, scholarship and friendship.

I would like to extend my thanks to the British Academy for funding the original research. I am also grateful to the staff at the British Film Institute and the Bibliothèque du film (BIFI) for arranging screenings and for help with finding materials.

Individuals who generously supplied films, articles and information include Margaret Atak, Viv Chadder, Hanna Diamond, Suzanne Langlois, Laurent Marie, Robert Murphy, Fabrice Montebello, Andrew Spicer, Robert Gildea and John Southall. Professor Jeffrey Richards has also been unfailingly supportive throughout in reading the manuscript and offering helpful suggestions. Special thanks are due to my dear friend Paul Mason for his typically good-humoured and well-informed comments.

Thanks also to my brother Michael, who was a constant source of support and encouragement during the course of this project, and to my son Joshua, who got far less of my company than he deserved as I completed the final draft.

Lastly, none of this would have been possible without my parents, who were there from the start. I dedicate this book, with love, to them.

Abbreviations

ACE	Alliance Cinématographique Européene
ACT	Association of Cinematograph Technicians
AN	Archives Nationales
BBFC	British Board of Film Censors
BFI	British Film Institute
BIFI	Bibliothèque de l'image – Filmothèque
BFPA	British Film Producers Association
CEA	Cinematograph Exhibitors Association
COIC	Comité d'Organisation de l'Industrie Cinématographique
CDCF	Comité de Défense du Cinéma Français
CLCF	Comité de Libération du Cinéma Français
IDHEC	Institut des Hautes Études Cinématographique
KW	*Kinematograph Weekly*
MFB	*Monthly Film Bulletin*
MOI	Ministry of Information
MPPA	Motion Picture Producers Association
NFFC	National Film Finance Corporation
PCF	Parti Communiste Français
PFR	*Penguin Film Review*
PRO	Public Record Office
SNCF	Société Nationale des Chemins de Fer Français
STO	Service de travail obligatoire
UFA	Universal Film AG

1

Britain and France and the Concept of 'Community'

This book is a comparative study of British and French cinema and society between 1939 and 1959. Although a relatively unexplored area, there are significant comparisons between the two countries both in socio-political terms and their film production. British cinema of the Second World War and the post-war era continues to attract attention, as demonstrated by recent contributions from Neil Rattigan, Robert Murphy, Christine Geraghty and James Chapman.[1] The collection of essays edited by Ulrike Sieglohr is a very welcome exploration of the representation of women in a variety of European cinemas.[2] Yet little comparative research of British and French cinemas has been undertaken. National cinemas have their own distinct identities, but each is also influenced by the mutual exchange of personnel. While the European presence in Hollywood is one of its defining characteristics, there has been little work about the influence European technicians had on the British film industry.[3] This is somewhat surprising, given that British film production, particularly during the 1930s, was dominated by European exiles.[4] Directors Marcel Varnel, Marc Allégret and Julien Duvivier, cinematographer Georges Périnal, composer Georges Auric and actresses Françoise Rosay, Simone Signoret and Micheline Presle all worked in British studios during the 1940s and 1950s. Furthermore, articles in the British and French film press indicate a strong mutual regard even during the isolation of the war years. The examination of this important alliance is therefore, in every sense, long overdue.

Of the three occupations by Germany of France, that of 1940–44 has proved to be the most fascinating and complicated by ties of friendship forged during the inter-war period.[5] Philippe Burrin describes 1940–44 in terms of an 'accommodation' with the Germans, an arrangement which was a necessary evil if the rigours of occupation were to be weathered.[6] Scholarly works on this era continue to appear, their titles reflecting the burdensome and sombre nature of the occupation.[7] Yet Britain and France have also had a complex history of entanglements, conflicts and alliances which has tended to attract military and political historians rather than social and cultural historians. In a military and political sense, the co-operation forged at the beginning of the Second World War deteriorated after France fell in June 1940. The French Cabinet rejected the British proposal of a union of both nations, affronted by the prospect of being a dominion. The *débacle* at Mers-el-Kébir, when the French refusal to scupper their fleet prompted the British to use force, which cost many French lives. However, Charles de Gaulle, leader of the 'Free French', depended on British goodwill, and Britain was eager to see France restored to ensure a balanced Europe after the war. At liberation there was a feeling that the French had too easily capitulated to defeat. In the drama *Went the Day Well?* (1942, Alberto Cavalcanti), Nora remarks, 'I haven't much sympathy for the French, they let us down so abominably'. While this does not reflect Ealing's customary support of the French, it indicates attitudes at this stage of the war. The French also felt betrayed by the British, so both regarded one another with a mixture of 'admiration, affection and resentment'.[8] In 1944, there was empathy for France, as *Picture Post* wrote: 'The future of France is linked closely with our own ... she will need the help – particularly the economic and industrial help – of her allies for some time to come'.[9]

Indeed, Britain and France had much in common in the first year of the war. Both populations were affected by enemy attack, which led to evacuation in Britain and *l'exode* in France. A sizeable proportion of men were conscripted, blackout was mandatory, and food rationing was in force. In Britain, popular culture – films, shows and songs like 'There'll always be an England' – uplifted the people, while in France, films entertained, the press were cheery and Maurice Chevalier sang that 'Paris will always be Paris'. Rural imagery was promoted by Vichy ideologues, just as British propagandists conceptualised Britain as essentially rural. Though the political situations were vastly different, writers evoked the countryside, and film-makers, in order to promote feelings of 'Englishness' and 'Frenchness' which would in contrasting ways conceal the realities of war and occupation.

Despite fluctuations in Anglo–French politics, the good relationship between the two film industries survived the war and beyond. Although the French were prohibited from making films about Germany's enemies, British studios had no such constraints upon them. Ealing was associated with typically 'British' films, but it also had a distinctly European dimension. In *The Foreman Went to France* (1942, Charles Frend), for instance, a factory foreman travels to France to prevent a piece of vital plant from being seized by the Germans. During his return journey, he finds himself caught up in *l'exode*. At the end, a group of *paysans* embarking for England sacrifice their belongings so that the machinery can be taken on board. Ealing made other films that celebrated the Anglo–French relationship and, like other studios, drew upon French expertise.

The banning by Germany of exports to enemy nations during the war provoked curiosity among British film-makers and critics about French film production. Alberto Cavalcanti visited Paris after liberation and concluded that the few new directors in France meant that films were in pre-war styles, 'remote and poetic'.[10] But important figures like Jacques Becker and Henri-Georges Clouzot made sharply contemporary films suggestive of the cultural and political divisions within Occupied France. At liberation, when foreign films were shown again, there was an explosion of interest in French film journals about British cinema. *Film français* surveyed British films of the previous five years, including *The Young Mr Pitt*, *The Man in Grey* and *Fires were Started*, and noted a new-found 'vitality'.[11] The following month the journal wrote of Britain's 'example to French cinema' in an article which praised the contributions made by film-makers, distributors and exhibitors to the war effort.[12] The effusive tone of this article suggests a vicarious desire to have achieved the same in France. In December 1946, *Cinémonde* announced that 'British cinema is going to conquer the world', and pointed to films like *Brief Encounter*, *This Happy Breed*, *Waterloo Road* and *The Way to the Stars* as evidence of an 'English school of filmmaking'.[13] Underlying the geniality, however, the old political antagonisms were not forgotten. When *Henry V* (1944, Laurence Olivier), with its defeat of the French at Agincourt was shown in September 1947, a year in which relations between the two nations had recovered a great deal of lost ground, the Ministère des Affaires Étrangères (Foreign Ministry) was concerned that it would compromise the alliance, even though the censor had passed the film. An official memorandum noted,

> It is not that the French monarchy is vanquished at Agincourt, nor even the spectacle in Technicolor of the rout which is most painful, but the depiction made with Shakespearian violence and crudity, yet also with consummate artistry, of the moral faults and weaknesses of the French … It is very serious

furthermore that comparisons could be made in the military field with a recent event.[14]

The Ministry objected less to the fact of the battle and more to the implication that the French lacked integrity and resolve in time of national crisis. By the autumn of 1947, French films which dealt with the recent past were about resistance and heroism, not defeatism. *Henry V*, albeit about a conflict long ago, was an untimely blow to French national self-esteem. Critics, however, concentrated more on its quality. *L'Écran français* noted that the film represented 'England's cultural and artistic heritage'.[15] *Cinémonde* pronounced it 'excellent'.[16]

Similarly, the esteem held by writers in the 'quality' press for French cinema is marked. During the war and beyond, *Sight and Sound* published regular surveys of French films and trends within the industry. Until its demise in 1952, *Sequence*, formerly the Oxford University Film Society's magazine, contained regular articles on French cinema by co-founders Lindsay Anderson and Gavin Lambert. Anderson made his critical debut in 1946 with an article entitled 'Some French Films – and a Forecast', in which he praised the small-scale, independent nature of French film production, compared with Rank's virtual monopoly in Britain.[17] The lay press also maintained a keen interest in all things French. Film critics C.A. Lejeune and Dilys Powell, 'the Scylla and Charybdis of movie criticism',[18] writing in the *Observer* and *Sunday Times* respectively, paid close attention to French films screened in London.

THE CONCEPT OF COMMUNITY

This book takes the idea of community as a way of understanding film and society rather than using class, which is far too restrictive. In *Class: Image and Reality*, Arthur Marwick addresses film as part of a range of source material, but his choice of *In Which We Serve* to illustrate the rigidity of wartime class structures is probably the most obvious example.[19] Neil Rattigan analyses class in British wartime cinema and finds, unsurprisingly, that the class consensus which was projected in films during 'the people's war' contradicted the reality of the class system.[20] Rattigan has inherent difficulties engaging with the notion of class divisions. He thus finds that in *In Which We Serve*, Hardy's address after Christmas dinner is a 'rather ridiculous speech' made comic by Hardy's 'pomposity',[21] whereas Jeffrey Richards writes, in a more sensitive assessment, that it is 'touchingly formal'.[22] Such an approach, which carries with it an inordinate amount of unconscious presupposition, tends to prohibit a more objective, insightful analysis. Moreover, his contention that 1950s war films were made to reinstate the middle classes after they had been displaced in wartime films by the working classes is arguable, given that production had always been under the control of middle-class businessmen.[23] Rattigan's thesis simply misses the nuances of films such as *The Cruel Sea* and *Ice Cold in Alex,* in which the officers, far from being heroic, are flawed and vulnerable. As Richards argues, historians now see class as increasingly one-dimensional, and only one of the 'bundle of identities', which people carry with them.[24]

This book will conduct the comparison through the concept of community. Defining 'community' is not a straightforward task. Joanna Bourke notes that historians define it as having 'elements of identification with a particular neighbourhood or street, a sense of shared perspectives, and reciprocal dependency'.[25] The conceptualisation of community has largely fallen to social scientists, for whom it is a fundamental societal structure. George A. Hillery's basic definition, formulated in 1955, still seems valid: 'A community consists of persons in social interaction within a geographic area and having one or more additional common ties'.[26] Communities are also formed through shared functions like work, so those within a factory, a hospital or a military base may have a deeper sense of communality than those defined by geographical factors.[27] Furthermore, community has connotations of benevolence. As Raymond Williams noted, 'unlike all other types of social organisation (state, nation, society etc.) it seems never to be used unfavourably, and never to be given any positive opposing or distinguishing term'.[28] As we shall see, British wartime films invariably conceptualised community in positive terms, their narratives joining together people from diverse backgrounds and locations into committed and cohesive forces. Conversely, some French film-makers operating under vastly different circumstances, took an opposing view of community and were unhesitant about exposing its more unpalatable elements.

In wartime, community tends to assume considerable significance. It provides a protective, reassuring structure at a time of great uncertainty and vulnerability. In this way, *Millions Like Us* (1943, Frank Launder and Sidney Gilliat) shows a young widow whose grief is absorbed by the rousing camaraderie of her fellow factory workers. 'Loss,' writes Andrew Higson of this final scene, 'is miraculously transformed into plenitude'.[29] Community also embraces the notion of social responsibility, which in potentially destabilising circumstances authorities instil to maintain social order. War on the one hand disrupts communities by instituting conscription and war work and necessitating evacuation from dangerous areas, but also creates new communities from the individuals involved in those processes.

Membership of a community is also linked to nationhood, which is particularly intense during times of national crisis such as war. Benedict Anderson has argued that the experience of nationhood, that of belonging to a nation, is a question of feeling part of an 'imagined' community.[30] One of the four determinants of nationhood he identifies is a sense of community, a 'deep horizontal comradeship' which expresses itself as a collective consciousness.[31] He also argues that nation states emerge less through military conquests than through language, education and mass communication. By these means, people come to know themselves as belonging to a distinct community. Film is clearly a form of mass communication, although Anderson cites only song, music, poetry and fiction.[32] Indeed literature, as Raymond Williams argues, must refer to 'knowable communities',[33] small recognisable units within which social interaction takes place. Similarly, film narrative is dependent on the delineation of 'knowable communities' and the relationship of people within them.

The notion of community was critical to British wartime culture. At a time of dislocation and disruption on a mass scale, the community and its concomitants, inclusion and shared experience, were deeply comforting. During the first two years of the war in particular, people of all classes were suffering in equal measure. The communal experience of 'the people's war' also provided a rich source of material for writers. James Hanley's *No Directions* describes a group of civilians during one night of the Blitz, and Robert Greenwood's *The Squad Goes Out* follows an ambulance crew stationed in Bermondsey.[34] Novels about evacuees invariably relate a successful outcome to the meeting of urban and rural. In Adrian Alington's *These Our Strangers*,[35] city evacuees Liz and Maud have an unhappy start in rural Payling Green, but are eventually protected by the Earl of Stainwater. Denis Ogden's fantasy play *The Peaceful Inn*, first performed in 1940 and filmed by Basil Dearden as *The Halfway House* in 1944 used community strength to cure the inn's troubled guests. Even Evelyn Waugh, who opposed the idea of the 'people's war' and wrote disparagingly about the antics of working-class evacuees in *Put Out More Flags*, could not actually distance himself from the notion of the wartime community.[36]

In a wider sense, war offered a unique opportunity for a radical reconceptualisation of the significance of the community in British society.

J.B. Priestley, the *vox populi* of the war, was a leading exponent of the communitarian ideal and co-founded the Common Wealth party in 1942. 'We must stop thinking in terms of property and power' he broadcast, 'and begin thinking in terms of community and creation'.[37] His Sunday evening 'postscripts', which reached 14 million people (40 per cent of the listening public),[38] reflected 'the real and everlasting spirit of our race'.[39] Priestley's broad Yorkshire accent added to his credibility as a national spokesman. In 1942 he wrote that the question to be asked after the war was not about wealth or poverty but 'whether we are going to be a mass of selfish, grabbing, grumbling, dreary individuals or a people with a *purpose*, co-operating for the common good'.[40] Priestley's wartime novels *Let the People Sing* (1942), about a campaign to save a small town's music hall, and *Daylight on Saturday* (1943), set in an aircraft factory, invoke these ideals. In his play *They Came to a City* (1944), the characters are given the choice of experiencing a new kind of society in a new city, or returning home.

In a physical sense, people were literally thrown together, as air-raids forced *en masse* gatherings in underground shelters. Although concerned parties feared that the shelters were unsafe,[41] the camaraderie within these subterranean communes was very real. In 1943, two years after the Blitz, Mass Observation reported that thousands of people were still making their nightly journey below ground because they missed 'not only shelter but a new society'.[42] War artist Henry Moore immortalised sheltering in a series of sketches, creating 'one of the abiding images of the Second World War'.[43] The notion of a 'national' community which emerged through shared experiences like the air-raids also had an ideological and political potency. As Labour MP Michael Foot recalled, 'There was a great community spirit during the war. It is the nearest thing I've ever seen in my lifetime to ... a democratic socialist state of citizens believing that they could have influenced ... what was going to be done and that the whole world could be changed by the way they operated.'[44]

The Labour Party's campaign in the 1945 election was indeed based on establishing a socialist state devoted to the welfare and security of its citizens. Its manifesto, 'Let Us Face the Future', announced a commitment to prioritising 'community' over 'private interests'.[45]

In France, the notion of community was more problematic, as the occupation brought division, prejudice and intolerance. 'Community' was nevertheless fundamental to Vichy ideology. The 'Rénovation Nationale', the new order conceptualised by Vichy's leader, Pétain, actually referred to an older rural, almost mythical, France, based on 'natural communities' devoted to family, work and region.[46] Women would return to the home, the birth rate would increase, and youth organisations would instil team spirit and a commitment to serve the community. The land itself, *le pays réel*, had regenerative powers. As Pétain said, the country would 'recover her full strength by re-establishing contact with the soil'.[47] Rural literature, new and re-issued, praised the noble *paysan* who worked the honest earth.[48] Films like *Monsieur de Lourdines* (1943, Pierre de Hérain) returned dissolute young men to their rural roots, and in *La Fille du puisatier* (1940, Marcel Pagnol), Vichy's pro-natalist policy and familial stability were satisfied within a rural setting.

As with most regimes intent on achieving total unity, Vichy sanctioned repression as well as inclusion, and declared war on communists, freemasons, anti-clericals, foreigners and primary schoolteachers who were accused by Pétain of indoctrinating children with pacifist ideas.[49] In both zones, anti-semitic material was disseminated through school text-books, documentaries, exhibitions, magazines and radio broadcasts, while new laws expelled Jews from industry, commerce and the arts. To a degree, antisemitic propaganda tapped into an existing mindset. When the German film *Jew Süss* (1940, Veit Harlan) was shown in 1941, French commentators reported that it was 'not a success',[50] but recent research has shown that in Lyon, Toulouse and Vichy, the film broke box-office records.[51] Pétain himself announced a repressive policy: 'There is no neutrality possible,' he said, 'between the true and the false, between the good and the evil, between health and 'sickness, between order and disorder, between France and anti-France'.[52] The collaborative nature of the Vichy regime, along with such official rigidity, divided the nation rather than unifying it. As Philippe Burrin writes, 'instead of "reconstructing the national soul" by filling it with memories of an invented "France", it left vivid memories of a very real France that continues to be a source of embarrassment and outrage'.[53]

One of the preoccupations of the late twentieth century was the 'quest for community'. Amitai Etzioni argues that in the West, where individualism has been a dominant ideological force, communitarianism is having an increasing influence on politicians of all persuasions.[54] Communitarians argue that there is a need to rebuild 'a sense of personal and social responsibility, a sense that we are not only entitled but also must serve, that the individual good is deeply intertwined with the needs of the common good'.[55] This longing for the restoration of old values suggests that while 'community' is essentially defunct, it is regarded with nostalgia. Attempts to rekindle the British wartime spirit in a modern political context have proved controversial. For example, Angus Calder's book *The Myth of the Blitz* was prompted in part by irritation at Margaret Thatcher's invocation of Churchillian rhetoric and the 'Dunkirk spirit' at the outbreak of the Falklands War in 1982.[56] Conversely, there is little desire for the kind of community so vigorously espoused by the Vichy government, an era which is being trawled on a massive scale by historians working in the field of the history of memory.[57] The myth which was celebrated in post-war literature and in film was that of the Resistance, which provided evidence of a national community during the country's most trying time.

The question to be posed with regard to post-war images of community in Britain is whether the community spirit which had been so carefully nurtured in wartime Britain survived the post-war years, or whether it became an anachronism. Certainly war literature describing cross-class collective action had given way to escape stories like *The Wooden Horse* and *The Colditz Story* which focused on individual officers rather than groups of ordinary men.[58] As Ken Worpole argues, the notion of freedom in these later novels is associated with escape from 'the collective living patterns of the prison camps', not participation in them.[59] 1950s war films have been seen as concentrating on the officer class, parodying working-class characters and marginalising women.[60] The definitive post-war film is *Passport to Pimlico* (1949, Henry Cornelius), which is nostalgic for wartime conditions and conjures up old alliances between Britain and France. Could the agenda of peacetime cinema have been so unambiguous given the increasingly sensitive approach of many wartime film-makers to the vital task of projecting 'the people's war'? Such a notion begs to be re-examined, for the myriad representations of community in post-war cinema demonstrate that British society was multi-layered and often at odds with the cosy depictions of the Ealing comedies.

As to France, how was community expressed by film-makers in the context of the painful legacy of the occupation? Stanley Hoffman has argued that while France as a political community was in disarray by 1946, other forms of community were stronger than they had been in the 1930s.[61] Vichy's youth organisations, the Corporation Paysanne and the Jeunesse Agricole Catholique, as well as the growing overall influence of Catholicism, were examples of institutions which had had a consolidating influence on the nation.[62] Yet there were searing divisions very near the surface. The visible and savage nature of the *épuration* and its failure even to define the 'crimes' its agents so ruthlessly punished was a response to the fact that Vichy and collaboration had been based on 'a silent and massive acquiescence'.[63] But the publication of hundreds of memoirs and diaries following liberation recounting tales of resistance suggested a desperate desire to convince the world and indeed the nation itself that France had not been a passive spectator.[64] Indeed the position adopted by the communists was that they had fought with the minority in the Resistance but had been assisted by the 'majority of the nation'.[65]

Communities themselves now faced up to four extraordinarily divisive years. As Albert Camus said in 1945, once the 'killers' had gone 'the French were left with a hatred partly shorn of its object. They still look at one another with a residue of anger.'[66] In his study of 'Peyrane' in the early 1950s, Laurence Wylie observed that the war had 'transformed the psychological atmosphere of the community'.[67] This, then, was the intricate social and political context in which film-makers were operating. Some films of the post-war years were criticised for their avoidance of present-day realities and for the fact that the quest for a 'quality' cinema had meant prioritising appearance rather than substance. Conversely, as this book will show, French post-war cinema very decidedly evoked the mood of its time, producing films which celebrated ordinary life and some which, as Gavin Lambert put it, had a 'new pessimism'.[68]

These introductory remarks have aimed to demonstrate that the concept of community is an invaluable way of looking at specific areas of social history. The exploration of community also provides us with the opportunity to enquire into its attendant elements, which collectively represent the essential issues with which society is constantly preoccupied. The polarised notions of belonging and alienation are recurrent themes in the films discussed, and offer an alternative perspective on the workings of two contrasting societies under severe pressure. Questions about the place of men and women within society can be asked by exploring the relationships between men as combatants, husbands and fathers and women as workers, wives and mothers, with their communities. Used as a prism through which to view society, the examination of community allows us to consider how the two cultures functioned. Cohesion and fracture, harmony and disorder, inclusion and exclusion, and the nature of social and national unity were issues brought into sharp focus during a period of war and peace and of struggle and reconstruction in Britain and France. The exploration of films of both countries between 1939 and 1959 will reveal that representations of community were complex and perceived as reassuring and welcoming, but also threatening and alienating. Film-makers raised questions about myths, ideals, identity, anxieties, conflicts and the wider social themes which resulted from wartime and post-war tensions.

Chapter 2 investigates the context in which film-makers were working during the war in Britain and the occupation in France. The notion of community was intrinsic to British wartime culture, and the chapter goes on to discuss the variety of ways in which it was interpreted on screen. Conversely, in 1940 France had suffered the worst and most rapid defeat in its history, its territory divided into the *zone occupée* and the *zone libre,* and its people embroiled in 'la guerre *franco-française*'.[69] The cinema of the occupation period has either been accused of being disengaged from reality or examined for elements of Vichy ideology, but these present a simplistic analysis of the meaning of this fascinating cinematic era. This chapter will argue that without resorting to either evasion or political endorsement, films were successful in suggesting the underlying tensions of a deeply divisive era.

Chapter 3 looks at wartime rural and urban imagery. British and French film-makers alike drew on a shared tradition of rural mythology in order to instil patriotism, even though France was predominantly rural and the vast majority of the British population lived in towns. To what extent therefore did existing cultural and demographic differences influence the kinds of films that were made? Furthermore, the invocation of the rural myth in British film, presenting a serene, unchanging world, actually accompanied a time of urban–rural conflict and physical disruption to the landscape. How did film-makers deal with these tensions when the need for national consensus was vital? Urban–rural friction was also at a height during the occupation in France, but rural films depicted *le pays* as the stable centre of French society. These films have been scrutinised for their Vichyite elements, yet with closer analysis they actually evince far more complex ideas about national identity and unity. Depictions of the urban world offer contrasting perceptions of the relationship of the capital to the wider nation. How did film-makers visualise London, a vast city with a socially and culturally diverse populace? More problematically, to what extent did French films reveal the difficulties of living in Paris, an occupied city?

Chapter 4 examines rural and urban imagery in post-war films. With the end of the war, how far was the southern English pastoral an appropriate image? Film-makers no longer constrained by a propagandist agenda were free to explore the rural hinterlands which had been neglected by wartime cinema. At a time of great change in the countryside, why did film-makers reject contemporary settings in favour of historical genres? In France, the increase in rural films in the post-war period suggests that *la campagne* was deeply important to forging national identity. How was this achieved at a time of increased urban–rural tension which had been caused by four years of mutual resentment? An exploration of some of these films will determine to what extent if at all they attempted to heal the breach between the two environments. The urban world was still represented by its capital cities. But now that the concept of consensus had been validated by the electorate itself, how did films portray the urban communities of Labourite Britain? After four years of occupation, Paris could once again be shown, but did producers engage with or avoid the recent past? In what ways did the 'film noir', a popular genre which emerged soon after the war, relate to the post-war settlement?

Chapter 5 looks at how film-makers approached the issue of de-mobilisation, which was crucial to the social, economic and political reconstruction of both nations. After six years of British films committed to the community ideal, how were ex-service personnel portrayed in the comparative isolation of civilian life? The proliferation of crime films involving war veterans is surely suggestive of a deep dissatisfaction. Indeed it has recently been argued that the contrast of a satisfying wartime experience with an unsatisfactory peace continued to influence the crime genre until the 1960s.[70] That these films were being produced in an era where the state was committed to the welfare of all might suggest a deep-rooted cynicism about the post-war settlement. But are there other forces at work here? In France, le retour had more painful resonances. Although some returning prisoners of war were heartily welcomed by their communities,[71] there was also some resentment that they were responsible for France's humiliating defeat and the subsequent occupation. The liberation also represented a crisis of masculinity, although it has been argued that membership of the Milice and support of Pétain had upheld masculinity, not undermined it.[72] Nevertheless, the presence of prisonniers and déportés whose return was even more troublesome threatened the notion of a national community which needed to be nurtured in the post-war years. Until Retour à la vie (1949, Henri-Georges Clouzot, Georges Lampin, André Cayette and Jean Dréville) no film had dealt directly with veterans and deportees.[73] However, other films which dealt less explicitly with the question of 'returning' were very effective in evoking the distressing business of returning to a country with an unhappy and contested history.

Chapters 6 and 7 deal with representations of British and Frenchwomen in the post-war context. In Britain, single and married women had experienced considerable independence during six years of conflict, managing to work with running a household, often single-handed. In considering women in the sense of their relationship with the community, with family and with men as lovers, husbands, fathers, brothers, this chapter seeks to widen existing research into women in post-war film. How did film-makers conceptualise the present for women; what kind of future were they proposing and what kind of femininity did they advocate? Was it simply a question of 'returning' them to the home, or were films actually offering a more complex picture? In France women had traditionally been a significant part of the national workforce, but they were still bound by the antiquated laws of the Code Napoléon, which subjected them to patriarchal control. Women were given the vote in 1944, and though equal rights were promulgated they were to a great extent paper statements. Post-war policy promoted motherhood above all. The chapter looks at the highly contradictory images offered by film-makers of women as contributors to the Resistance movement, as willing collaborators, as mothers and home-builders and, with the 1950s, as increasingly 'sexualised' objects on screen.

Chapter 8 pulls together the themes discussed in the previous chapters and come to some conclusions about the ways in which community was represented in respect of those themes.

2

Film Industries at War:
Projecting 'Community'

On the outbreak of war, the British and French governments adopted similar policies towards their film industries. Cinemas were closed in anticipation of enemy bombardment, British cinema was put under the control of the Ministry of Information (MOI), French cinema under the Commissariat de l'information. After June 1940, the Vichy government established the Comité d'Organisation de l'Industrie Cinématographique (COIC), supervising production in both zones. Far from wilting under these apparent constraints, both industries thrived so well that the period has been deemed a 'Golden Age' of British and French cinema. However, the distinctions between the two cinemas were consonant with the political contexts in which they operated. British cinema had one major function: to visualise 'the people's war',[1] at the heart of which was the notion of 'community'. France, however, was ideologically divided, and national solidarity was at the very least a tenuous notion. For film-makers, whether employed by the German-run Continental Films, operating under the COIC, as clandestine members of the Comité de Libération du Cinéma français (CLCF), or openly pro-Vichy, projecting 'community' was a complex business. As we will see, films of the occupation were the antithesis of British 'realism'. They drew for the most part on 'escapist' genres: *policiers*, histories, thrillers, dramas and allegories, seemingly far removed from current realities. Yet many of them provide insights into film-makers' representations of community in an era when, unlike Britain's apparent solidarity, the French were 'against the French'.[2]

In September 1939, British studios were requisitioned, British-based American production companies reduced their activities to a minimum, independent producers closed, and Wardour Street's distributors moved out to the countryside.[3] Parisian theatres were subject to an 8 pm curfew and production on 20 films was stopped as actors and technicians were mobilised. Only three of the 30 Paris studios remained open, and St Maurice and Pathé were commandeered.[4] Film personnel not already conscripted, including directors Jean Grémillon and Louis Daquin, left Paris for the south. Indeed the Victorine Studios in Nice, where Marcel Carné's *Les Visiteurs du soir* (1942) and some scenes of *Les Enfants du paradis* (1945) were filmed, were promoted as an alternative venue to Paris.[5] However, within two weeks of the outbreak of war, both governments realised the importance of film as a morale-raiser. *Kinematograph Weekly* pointed out that the pubs were now full of disgruntled film-goers and that 'the time for re-opening the kinema – and the theatres and the music halls – has become an urgent public necessity'.[6] After protests from the British Film Producers Association (BFPA) and the Cinematograph Exhibitors Association (CEA) coupled with the absence of air attacks, cinemas were re-opened. The American companies Warner Brothers, MGM, Twentieth Century Fox, RKO and Columbia, realising that the industry would survive despite the war, stepped up production. In France, the prospect of demoralised soldiers and bored civilians also convinced the government to re-open the cinemas.

Whereas pre-war French cinema had a worldwide reputation and had little need for state assistance, the British government had taken steps to protect domestic production under the Cinematograph Acts of 1927 and 1938 by which exhibitors and renters were obliged to show a percentage of British films.[7] In autumn 1939, however, such was the atmosphere of uncertainty about the role that film might play in the prosecution of the war, consideration was given to ceding all production to Hollywood for the duration.[8] When a deputation from the Association of Cinematograph Technicians (ACT) approached the MOI about ideas for film propaganda, they were told that 'directors and technicians were not needed'.[9] Months later, the MOI's Home Morale Emergency Committee, concerned about the effects of air-raids on the public mood, noted, 'Tell actors that they are counted upon to keep people cheerful, lead singing etc.', a directive which indicates the superficial attitude of the government towards the entertainment industry in general.[10]

Nevertheless, the shift in official response was brought about by the wartime achievements of the British film industry. The MOI has been criticised for incompetence by contemporaries and historians, but its wartime role has been reassessed by James Chapman, who argues that despite early difficulties the Ministry recognised that documentary and commercial feature films were essential to the propaganda programme.[11] Crucially, at a time of shortages, cinema-going, which was convenient and comparatively inexpensive, steadily increased in popularity, rising from pre-war levels of around 19 million weekly spectators to 30 million in 1945.[12] Audiences too were displaying increasing interest in British films, as letters to *Picturegoer*, the leading popular film journal, reveal. Readers claimed that '*Convoy* [1941, Pen Tennyson], *Saloon Bar* [1940, Walter Forde], *Gaslight* [1940, Thorold Dickinson] and *Pastor Hall* [1940, Roy Boulting]…are easily as good as the more lavish American films',[13] and pointed out that 'Technically, the British film is equal to the American productions'.[14] By 1943, the MOI was sufficiently convinced of the effectiveness of feature films for propaganda purposes that it commissioned a survey on 'The Cinema Audience', which revealed that 70 per cent of adults visited the cinema and one seventh went once a week or more.[15]

Initially, the Films Division of the MOI was only concerned with the censorship of newsreels, noting that while 'the question of news reel films is one of vital importance to the work of this Division', it was 'unnecessary' to censor 'ordinary interest or feature films'.[16] However, the appointment of Sir Kenneth Clark as head of the Films Division in January 1940 changed official attitudes. As Clark told *Kinematograph Weekly*:

> We must on the screen, tell our own people, tell our Empire, tell the whole world what we are doing to win the war, bring home the great national effort and the sacrifices we are making…What we are fighting for must be put over on the world by indirect methods, of which the filmic world is one…no film is good propaganda unless it is good entertainment.[17]

The MOI's 'Programme for Film Propaganda' identified three key themes which should be incorporated into documentaries, newsreels and feature films: 'What Britain is fighting for', 'How Britain fights' and 'The need for sacrifices if the fight is to be won'.[18] Nearly 1400 short films were made by the Crown Film Unit and commercial companies which attempted to espouse these ideals.

Yet the Films Division was also aware that 19 million weekly cinema-goers wanted primarily to be entertained. The MOI secured the co-operation of the Air Ministry for Alexander Korda's production *The Lion Has Wings*, released in November 1939, and though it was an uneven concoction of actuality footage and dramatic scenes, it was highly profitable, yielding £25,140 for the Treasury.[19] During Clark's tenure, the MOI decided to subsidise a weightier project, Michael Powell and Emeric Pressburger's *49th Parallel* (1941), the only wartime feature to receive direct government backing. *49th Parallel* demonstrates 'What Britain is fighting for', and was also intended to persuade the US to enter the war. The film addresses conflicting ideologies on a grand scale: National Socialism, represented by a group of Nazi submariners, who, after their vessel is destroyed in Hudson Bay, encounter three 'democratic' communities during their journey to reach neutral America; an Eskimo trading post, an émigré Hutterite settlement and an intellectual Englishman who is researching Sioux culture. Of these groups, the Hutterite community most powerfully embodies democratic ideals. They welcome the Nazis, who, posing as itinerant farm labourers, are helping them with the harvest. One evening, during an electrical storm, Lieutenant Hirth (Eric Portman) seizes an opportunity to address his hosts. Against a dramatic backdrop of forked lightning, he stands alone and speaks of another tempest. 'There is a new wind blowing from the East,' he proclaims, 'a great storm coming across the sea, a hurricane which will sweep aside all the outmoded ways of life and mark the beginning of a new order not only for Europe but for the whole world!' His voice rising, Hirth demands that his 'Brothers – Germans!' support 'the greatest idea in history, the supremacy of the Nordic race!' Finishing his speech with a rousing 'Heil Hitler!', he sits down having stunned his audience into silence. Peter's (Anton Walbrook) calm, controlled but equally forceful reply to the Nazi's harangue explains the Hutterites' benevolent but potent philosophy. Forced to leave Germany because of racial, political or religious persecution, now 'all have found in Canada security, peace and tolerance and understanding which in Europe, it is your Führer's pride to have stamped out! 'No,' he quietly concludes, 'we are not your brothers!' The Hutterite community is thus used to present a powerful ideological standpoint, that peace and tolerance is morally superior to Nazi aggression.

The notion of 'community' itself did not, however, dominate film-makers' thinking in the early months of the war. Given that during the 'phoney war', nearly half the films released were comedies, the emphasis was clearly on distraction. Mass Observation noted that 'topical films are well received, provided that they are not excessively realistic or particularly unpleasant. Comedies about this war are much more popular than dramas.'[20] As we shall see, the 'realist' drama became one of the defining characteristics of Britain's wartime cinema. The studio most associated with the projection of 'realism' was Ealing. As Charles Barr notes, by 1942 'the broad congruency between the Ealing community and the "national community" is already operating'.[21] Ealing's 'community ethos' was already in evidence, however. In deference to the war situation, the ending of *The Proud Valley* (1940, Pen Tennyson), set in a Welsh mining village, was changed. Instead of the miners striking and forming a co-operative when the mine is closed, the revised ending shows the men working with the managers to keep the pit open. Worker–employer conflict is thus replaced by cross-class community spirit, which was consonant with wartime culture and the notion of 'the people's war'.

The plight of the French was not forgotten, however. While some films featured Russians, in *Tawny Pipit* (1944, Charles Saunders and Bernard Miles) and *The Demi-Paradise* (1943, Anthony Asquith), and a Czech in *The Gentle Sex* (1943, Leslie Howard and Maurice Elvey), at Ealing Studios an Anglo–French community spirit was being generated. Ealing not only forged and maintained connections between the two film worlds, but supported the French in the films themselves. The director Marcel Varnel, who had worked with those most 'English' of comedians, Will Hay and Arthur Askey in the 1930s, joined Ealing in 1940 and directed George Formby in *Let George Do It* (1940) and *Turned Out Nice Again* (1941), and Will Hay in *The Ghost of St Michael's* (1941). Other Ealing productions had distinct Anglo–French storylines, *The Foreman Went to France* (1942, Charles Frend) being the first wartime example.

The next two films involved the French actress Françoise Rosay, then in her fifties and a highly respected *grande dame* of the acting world. Rosay and her husband, director Jacques Feyder, had taken refuge in Switzerland during the occupation, and when summoned back to France by the Vichy authorities, she refused. Rosay spent some time performing in theatre in Tunisia, but left when it was occupied by the Germans in 1942. Her subsequent work on radio in Algiers, which was unpaid to rebuff accusations of collaboration, involved exhorting the French audience to 'rally to the French cause'.[22] In 1943, Rosay came to England and was introduced to Michael Balcon, the head of Ealing, by her old friend director Alberto Cavalcanti. The first two films made for Ealing make good use of her nationality while also promoting Anglo–French understanding. In *The Halfway House* (1944, Basil Dearden), she plays a mother in mourning for her son, who has been killed in a naval battle and whose marriage to an English sea captain (Tom Walls) is foundering under the weight of their mutual but unshared grief. When she organises a séance, he turns away in disgust. The soothing and spiritual atmosphere of the 'ghostly' inn, and the efforts of the 'dead' proprietors, who guide their guests to the root of their problems, help her come to terms with her loss and repair her marriage. Her 'Frenchness', emphasised by her strong accent, designates her firmly as an outsider, as does her seemingly isolated anguish, but she is gently brought into sharing her troubles with the inn's equally troubled community.

Screenwriter T.E.B. Clarke recollected that after the film's release a script had to be found in order to prevent Rosay being lured away by another studio.[23] The result was *Johnny Frenchman* (1945, Charles Frend), in which Rosay, again partnered by Tom Walls as Nat the harbourmaster of Trevannick, portrays Florrie, the doughty matriarch of a Breton fishing village, Lanec. The rivalry between the two communities is encapsulated in the wrestling match between Florrie's son Yan (Paul Dupuis), who joins the Free French on the outbreak of war and Bob (Ralph Michael), one of the local fishermen, over the love of Nat's daughter Sue (Patricia Roc). Florrie's bravery, however, ultimately resolves the feud between Lanec and Trevannick. *Johnny Frenchman* was shot in Mevagissey in Cornwall during the summer of 1944, where boats belonging to Breton fishermen who had left France in 1940 were used.[24] During filming, news came of the liberation of France, and Balcon recalled, 'Somebody produced champagne (pretty scarce then) and we toasted Françoise who was much moved. Then we all sang the Marseillaise. Happy though the occasion was, it was also a kind of goodbye, for we realised that now, at long last, Françoise would be on her way home to her beloved France.'[25]

A feature on Rosay in *L'Écran français* the following year mentioned *The Halfway House* and *Johnny Frenchman* and showed her, as a newly enfranchised Frenchwoman, placing her voting-slip in the ballot box, calling her 'a great and active citizen'.[26] *Johnny Frenchman* was put on general release in August 1945, and the press book sent to film renters suggested, 'If there are any veterans of the Free French in your community, get them interested in this tribute to their efforts which did so much to win the war'.[27] Ealing therefore made a considerable contribution to promoting a union between the two nations, and continued to do so after the war.

Meanwhile, as the idea of the 'people's war' became absorbed into popular culture, film producers from various companies engaged with the idea of a common community. 'The war film discovered the common denominator of the British people,' wrote Roger Manvell in 1947.[28] In contrast to the distinctly middle-class perspective of *The Lion Has Wings*, British cinema began to address ordinary people. Films projected the national interest while also acknowledging private interests and desires by juxtaposing the documentary style, which dealt with 'public' issues, with narrative fiction, which addressed the 'private'. The result was the 'realist' film.[29] This fusion of stylistic techniques was evident in films like *In Which We Serve* (1942, Noel Coward and David Lean), *The Bells Go Down* (1943, Basil Dearden), *Millions Like Us* (1943, Frank Launder and Sidney Gilliat) and *The Way Ahead* (1944, Carol Reed). In each of these, disparate individuals from different social backgrounds are moulded into cohesive, efficient, committed units in the navy, the fire service, a factory and the army respectively. In these films and others, the nation is represented by recognisable communities of people with whom wartime audiences could easily identify.

The films mentioned above were produced by various companies, yet all of them were linked to some extent to J. Arthur Rank. Rank was the dominant figure in the industry, and owned Pinewood, Denham and Elstree Studios, Gainsborough Pictures and General Film Distributors. He was a major shareholder in Gaumont-British, which had a chain of cinemas, and was chairman of the Odeon circuit. In short, the Rank Organisation controlled half the total British studio space and owned over 600 of the country's 4850 cinemas.[30] Despite the monopoly held by Rank, for which he was heavily criticised after the war, film-makers working within his ambit were able to produce ambitious and creative films. In 1942, Rank established Independent Producers, a conglomerate of film-making companies. Excelsior and GHW were joined by the Archers, Michael Powell and Emeric Pressburger, then Cineguild, comprising Ronald Neame, David Lean and Anthony Havelock-Allan, Frank Launder and Sidney Gilliat of Individual Pictures and Leslie Howard. Yet within the diverse output produced within the liberating atmosphere of Independent Producers, the films exuded patriotism and consensus. Even the semi-autonomous Gainsborough Pictures, which became associated with period melodramas, still produced 'populist realism' under the guidance of Ted Black, such as *Millions Like Us* and *Waterloo Road*.[31]

Although costume dramas were despised by the critics for their lack of contemporary content, they did tackle current issues. *Fanny By Gaslight* (1944, Anthony Asquith), based on Michael Sadleir's wartime bestseller and set largely in the 1880s, is particularly suggestive of social change.[32] Prospective politician and aristocrat Harry Somerford (Stewart Granger) falls in love with Fanny Hopgood (Phyllis Calvert), the illegitimate daughter of his employer, a Cabinet Minister. His sister tells Fanny that marriage would mean 'the ruin of his career, which depends so much on social connections', but he refuses to give Fanny up. Harry's mother asks in astonishment if he believes that class distinctions should be done away with, to which he replies, 'They will be done away with. A hundred years from now there'll be no such thing. If your high-bound friends don't like it, so much the worse for them.' None of this dialogue is in the novel, which suggests that the idea of a 'levelling' of the classes had intensified during the war. Similarly, the storyline of *The Wicked Lady* (1945, Leslie Arliss) bears little resemblance to the Britain into which it was released in December 1945, but its portrayal of Lady Barbara Skelton (Margaret Lockwood) defying convention in order to pursue a more exciting lifestyle was a satisfying one for female spectators, many of whom had experienced great independence during the war. Gainsborough's costume films have in common the female outsider; Fanny is barred from a respectable marriage because of her lack of breeding, and the maverick Barbara fits uneasily into the rigid aristocracy into which she has married.

For those films which dealt head-on with current events, the wartime community of British film was not just a geographical entity. Ships, barracks, factories, training camps and aerodromes each functioned as a form of 'no-man's land' into which characters were gradually assimilated. Geoff Brown argues that the earliest of these films, *In Which We Serve*, 'enthroned realism as the preferred national style'.[33] More importantly perhaps, it was the first film to pay equal attention to the depiction of officers and men. Whereas earlier naval dramas like *Convoy* and *Ships with Wings* (1941, Sergei Nolbandov) had conceptualised the war as being fought by the officers, *In Which We Serve* symbolises the 'levelling' of classes, which has been promulgated as one of the major changes brought about by total war.[34] The opening scene uses documentary footage of a busy shipyard, and a narrator (Leslie Howard) tells us that 'this is the story of a ship'. As Jeffrey Richards suggests, HMS *Torrin*, whose crew represents all classes, acts as a metaphor for Britain.[35] Indeed, as Noel Coward visited HMS *Nigeria* and HMS *Shropshire* for background material, he was struck by the notion that a ship's company was a discrete microcosm of society. 'The feeling was,' writes his biographer, 'of a country town whose inhabitants were now bound together in a common endeavour springing not from a grandiose concept of "King and Country" but rather from a much simpler and more immediate need to preserve their community at all costs'.[36]

At the beginning of the film, the *Torrin* has been sunk off Crete and the exhausted survivors are hanging onto a Carley float. The narrative focuses on three of the crew, Captain Kinross (Noel Coward), Chief Petty Officer Hardy (Bernard Miles) and Able Seaman Blake (John Mills). Up to their necks in oily water, rank (and class) is forgotten as German planes fire indiscriminately at them. In a series of flashbacks, they remember the past at home and at sea. Blake and Hardy fondly recall Christmas dinners, and the speeches in which they had both expressed their deep devotion to the Navy and the *Torrin*. Alix Kinross (Celia Johnson) delivers a moving speech about the Navy wife's biggest rival, her husband's ship. 'It's extraordinary,' she says, 'that anyone could be so fond – and so proud – of their most implacable enemy – this ship'. Devotion to the ship is paramount. When a terrified young stoker (Richard Attenborough) abandons his torpedo station, his shipmates shun him and he tries unsuccessfully to drown his sorrows. Yet when he later redeems himself, he is brought into the fold not only as a member of the *Torrin* but, as the Captain assures him in his dying moments, as a brave man of whom his family can be proud. At the end of the film, Kinross is bidding goodbye to his remaining crew in the shipyard. This final scene encapsulates the emotional restraint which runs through the entire film: in Alix's speech, in the farewell scenes between the Hardys and the Blakes, in Kath Hardy's stoicism during the Plymouth Blitz, in Hardy's reaction when he hears of her death, and in the rescue of the British Expeditionary Force, 'our brothers-in-arms', from Dunkirk. The emotional control and understatement which distinguishes *In Which We Serve* from earlier productions were the characteristics of the 'quality' film.[37]

Critics, film-makers, politicians, the public and even royalty identified with *In Which We Serve*. In 1947, Dilys Powell recalled, 'The experiences of civilian and fighting men were presented as essentially one, bound together by ties of human love and devotion; nobody but felt he had a stake in this drama'.[38] Cinemagoers admitted to powerful reactions to the film. One viewer questioned by Mass Observation said that 'it made me feel I would die for the Senior Service', another that it was 'truly British [and] I could visualise it happening to me'.[39] A 24-year-old woman wrote that *In Which We Serve* and *This Happy Breed* (1944, David Lean),[40] showed that 'these people were us, were our Fathers and Mothers after the last war, were our husbands and brothers in this war'.[41] The Russian director Vsevolod Pudovkin felt that it distilled the English character: 'The picture is English through and through. You can see the face of the real England.'[42] Churchill had the film screened several times, and the Royal Family, who had visited the set at Denham, saw it at Buckingham Palace. 'Although the ship is lost,'

George VI told Noel Coward, 'the spirit which animates the Royal Navy is clearly brought out in the men'.[43] *In Which We Serve* was and still is a stirring film the tenor of which rests on understanding and sympathy between the classes. The community of HMS *Torrin* demonstrates above all that, according to wartime cinema culture, comradeship transcended class divisions.

Other films drew together civilians from diverse backgrounds and moulded them into equally formidable forces. *The Gentle Sex* and *The Way Ahead* are comparable in that they concern, respectively, the recruitment of women to the Auxiliary Territorial Service (ATS) and conscription to the army. *The Gentle Sex* has tended to be neglected in favour of *Millions Like Us*, the story of a group of girls who are mobilised to work in an aircraft factory.[44] They are to an extent companion pieces, in that they were made with the co-operation of the MOI to encourage the recruitment of women into less glamorous occupations than the Women's Royal Naval Service (WRNS) or the Women's Auxilliary Air Force (WAAF). In the early part of the war, volunteers to the Auxiliary services tended to be upper-class women in search of adventure,[45] but the introduction of female conscription in December 1941 involved all classes. *The Gentle Sex* shows a group of women from diverse social backgrounds who experience a new-found camaraderie in the ATS: Ann (Joyce Howard), a Colonel's daughter, Dot (Jean Gillie), a 'good-time girl', Maggie (Rosamund John), a down-to-earth Scotswoman, Betty (Joan Greenwood), an only child, Joan (Barbara Waring), a stand-offish dancing teacher, Gwen (Joan Gates), a Cockney waitress, and 'foreigner' Erna (Lilli Palmer), a Czech refugee. The film celebrates the closeness of the female community, who train together and then separate to do their different jobs. Four of them become convoy drivers, the other three gunners. One night during a Blitz, there are casualties at the gun site, and the women, as the press book describes, 'are re-united in their common desire to do their jobs as women-at-war'.[46] By the end, the wise and compassionate Maggie has realised that Joan's brusque manner is due to insecurity, and she ensures that Joan is accepted.

One area covered by the MOI's 'Programme for Film Propaganda' regarding feature film was that part of the 'British life and character' was 'sympathy with the underdog'.[47] The community of women in *The Gentle Sex* collectively represents Britain, but refers also to the displaced European, Erna. While Joan is quickly marginalised through her inexplicable moroseness, Erna is completely accepted by the group. When returning by freight train from an all-night driving job, Joan blithely remarks on the 'efficiency' of the Nazis and Erna retaliates, explaining that the Gestapo shot her father 'for fun', tortured her brother and arrested her fiancé. 'You don't know the filth of the Gestapo,' she tells Joan, 'you don't know the slavery, the misery, the degradation'. With these words the train's whistle shrieks and we are suddenly reminded of another aspect of what Britain is fighting for, the defence of 'the underdog', the victims of Hitler's tyranny.

Other films similarly demonstrate that British communities are only too willing to accept outsiders. *Tawny Pipit*'s 'foreigners' are two rare birds who come to nest in the village of Lipsbury Lea and are protected from egg thieves by the villagers. The significance of birds during the war was that, according to ornithologist James Fisher, they were 'part of the heritage we are fighting for'.[48] The protection of the birds by the village community against wrongdoers is metaphorically the defence of democracy against invaders. The theme was reprised in 1954 in Group 3's *Conflict of Wings* (John Eldridge), this time with a Cold War setting, as villagers try to prevent their bird haven from becoming an RAF rocket-launching site. At the end of *Tawny Pipit*, the village welcomes a famous Russian woman pilot, Olga Bokolova (Lucie Mannheim), who has shot down 100 German planes. Originally a farmer's daughter, she explains that both the farm and her parents have disappeared, but she will fight 'to the last' to win back the cornfields. Love of the rural is presented as a common bond between the two nationalities, while the pastoral setting evokes a sense of peace and neutrality. This scene also stresses the role of women in the war, through Nancy (Jean Gillie), a land girl whose brief exchange with Olga suggests a camaraderie which transcends questions of nationality.

The nurturing of male camaraderie is central to *The Way Ahead*. Noting the success of *In Which We Serve*, Minister of Information Brendan Bracken asked Noel Coward to undertake a similar project for the armed services, but Coward declined due to his lack of knowledge of the army.[49] However, Eric Ambler and Peter Ustinov had scripted *The New Lot* (1943, Carol Reed), a training film commissioned by the Directorate of Army Psychiatry in order to counter 'fatalistic bloody-mindedness' among new recruits.[50] Joined by Major David Niven, who was also concerned about morale, and Carol Reed, they worked on a full-length version together. But, Niven cautioned, 'the movie-going public...after three years of War can smell pure propaganda a mile off'.[51] The object of the film was to make the audience say, 'There, that's what our Bert is doing. Isn't it wonderful?'[52]

In his role as Lieutenant Jim Perry, a garage mechanic, David Niven forgoes his star status. A member of the Territorial Army, Perry takes charge of the new recruits in the Duke of Glendon's battalion. Seven men are called up: Davenport (Raymond Huntley), a department-store manager; Parsons (Hugh Burden), his sycophantic assistant; Brewer (Stanley Holloway), a boilerman at the House of Commons; Luke (John Laurie), a farmer; Lloyd (James Donald), a rent collector; Stainer (Jimmy Hanley), a car salesman; Beck (Leslie Dwyer), a travel agent. Its narrative is a familiar one, that of individuals welding together to become a unified whole. During their training the reluctant conscripts grumble and complain under the watchful eye of Sergeant Major Fletcher (William Hartnell), a 'regular' and a tough disciplinarian. Lieutenant Perry appears more sympathetic to the men, but when Stainer and Lloyd effectively sabotage a training exercise, he gives them a thorough 'dressing down'. Perry reminds them that the battalion's cap badges signify battle honours first won against Napoleon in 1809, and 'Salamanca, Orthez, Waterloo, Alma, Sebastopol, Tel-el-Kebir, Mons, Ypres, Somme…' The potent invocation of military tradition and heritage succeeds in making the men feel guilty. Yet Perry does not intend to report them, saying that Captain Edwards is 'already depressed enough to think that it was his company that let the whole battalion down'. This act creates a distance between him and his superiors and helps to preserve the albeit precarious relationship between himself and the men.

After the Lieutenant unexpectedly encounters the men at Mrs Gillingham's house, where they go to have tea and baths, their relationship moves into a different phase. The recruits recognise in Perry a firm but humane commander, and he wins their respect, loyalty and affection, as indeed many soldiers experienced with their officer.[53] Perry also demonstrates that being in the services has a great advantage. When Parsons reveals that he is in debt, Perry counsels him, 'You're not alone any more against anyone, Germans or furniture shops'. Thanks to Perry's influence with the Colonel, Parsons receives a war emergency grant and 48 hours' leave. Nurtured by army camaraderie, and the unfailing confidence of Sergeant Fletcher in their abilities, the raw recruits become a highly professional team. They prove themselves to be so committed that when they are torpedoed en route to North Africa they are crushed by disappointment. Their second chance soon comes, and in a small Tunisian village they dig trenches by day and while away the evenings until the time comes to confront the German army. Their transition from separate individuals to a cohesive force is crystallised in a short sequence in a café when a crackling BBC voice comes through on the wireless, describing an English harvest: 'Yes, it's been a good year all round in Berkshire… potatoes and sugar beet look like coming on nicely'.

The men stop their chatter, lower their darts and their glasses and listen intently, suddenly transported back home. Even the hard-bitten Sergeant Fletcher appears moved by the announcer's words, and on entering the room Perry is struck by the extraordinary hush. Rural imagery and patriotism were powerfully interlinked by wartime culture and propaganda. The rather unromantic reminder of root vegetables in *The Way Ahead,* as well as more pastoral 'snapshots' in films like *The Captive Heart* (1946, Basil Dearden) where the protagonists are also far from home, are deployed to illustrate 'What Britain is fighting for'.

The critical reception of *The Way Ahead* was very positive. The mood of the country, however, had changed in the eighteen months between the original idea and the film's release in June 1944. Following the D-Day landings and the near-assurance of an Allied victory, there had been a revival of patriotism, and public attention had shifted to demobilisation and the future. But the film served another purpose. Reviewing *The Way Ahead,* C.A. Lejeune wrote that she hoped that 'somewhere, in some office, at this moment, some man of good sense is planning a film to show how a good soldier can be turned back into a good civilian'.[54] In 1944 *The Way Ahead* had succeeded in suggesting that a good soldier was one who learned to put community interests before private concerns. Six years of wartime film had presented communality as an ideal which many critics and writers hoped would influence and shape Britain's post-war reconstruction. However, while the idea of community had been a powerful and pervasive force for wartime film-makers, post-war cinema seemed to suggest that without the war as a motivating factor it was a profoundly difficult concept to transfer into the post-war environment.

Communities were less easily conceptualised and projected onto the screen by film-makers in Occupied France. The British were in conflict with a single aggressor, which made the task of engendering solidarity comparatively straightforward, but during the Vichy era the French were divided by a *guerre franco–française.*[55] In 1939, the attitude of the French government towards its film industry was unambiguous: the Commissariat de l'information directed that films should be 'healthy and optimistic'.[56] A list of prohibited films was drawn up, including Jean Renoir's pacifist masterpiece *La Grande illusion* (1937) and Marcel Carné's 'morbid' *Quai de brumes* (1938) and *Hôtel du Nord* (1938), with their 'doomed lovers…urban backstreet squalor and an all-pervading air of fatalism'.[57] Renoir's trenchant class satire *La Règle du jeu* (1939), was an example of films which were 'depressing, morbid, immoral and distressing to children', banned by a directive issued in October 1939.[58] As in Britain, during the uncertain days of the *drôle de guerre*, film-makers were encouraged to entertain and divert audiences rather than bombard them with propaganda. Consequently, out of 35 films made between September 1939 and May 1940, 16 were comedies.

The entry of the Germans into Paris in June 1940, however, threw the film industry into confusion. Production was curtailed, and leading directors and actors including Julien Duvivier, René Clair, Jean Gabin, Charles Boyer and Michèle Morgan left for Hollywood. For Jewish personnel, the Nazi invasion had more sinister implications. A law of October 1940 prohibited Jews from working in any branch of the cinematographic industry,[59] although designer Alexandre Trauner and composer Joseph Kosma among others were able to continue working under Marcel Carné's protection by using pseudonyms. Under the circumstances, their contribution to the making of *Les Enfants du paradis* was a triumph against all the odds. The COIC officially sanctioned antisemitism in 1941 by ordering *l'assainissement*, the 'purification', of the profession. Despite the occupation of Paris and the relocation of some people like Carné and writers Jacques Prévèrt and Charles Spaak to the South, the capital remained the centre of the film industry.

Foreign productions, apart from German films, were now banned in the occupied zone. As American films had comprised almost 52 per cent of the total screened in 1936,[60] domestic film production assumed greater significance. The Germans established Continental under the leadership of producer Alfred Greven, a former director at Berlin's renowned UFA studios, with Joseph Goebbels in overall control at Propaganda Staffel. As *Le Film* announced, Continental quickly secured the services of five well-known directors and two actors.[61] When Goebbels saw Continental's *La Symphonie fantastique* (1941, Christian-Jaque), a 'biopic' of Berlioz, he was disconcerted by its nationalistic theme. 'I have sent for Greven,' he wrote in his diary, 'to give him absolutely clear and unmistakable directives to the effect that for the moment, so far as the French are concerned, only light, frothy and if possible, rather unsophisticated pictures are desired...there is no reason why we should encourage their nationalism'.[62] Greven announced on his return that 'none of Continental's films will have the slightest political tone and all manner of propaganda will be firmly excluded'.[63]

Despite Goebbels's desire to 'suppress' French cinema, the German authorities were in fact anxious to maintain its high reputation in order to create a 'European' film industry capable of competing with Hollywood.[64] In this respect, as Colin Crisp argues, the flourishing of the industry during the occupation was not paradoxical but 'perfectly logical'.[65] Notwithstanding his intention to produce entertainment rather than propaganda, Greven ensured that Continental emerged as a powerful vertically integrated concern. It owned the studios and processing laboratories of Paris-Studio-Cinéma, distribution handled by UFA's subsidiary Alliance Cinématographique Européene (ACE) and exhibition by an affiliated company. Continental was amply funded, well supplied with film stock and equipment, and was thus a very attractive company to work for.

The disadvantage of working for Continental would only become apparent at liberation. Former employees were automatically assumed to have been collaborators, and punishments meted out to actors and technicians ranged from suspension to imprisonment. But as actor Pierre Fresnay recalled, the COIC had explained to film personnel that because the Germans had threatened to stop French production if Continental did not go ahead, working for the company was their 'patriotic duty'.[66] In the event, just as British film-makers operating under the Rank umbrella enjoyed un-precedented artistic and economic freedom, so too did Continental's directors. The 30 diverse films made by Continental during the occupation,[67] more than any other single company, by no means constitute the light-hearted escapism Goebbels had envisaged. In contrast to the grandiose and self-laudatory theme of *La Symphonie fantastique*, other films with less patriotic storylines offered far more subtle interpretations of national identity.

In the *zone libre*, the Vichy government established the COIC in November 1940 under a former director of ACE, Raoul Ploquin, and it was to take control of the industry until liberation. Colin Crisp argues that the COIC provided for the first time 'a reliable organisational framework' for French cinema, which laid the foundations for the post-war film industry.[68] It established censorship procedures, founded a film school, the Institut des Hautes Études Cinématographiques (IDHEC), and provided generous funding for the national archive, the Cinémathèque Française. In February 1941, Ploquin secured an agreement that films made in Vichy would also be shown in the *zone occupée*, provided that Vichy cinema programmes included a German newsreel. The COIC also provided low-interest loans to producers through the Crédit Nationale and, like the MOI in Britain, it financed short films and documentaries. Compared to the impoverished conditions in which film-makers had worked during the 1930s, there was an atmosphere of vitality and creativity. By September 1941, Ploquin was able to tell the Comité that 'French cinema...will show the entire world the prestige of the French spirit'.[69]

The films produced under the aegis of the COIC have been scrutinised for elements of Vichy ideology. Georges Rouquier's documentaries about rural artisans, *Le Tonnelier* (1942) and *Le Charron* (1943), were consonant with the 'educative mission' of the Revolution Nationale,[70] which venerated modest family enterprises, small-scale producers. Many years later, Rouquier claimed that rather than subscribing to Vichyite ideals these films affirmed national identity at a critical time when 'we were, really no longer ourselves'.[71] The 220 feature films produced during the period have, however, attracted most attention. Some historians claim that the term 'Vichy cinema' is misleading, since it tends to suggest a discrete period of film-making which ended with liberation. Jean-Pierre Jeancolas argues that there is a continuity before and after Vichy.[72] According to Jacques Siclier, the presence of pre-war actors and technicians indicates that 'Vichy' cinema was merely a continuation of the 1930s.[73] However, in 1944 critic André Bazin identified a 'pleiade of young technicians' who had emerged during the occupation, among them directors Henri-Georges Clouzot, Louis Daquin and Jacques Becker.[74] As will become clear, the work of these film-makers often had a contemporaneous edge. Some of the themes of Vichy production were distinctly pre-war, such as in *La Fille du puisatier* (1940, Marcel Pagnol) and *Le Voile bleu* (1941, Jean Stelli). These strongly pro-natalist films refer both to Pétain's cultivation of motherhood and the family as well as reflecting existing concerns about depopulation which Daladier's Code de la famille had sought to redress in 1939.[75] Conversely, other films constituted a *cinéma d'évasion* because of their allegorical or historical content. In 1946, Lindsay Anderson attributed these films to the 'impossibility under occupation conditions of making realistic films on contemporary subjects'.[76] Yet he added that while films like *Les Visiteurs du soir* and *L'Éternel retour* (1942, Jean Delannoy) were dismissed by some as merely escapist and defeatist, 'there seems no reason to suppose that fundamentals should not be as successfully reached through fantasy and myth as through realism and sugar-coated social propaganda'.[77] Film-makers working for both Continental and production companies under the aegis of the COIC were indeed able to reach those 'fundamentals' through a diversity of genres.

Henri-George Clouzot's contribution to Continental is of considerable significance. Clouzot adapted Simenon's novel *Les Inconnus dans la Maison*

(1941, Henri Decoin), a film banned at liberation because of its anti-semitic content, and *Les Dernier de Six* (1941, Georges Lacombe), based on a *roman policier* by Stanislas-André Steeman. Both of the films he directed are particularly suggestive of ambiguity within the community: *L'Assassin habite au 21* (1941), adapted from another Steeman thriller, and *Le Corbeau* (1943), based on a real-life incident about a small town besieged by anonymous letters. *L'Assassin habite au 21* evokes an 'oppressive atmosphere triumphant with ambiguity' which is a characteristic of the *cinéma policier* of the 1940s.[78] François Guérif argues that *policiers* contribute to the cinema of 'evasion' just as much as fantasies, historical stories and allegories.[79] Certainly, *policiers* are melodramatic rather than realistic, but the satire within *L'Assassin habite au 21* is as effective as that in Renoir's *La Règle du jeu*, though it has different emphases. A large part of Clouzot's film takes place in a *pension* where a group of decidedly eccentric people live in complete disharmony. Renoir's film shows the bourgeoisie being able to maintain appearances by the application of certain rules, and as a whole it functions as a metaphor for the imminent collapse of that system. In *L'Assassin habite au 21*, the mutual mistrust of the *pensionnaires* symbolise the disquieting circumstances of living in an occupied and divided city.

There are references to danger in the city and danger within the *pension*'s community. In a *quartier* of Montmartre, four murders have been committed by the mysterious 'M. Durand', who leaves his calling-card next to his dead victims. Commissaire Wens (Pierre Fresnay), informed that the murderer lives at the Pension Mimosas, disguises himself as a *pasteur* and goes to investigate. He contrives to 'chat' to each of the residents. Colin (Pierre Larquey), a *petit bourgeois* who spends his time making puppets, the latest being a faceless 'M. Durand', quickly dispels any suggestion of solidarity amongst the boarders by telling Wens that they are all odd: Mademoiselle Cuq (Maximilienne) is 'potty'; Docteur Linz (Noël Roquevert) an unconvicted abortionist; Lallah Poor (Jean Tissier) is a complete mystery, and he alludes to an illicit affair between the blind ex-boxer Kid Robert (Jean Despeaux) and his nurse. 'What a menagerie!' he exclaims. 'Still,' he adds, 'one shouldn't speak ill of one's neighbours, should one?'

The narrative resonates with notions of guilt and duplicity, and an atmosphere of *déséquilibre* reigns at the *pension* itself. The alcoholic ex-colonial Linz quarrels with Cuq over the bathroom, and then with Colin about his morning whisky. Lallah Poor's apparent affinity with his fellow *locataires* is wholly negated by the fact that he is a magician who lives by facades and trickery. While the *pension* resounds with misgivings and dis-agreements, Wens's reference to Paris is direct in its suggestion of the enemy occupation. 'The faithful city,' he intones during grace, 'has become a whore. Where murderers now lurk was once the home of equity and justice.' His language invokes the idea of revenge, as he adds gravely, 'But darkness will not always reign on the earth where now there is anguish. For as the Lord says I will take satisfaction from my adversaries and vengeance from my enemies.' Yet despite the suggestion of invasive hostile forces, culpability for the murders ultimately rests on insiders rather than outsiders. 'M. Durand' is revealed to be a trio, comprising Colin, Lallah Poor and Linz, who since boyhood have been united in *malfaisance*. The name of the *pension* may well be a reference to Jacques Feyder's 1934 film *Pension Mimosas,* in which the landlady of a seaside boarding house (Françoise Rosay) oscillates between sparkling gaiety in public and profound melancholia in private, suggesting that a person's true nature is never really obvious. The little community in *L'Assassin habite au 21* is similarly unknowable and operates as a microcosm of an occupied nation in which the old certainties are no more.

Le Corbeau, Clouzot's next project, was vilified as being anti-French and was banned at liberation. Although most of Continental's productions were based in Paris, the provincial setting of *Le Corbeau* shifts the emphasis squarely away from the capital. While Paris was traditionally the location of the *policier*, the suggestion of provincial wickedness was deeply unpalatable. In *L'Écran français*, Georges Sadoul roundly denounced the 'cripples, the amoral people, the corrupters who in *Le Corbeau* dishonour one of our provincial towns'.[80] At liberation, the Comité Regional Interprofessionnel d'Epuration summoned Clouzot before them, and he was initially suspended for life, while the film's leading actors Pierre Fresnay and Ginette Leclerc were both briefly imprisoned. In 1945, the Centre Catholique du Cinéma (CCR), judging it 'painful and unyielding and unremittingly morbid in its complexity', gave the film a maximum amount of six points, which classified it as 'essentially pernicious in its social, moral or religious point of view'.[81] As recently as 1979, Louis Daquin, a member of the Comité de Libération du Cinématographie Français (CLCF) was unrepentant about his condemnation of the film as furthering the German cause.[82] In fact, despite claims by contemporary film critics that UFA had gleefully shown *Le Corbeau* in Germany under the title *A Little French Town* as part of its anti-French propaganda campaign, a letter in the production file indicates that the company refused to distribute it. In October 1944, a representative of the Sécurité Militaire wrote to the head of the Commission d'Epuration du Cinéma and confirmed that UFA had rejected the distribution, stating that the film 'did not conform to German mentality'.[83] *Le Corbeau,* however, was extremely successful at the box office throughout France,[84] and is a finely crafted film, regarded as one of the outstanding productions of the occupation.

The controversial subject of *Le Corbeau* was anonymous letters. It was rumoured that by 1942, the work of *corbeaux,* anonymous letter-writers, were arriving at the Kommandatur headquarters in Paris at the rate of 1500 a day.[85] In addition, the Vichy authorities, who actively encouraged informing, received an estimated three to four million letters during the regime's existence.[86] Jean Dutourd dealt with this in his satirical novel *Au Bon Beurre* (1952), about the collaborationist proprietors of a *crémerie*. Julie Poissonard writes to the Général de la Commandature informing him of an incident which would 'revolt the honest hearts of the French people', the presence in her neighbourhood of an escaped prisoner.[87] Having given explicit details of the unfortunate man's whereabouts, she concludes by offering cordial greetings from 'a Frenchwoman who does not sign, for reasons you will understand'. After posting the letter, she feels 'lighthearted and calm', and sleeps well.[88]

Poison pen letters were not unique to the occupation, however. Louis Chavance's script for *Le Corbeau* was actually based on the case of Angèle Laval, who in 1917 composed 1000 malicious letters to inhabitants of Tulle, with some tragic consequences.[89] Chavance wrote the scenario in 1937 after some thorough research on *anonymographie*. He closely studied a monograph by Dr Edmond Locard, who had interviewed Laval and revealed that the Tulle affair had led to an epidemic of at least twenty other similar incidents nationally.[90] Reviewing *Le Corbeau, L'Illustration* wrote that the theme was not new but was topical at a time when 'denunciations and threats of all kinds are each day becoming more numerous'.[91] The community of Saint Robin, which soon resonates with suspicion and hatred, provides a potent allusion to the divided nature of Occupied France.

The opening caption, 'A little town here or there', confers universality to the story. In this town, no-one is innocent, not even the children. The rather unpleasant Rolande (Liliane Maigné) enjoys eavesdropping, and a little girl surreptitiously extracts a letter from her pocket. The 'caring' professions are staffed by disturbed individuals. A nurse, Marie Corbin (Hélèna Manson), has been depriving François, a cancer patient, of morphine injections in order to satisfy her ex-fiancé Dr Vorzet's craving, while Vorzet's wife Laura (Micheline Francey), a hospital visitor, is ultimately exposed as a jealous neurotic. The main protagonist of the film is physician Dr Germain (Pierre Fresnay), who is also an outsider, and as such automatically a suspect. Similarly, in Paul Stein's British film *Poison Pen* (1939) the 'foreigner' in the village, Connie (Catherine Lacey), is similarly the first to be put under suspicion. The persecution is such in both films that the innocent Connie hangs herself and Germain resolves to leave town.

At the beginning of *Le Corbeau*, 'Au Frontière du mal',[92] Germain emerges from a farmhouse with bloody hands, having attended a childbirth case. 'The mother is saved,' he tells *grandmère*, but the baby is dead. In prioritising the mother over the child, he contravenes Vichy ideology, which stressed the family and children, made abortion a crime, and imposed a death penalty on abortionists.[93] At the hospital, Dr Bertrand (Louis Seigner) remarks that it is the third such case Germain has handled, and word soon spreads around the town. A 'pregnant widow' sent by Germain's scheming colleagues comes to him for an abortion, which he refuses to carry out, and the local haberdasher refuses to let him treat her niece. Germain eventually reveals that because of the tragic death of his own wife in childbirth, his practice is to save the mother in preference to the child. But by this time his reputation is thoroughly tarnished and he is under constant suspicion.

The definitive scene in the film is one in which Vorzet explains to Germain the ambiguities within human nature. In the dimly lit schoolroom, he says to Germain accusingly, 'You think people are all good or all bad'. He swings a light bulb back and forth, which illuminates a globe. 'You think that the good is light and bad is darkness. But where is the light? Where is the dark? Where is the frontier of evil? Do you know which side you are on?' Vorzet's questions reflect on the whole nature of the occupation, and his language evokes 'darkness' in the nation's past, but also, more significantly, its present. Indeed the dialogue contradicts Pétain's words, mentioned in the introduction: 'There is no neutrality possible between the true and the false, between the good and the evil, between health and sickness, between order and disorder, between France and anti-France'.[94] The concepts of light and dark are also represented in the film's two main female characters, Denise (Ginette Leclerc), sensual and dark-haired, the antithesis of Vichy femininity, and Laura, blonde and seemingly virtuous. Vorzet tells Germain that he is not immune from corruption, although Germain indignantly professes to know himself. Thus far Germain has maintained a firm moral position, but his certainty now begins to falter.

Confusion and ambiguity permeate the narrative of *Le Corbeau*. At the end of the film, Germain suspects that both the women who profess to love him are 'Le Corbeau'. Ultimately, the notion that good and evil are discrete concepts is obfuscated by the revelation that the seemingly benign Dr Vorzet is the true culprit. Even Laura is guilty of writing the first letter because of her jealousy about Germain. The suspicion pervading the community is expressed in one of the film's most striking scenes. François, distraught at his terminal illness, has cut his throat. During his burial, the town prefect talks of vengeance against 'l'oiseau noir! Le Corbeau!', his words appearing to be directed towards Marie Corbin. All eyes turn on her, and Marie, suddenly vulnerable and isolated, runs off panic-stricken through the town's empty streets, followed by the rumble of a pursuing crowd. As we shall see, the harrying of those perceived to be 'guilty' would assume greater significance after liberation, when collaborators were identified and punished in public places. In particular, women deemed to be guilty of 'horizontal collaboration' by unofficial *épurateurs* were publicly chastised; their heads shaved, they were forcibly paraded through crowded streets in a 'carnivalesque' fashion.[95] In *Le Corbeau*, the mob acts as a symbol of deep-rooted violence and resentment, and Marie, the single woman deprived of her true love, is a convenient target. Similarly, *Poison Pen* resorts to stereotype when the deeply maternal but childless spinster Mary (Flora Robson) is revealed as the writer. In *Le Corbeau,* the aged Vorzet, by implication also sexually inactive, proves to be the culprit, thus placing an accusatory emphasis on society's elites. The accompanying suggestion of shifting culpabilities amongst the town's population gives the film historical plausibility. Indeed, the all-pervasive complexity and uncertainty of character and situation encapsulates the moral ambiguity of the period. The lack of clearly delineated 'heroes' and 'villains' within a single community anticipates the truly nebulous reality behind the notions of 'resistance' and 'collaboration' which would have to be confronted at liberation.

Other films, however, offered alternative images of community to Clouzot's pessimism. *Le Ciel est à vous* (Jean Grémillon), released four months after *Le Corbeau,* was hailed as its antidote. Like *Le Corbeau*, its location removes it from Paris, but its community contrasts with Saint Robin. Based on the true story of Andrée Dupeyron, who broke a flight record in 1937, the story concerns Pierre Gauthier (Charles Vanel), a veteran of World War One, and his wife Thérèse (Madeleine Renaud), who run a garage in Villeneuve-sur-Loire. They become consumed by a passion for flying, and Thérèse eventually wins a record on a solo flight to North Africa, an achievement celebrated by the whole community. In an article in *L'Écran français*, Georges Adam and Pierre Blanchar delightedly announced that 'Le

Corbeau has been plucked'.[96] People will recognise in it, they declared, 'the true French…their blood, their honesty'.[97] Grémillon's clandestine membership of the CLCF has resulted in the film's being identified as a key cinematic statement about national identity, heroism and freedom. Yet its producer was Raoul Ploquin of COI, and it was premiered before Pétain, his wife and ministers at Vichy in February 1944.

The most obvious paradox of *Le Ciel est à vous* has been noted.[98] Thérèse is introduced as a good wife and mother whose principal activities are helping her husband with the business and caring for their two children. In short she is an ideal example of Vichy womanhood, and was identified as such by both the Resistance and right-wing press. *L'Écran français* described her as 'modest and courageous',[99] and *Les Nouveaux Temps* called her 'a good housekeeper and mother' who, on successfully landing in North Africa, 'thinks only of her husband and children'.[100] Yet Thérèse faces the consequences of being an 'absent' wife and mother. Arriving home after three months working in Limoges, she finds that her son Claude has had a bicycle accident, and Pierre is spending all his time at the aerodrome. She refuses to allow her daughter Jacqueline to study piano at the Paris

1. *Le Corbeau* (1943, Henri-Georges Clouzot), with Pierre Fresnay (right) and Ginette Leclerc. © 1942 Studiocanal Image.

Conservatoire and is complicit in the decision to sell the instrument to help buy an aircraft, although in deference to Vichy family dynamics she delegates the task of telling Jacqueline to Pierre.

As if to reiterate the theme of neglect, the town's orphans appear in four sequences during the film, none of which have any bearing on the narrative but rather symbolise isolated children. A handwritten version of the script mentions their three (sic) appearances and intriguingly notes that the orphans signify an 'element of suspense'.[101] As Pierre, Claude and Jacqueline make their way home from the station on his return from the aerodrome, where he has waited in vain for news of Thérèse, the orphans literally block their path, singing 'all the bells begin to ring, here go the abandoned children'.[102] The Gauthiers stand and wait for them to pass before they move on. This sequence has an elliptical effect, allowing time for the audience to consider the significance of the reappearance of the orphans. Yet none of the contemporary reviews available remark on Thérèse's blatant neglect of *le foyer* (the home). It was nearly thirty years later, in 1972, that *L'Écran français* identified Thérèse not as a Vichy heroine but rather a woman prepared to sacrifice her home and family to fulfil her personal ambition.[103]

Yet even more than the confusing Thérèse, the response of the community towards the Gauthiers is suggestive of the contradictions and complexities at work in society. At the opening of the aerodrome, the president of the club and *conseiller* Dr Maulette (Léonce Corne) makes a speech in which he says that 'we live in a little town, but we are proud to undertake a great idea and show by it that we do not lack vitality and courage'. The importance of the aerodrome to the town and flying, with its connotations of openness and freedom, provides a considerable contrast to the nefarious activities in *Le Corbeau*. Yet the local bureaucrats do not initially support the Gauthier's ambitions. The members of the Conseil Municipal persuade the *maire* that they should not receive funding for their flying because it will not serve the community interest. Furthermore, M. Dubois insists that 'a woman's place is in the home'. While bureaucratic objections are not unexpected, the reaction of the local people is decidedly ambiguous. Although the film has attracted attention because of contradictory discourses about women, the threatening atmosphere summoned up during Thérèse's absence has not been noted. When Pierre returns home having had no news of Thérèse, their home is besieged with phone calls berating both of them for their foolhardy escapade. Pierre's mother-in-law, Mme Brissard, complains that their so-called 'friends' say nothing out loud but in private carp and criticise. Pierre's anxiety reaches its height when he believes that the locals who have amassed outside are about to attack him, and he arms himself with a hammer. Although the assembled crowd wishes only to break the good news about Thérèse's safe arrival, it appears potentially dangerous. This scene suggests a fundamental instability within the community, which manifests decidedly shifting loyalties towards its fellow inhabitants. So even in a film which purported to show French heroism and solidarity, the ambiguities are clearly present. Furthermore, despite the heroic heights literally reached by Thérèse, Dr Maulette is killed when his aircraft crashes, suggesting that freedom can also mean danger. As we will see later, even films addressing problems inherent to their historical contexts tend to repress rather than resolve them. In *Le Ciel est à vous*, we need to ask whether the heroic nature of the ending is actually sufficient to efface the memory of the dislocation caused by Thérèse to her family?

One of the characteristics of cinema during the occupation is its lack of contemporaneity. *Le Ciel est à vous* and *Le Corbeau* are amongst those films which have been identified as avoiding the present by being located in a 'contemporain vague'.[104] As Alan Williams notes, the use of enclosed, isolated communities became something of a stereotype in film of the period.[105] Examples include Jean Grémillon's *Lumière d'été* (1942), an exposé of bourgeois hypocrisy reminiscent of Renoir's *La Règle du jeu*, which is set in a remote mountainous region; *L'Éternel retour* (1942, Jean Delannoy), a modern version of Tristan and Isolde based in a chateau, and *Les Anges du péché* (1943, Robert Bresson), set in a convent. Yet these and other 'escapist' films are able to convey contemporary realities very successfully. *Les Enfants du paradis* (1945, Marcel Carné), for instance, ostensibly a tribute to nineteenth-century Parisian theatre, is a prodigious piece of filmmaking in which the central protagonist, the enigmatic and independent Garance (Arletty) has been interpreted as a symbol of national freedom.

Most suggestive of the indomitable spirit of a captive France is undoubtedly *Les Visiteurs du soir* (1942, Marcel Carné), a mediaeval fable set in a shimmering white chateau. An expensive 'quality' production which won the COIC's Grand Prix du Film d'Art Français in 1942, it had a considerable impact at a time when many people believed that French cinema would not survive. André Bazin wrote in 1944, 'even as we listened to the demon of despair,' 'there was already being erected under the sky of Provençe the great white chateau that Marcel Carné was to make the bastion of our hopes'.[106] At first sight, the film appears to be an exploration

2. *Le Ciel est à vous* (1944, Jean Grémillon), with Madeleine Renaud. BIFI.

of good and evil. Two emissaries of the devil, Dominique (Arletty) and Gilles (Alain Cuny) ride over a desolate landscape to a chateau where the betrothal is being celebrated of Baron Hugues's (Fernand Ledoux) daughter Anne (Marie Déa) and Chevalier Renaud (Marcel Herrand). Their mission is to use their charm to seduce the couple and destroy their happiness.

Yet this is not a harmonious and innocent community waiting to be despoiled. It is, like France itself, riddled with contradictions, cruelties and ugliness. Just outside the chateau, the envoys meet a man who is distraught at the death of his beloved performing bear. An innocent beast who had given people so much laughter over the years, he has been pierced by an arrow shot 'in fun' by a bored guard. Inside the walls they soon discover that Anne and Renaud do not love each other, and while she is gentle and loving, his passions are hunting and war. The love felt by one of the maids, Louison, for Anne's page remains unrequited because Louison is ugly, and the panoply of entertainment in the chateau includes the dramatic unveiling of three hideously disfigured dwarfs. The Baron Hugues, although outwardly a grieving pious widower, succumbs easily to Dominique's charms and does not hesitate to imprison his daughter when she publicly confesses her love for Gilles. Dominique succeeds in making Renaud fall in love with her, and arouses Baron's jealousy to such an extent that they have a jousting match during which Renaud is killed. Gilles falls in love with Anne and the devil himself (Jules Berry) is forced to intervene, but when he sees that they will not betray each other, he becomes enraged and turns them to stone. Yet beneath their petrified forms, their hearts continue to beat. While the outward manifestations of piety and loyalty have been tested and found wanting, there is nevertheless, in the midst of chaos, constancy and vitality, in sum a perfect metaphor for a nation which survives despite myriad inner complexities of enemy occupation.

The manner in which community was expressed in British and French cinema was consonant with the distinctive socio-political contexts in which film-makers were operating between 1939 and 1945. During the 'phoney war', diverting and entertaining films were made under the auspices of the MOI in Britain and the Commissariat de l'information in France. Yet within months, the MOI had recognised the value of feature film as propaganda and Britain's film-makers quickly became involved in conveying the idea of a national community. Indeed 'community' became one of the dominant characteristics of wartime cinema. Ambitious productions like *49th Parallel* demonstrated that democratically run communities could present formidable opposition to Nazism. In *In Which We Serve*, the ship is the community, its crew representing a microcosm of the British nation. A range of films including *Millions Like Us*, *The Gentle Sex* and *The Way Ahead* showed individuals with their own troubles and idiosyncrasies gradually becoming responsible, committed team members devoted to a common cause. 'Community' was an apposite, accessible but essentially artificial construct in the wartime context, and as subsequent chapters will show, its conceptualisation was to prove challenging for post-war film-makers.

While French cinema of this era has been scrutinised for its 'Vichy' elements, it is more illuminating to look at the ways in which films projected the ambiguities and tensions of community. Expressing community was problematised by the fact that French film-makers were not motivated by a cohesive national ideology, as were their British *confrères*. Unlike British wartime films, there were few 'realist' productions which referred to contemporary issues, but rather a wealth of 'escapist' genres, *policiers*, comedies, fantasies, allegories and historical dramas. The tensions and divisiveness of daily life were nevertheless evoked within this diversity of genres by both the German-run Continental and by other companies operating in both zones. Within the narrative of *L'Assassin habite au 21*, the reality of the occupation is implied through the *locataires* who live in a claustrophobic atmosphere charged with suspicion and uncertainty. *Le Corbeau*, probably the most controversial film of the period, not only refers to the real prevalence of *anonymographie* but, more disturbingly, the innate cruelty of human beings. Even *Le Ciel est à vous*, the film interpreted as *Le Corbeau*'s curative, features a mob almost as sinister as the invisible rabble who pursue Marie Corbin through Saint Robin's cobbled streets. When the devil's envoys visit a chateau in *Les Visiteurs du soir*, intent on corrupting innocence, they find a community infused with cruelty and deceit. Yet the final Manichaean conflict between the devil and the two lovers dispels earlier uncertainties and doubts and affirms that France will survive in spite of restraint and imprisonment. As we have seen, images of community in film of the occupation were far removed from the unambiguous statements of solidarity evident in British film. In what should perhaps have been a time of absolutes, of villains and heroes, of collaboration and resistance, film of the period suggested a more convoluted reality.

3

Countryside and City, *Paysage et Patrie* at War

By the time Paris was taken by the Germans in June 1940, the historic towns of Calais, Lille, Amiens, Beauvais and Rouen had already been damaged by aerial bombardment. Turning its attention to Britain, the Luftwaffe steadily bombed London, Coventry, Southampton, Birmingham, Bristol, Plymouth and Manchester between September 1940 and January 1941[1] and Glasgow in March 1941. The countryside obviously became a safe haven for British and French townspeople, though the demographic and cultural distinctions between the two were marked. Only one fifth of the British population lived in country areas, while about a third of French people lived and worked in rural *communes*. Furthermore, the character of industrialisation in France meant that urban ties with the countryside had persisted into the twentieth century, whereas in Britain, Europe's most urbanised nation, town and country were more sharply defined. During the war, the tensions between urban and rural quickly emerged. For six years, Britain's countryside was besieged by outsiders, from service personnel to itinerant travellers, during what has been called a 'war of movement'.[2] In 1940, the exodus in France exposed an uneasy relationship between town and country, and indeed anticipated the greater *dépaysement* which was brought about by the occupation. Throughout, Pétain desired that France should be 'what it should never have ceased to be, an essentially agricultural nation'.[3] Consequently, rural France and its populace were subjected to four years of ideological exaltation while the city, represented by Paris, occupied a more ambivalent position within the public consciousness.

Rural Britain represented not only safety, but was also perceived as the location of national strength.[4] The countryside was deployed to inculcate patriotism, drawing on a long tradition in popular and high culture in which rural was analogous to national.[5] Pastoral imagery was there in radio broadcasts, films, novels, songs, poems, paintings, posters and advertisements. In some cases, there was a change from pre-war depictions of the rural. Whereas the film *Poison Pen* (Paul Stein), released in July 1939, paid scant attention to scenery and concentrated on the small-mindedness of village life, within a few weeks films started to be made that focused on the rural as the locus of benevolence and tolerance. The rural myth was, however, firmly located in Southeast England. When Rachel Knappet went to work as a land girl on a farm in Lancashire, her friends teased her for choosing a landscape of 'coal mines and factories', rather than of meadows and trees.[6] While film-makers rarely departed from the Southern English pastoral during the war, the imagery itself became more subtle and, as will be seen, shifted from the middle-class perspective evident in early wartime productions. The visualisation of urban Britain was even more focused. Film-makers largely neglected the provinces, while Britain was represented by London, particularly with the onset of the Blitz in September 1940. The geographical and cultural breadth of the city required its reduction on screen into small but recognisable communities in films like *The Bells Go Down* (1943, Basil Dearden), *This Happy Breed* (1944, David Lean) and *Waterloo Road* (1945, Sidney Gilliat), communities which, along with their inhabitants, came to function as metaphors for the nation.

The use of pastoral imagery was part of Vichy's efforts to revitalise the real 'France', to reconstruct a national spirit based on a mythologised rural past. One of the paradoxes of Vichy, however, was that while the new regime idealised the countryside and its cultivators, lack of food was alienating urban people from rural dwellers. In 1939, when conscription had deprived agriculture of two million men, farmers in the Loire were reported to have shouted abuse at townspeople whom they observed leisurely walking, fishing or picking mushrooms.[7] In May 1940, as the German army approached Paris, an estimated six to eight million refugees flooded the roads heading south and west.[8] Those with relatives in the countryside made the most of their connections; others simply fled for its safety. Peasants sold wine, water and milk at inflated prices, in revenge, it was said, for being mocked as inarticulate 'clodhoppers'.[9] Yet rural France was also the territory of the Resistance, which extended its influence into the countryside after France was entirely occupied in November 1942.[10] The *Maquis* who hid there in order to evade the compulsory Service de travail obligatoire (STO), owed much to the peasantry for their subsistence and survival.[11] The films that emerged from the period indicate the considerable complexities at work, yet as we shall see invariably referred to Paris, suggesting that on some level national unity still existed within a fractured country.

In Britain, rural depopulation, which had long exercised those concerned with the physical and cultural demise of the countryside, abated even before war was declared. In June 1939 two million people voluntarily left London, and on 1 September, the government's scheme moved a further one and three quarter million people into safe areas. The *Daily Mail* declared it 'the greatest organised movement of a human population in the world's history'.[12] In total, nearly four million people moved from town to country between 1939 and 1945, almost 9 per cent of the population.[13] However, the reality of rural life did not necessarily conform to visions of the countryside that existed in urban imaginations. Indeed the experience exposed deeply entrenched and often stereotypical views which rural and urban dwellers held of each other.

Although rural France and rural Britain have distinct identities and histories, both follow a similar trajectory in the way they have been culturally defined. From the depression of the 1880s, British ruralists, repelled by the 'materialism' of urban life, proposed a vision of England which was essentially rural. Rural represented 'peace, innocence and simple virtues', while the city was denounced for its 'noise, worldliness and ambition'.[14] Similarly, late-nineteenth-century French literature extolled the simple *paysan* and suggested that the immutable basis of society was in the land.[15] Country people who migrated to the town for work did not sever ties with their rural roots, and so had a special attachment to *le pays* which still persists.[16] During the inter-war years, rural mythologising reached its apotheosis as politicians emphasised the rural as the repository of noble virtues. Though Britain's countryside was conceptualised as 'neatly quilted with a green patchwork of fields', in reality it was 'one of the most dilapidated landscapes in Western Europe'.[17] Similarly, in France, when Marcel Pagnol's rural dramas on stage and screen were at the height of their popularity with urban audiences, large numbers of *paysans* were actually impoverished and demoralised.[18]

In Britain, the war quickly disclosed long-standing misconceptions between town and country. Urban dwellers resented country folk, who seemed to be well-fed and sheltered from bombs, while farm workers who spent seven days a week labouring from dawn until dusk took umbrage at townspeople taking leisurely country walks.[19] Yet urban populations were soon aware that the real business of the countryside was growing food. Ten million acres of grassland were ploughed up to be planted with crops, and seventeen million acres of moor and marshland, some unused since Saxon times, were utilised for food production.[20] By 1945, much of Britain's terrain was transformed. Civilians joined initiatives like the 'Lend a Hand on the Land' campaign, while the Women's Land Army, whose mainly urban conscripts totalled over 80,000 by 1943, stressed the idea of 'back to the land' in their official song.[21] As Angus Calder noted, 'the war broke down the barriers between the producers and consumers of bacon and eggs, potatoes and greens'.[22]

Of the urban–rural confrontations, evacuation was the most controversial, and has been interpreted as a major cause of social disruption.[23] For instance, much of the administration was carried out by ex-military men, experts in the field of organisation but insensitive to the huge emotional impact evacuation had on the children themselves.[24] Some evacuees found country life a happy experience, but others missed the amenities of the town and the bustle and communality of close-knit urban neighbourhoods.[25] The press was scathing, describing the evacuee child as 'filthy, verminous, incontinent, ungrateful and thoroughly ill-mannered', and mothers as missing the 'regular nights at the pictures [and] the fish and chip shops'.[26] Even the liberal *News Chronicle* claimed that 'householders are tired of housing dirty guests with dirty habits; of women who quarrel in the kitchens or who are always grumbling'.[27] Richard Titmuss concluded that the attendant revelations about urban poverty 'aroused the conscience of the nation',[28] which confirmed the need for a welfare state. Research has nevertheless shown the extent of social conscience, in that the middle classes were particularly guilty of avoiding reception duties.[29] As *Picture Post* revealed in November 1940, poor families who were already overcrowded took in evacuees, while big country houses stood empty.[30] Clearly the experience of urban people indicated that there was little correlation between rural romanticising and reality.

Film-makers conforming to the idea of 'the people's war' depicted the relationship between evacuees and householders as non-confrontational. The film evacuee, invariably a Cockney, was comical, adaptable and plucky. In *Tawny Pipit* (1944, Bernard Miles and Charles Saunders), two rare birds are found nesting in a field, and a recuperating RAF pilot and his nurse notice that two boys are about to steal the eggs. When they discover the boys are evacuees, they exchange sympathetic glances and successfully enlist their help in a campaign to protect the birds. In *Went the Day Well?* (1942, Alberto Cavalcanti), evacuee George Truscott (Harry Fowler) becomes a hero in his adoptive community by escaping from the manor house where he and other evacuees are being held hostage by German paratroopers and summoning help, even though he has been wounded. The evacuees' hostess, Mrs Fraser (Marie Lohr), ultimately sacrifices her life for her charges when a grenade is thrown through the window. These gestures correspond with the ethics of the 'people's war', in which class differences are replaced by social cohesion and a collective sense of responsibility. It was only in the post-war period that film-makers tentatively addressed the sociological implications of evacuation.[31] Ultimately the rural myth informed wartime film, and as cinema attuned itself to its audience it was used as effective propaganda, as it had been in earlier periods of national crisis.

During the Great War, writers had juxtaposed notions of patriotism and sacrifice with visions of rural England which had created a unifying myth.[32] A generation later, poets still drew on rural imagery that was often aimed at servicemen.[33] Literary anthologies produced for the forces invariably included sections devoted to rural poetry and prose intended to evoke notions of 'home'.[34] Frank Newbould's posters produced for the Army Bureau of Current Affairs were entitled 'Your Britain: Fight for it Now', and showed picturesque village greens and sweeping vistas of the South Downs, conceptualising England as a rural arcadia. In his Sunday evening broadcasts, J.B. Priestley engaged in similar discourses, as he mused on 'the loveliness of our gardens and meadows and hills'.[35] The rural world was captured on a populist level, however, by the song published in November 1939 that began, 'There'll always be an England while there's a country lane, wherever there's a cottage small beside a field of grain'. First heard during the 'phoney war', when people needed some motivation, its appeal was immediate and widespread. When the King and Queen visited the bombed East End in September 1940, the *Daily Mirror* reported that the cheering crowd began to sing it.[36] Behind a lyric that might appear incongruous with urban living was an invocation of the ideal community, resilient, timeless, peaceful and rural.

The countryside provided an antidote to the disruption, destruction and noise of war. A Mass Observation report on letters to *Picturegoer* in 1940 includes one from a London reader who wrote, 'It might prove a godsend to millions of harassed folk if the cinema would show us a few pictures of peaceful English landscapes and the quiet happenings of a typical English village in the autumn...'[37] Apart from its connotations of tranquillity, the countryside was a site of patriotic feeling. Another *Picturegoer* reader attached ideological importance to rural imagery. 'Show us the country we love,' he wrote, 'the country we believe is worth fighting for. Producers – show us England.'[38] These filmgoers' requests indicate that the MOI had correctly identified at least one key issue of the war which could be successfully addressed by film-makers using rural scenes: what Britain was fighting for.[39]

The Lion Has Wings (Brian Desmond Hurst, Michael Powell and Adrian Brunel), released in November 1939, was designed to demonstrate the strength of air defences. Significantly, it conceptualises the nation as essentially rural, beginning with a sweeping shot over fields of oast houses and country churches while a voice announces, 'This is England, where we believe in freedom'. In the final scene a Red Cross nurse (Merle Oberon) and her RAF officer husband (Ralph Richardson) sit by a tree-lined river. 'We must keep our land … we must keep our freedom,' she says, 'we must fight for what we believe in – truth and beauty and fair play'. The film articulates democratic ideals within a carefully recreated rural setting, although the *New Statesman*'s critic wrote that he would have preferred 'a less misty explanation' of why the 'Lion' was using his wings.[40] Despite mixed reviews, *The Lion Has Wings* was generally well received by audiences, and was the third-most-successful British film of 1939. However, its propaganda element was considered too laboured,[41] and it certainly exudes a middle-class air, as Graham Greene sardonically noted: 'As a statement of war aims, one feels this leaves the world beyond Roedean still expectant'.[42] The film exemplifies an early tendency of propagandists to divide the nation into 'us and them' that was soon abandoned by the MOI as being too condescending.[43] In the context of what had become by the summer of 1940 a 'people's war', film subsequently focused on the notion that the countryside belonged to everybody.

The Dawn Guard (1941, John and Roy Boulting), an MOI short, exemplifies this idea and acknowledges the discoveries made about urban poverty through the evacuation process. Two farmers on Home Guard patrol stand on a hill, and the younger man (Bernard Miles) tells his older companion (Percy Walsh) that peace must bring full employment, an end to slums and 'no more half-starved kids with no room to play in'. His speech is intercut with shots of children running around in narrow urban alleyways, then to others playing in a field. This notion of 'a brave new world' articulated on a hilltop effectively distances the speaker from the everyday world while giving him an air of authority. As Raymond Williams writes, 'the idea of landscape implies separation and observation',[44] and this was a device used in several wartime films containing a social or political

message. In Ealing's *They Came to a City* (1944, Basil Dearden), based
on J.B. Priestley's play about a post-war Socialist Utopia, Priestley, the
figure of authority, talks to a soldier and his girlfriend about the ideal
community on a hillside. In a scene in *Millions Like Us* (1943), Frank
Launder and Sidney Gilliat employ a rural setting to enable two factory
employees from different classes to discuss the possibility of marriage.
Upper-class Jennifer (Anne Crawford) and lower-middle-class Charlie
(Eric Portman) have a picnic on a hill high above the factory. He speaks
bluntly: 'The world's roughly made up of two kinds of people – you're
one sort and I'm the other. Oh, we're together now there's a war on – we
need to be. What's going to happen when it's all over?' The abstract setting
underlines the fantasy of the romance while also permitting a serious
dialogue about class relationships which would rarely have arisen in a pre-
war film.[45] The artificiality of the scene also avoids commitment to a
definite solution,[46] and is echoed in *A Canterbury Tale* (1944, Michael
Powell and Emeric Pressburger) when magistrate Thomas Colpeper (Eric
Portman) tells shop girl (Sheila Sim) that the war has caused an 'earthquake' in which anything might happen.[47] Again the pastoral setting
conveys a detachment and an exclusivity that precludes long-term resolution
of the issue under discussion.

Despite the increasing reputation of British films, most of the films seen
during the war were American.[48] *Mrs Miniver* (1942, William Wyler) is set
in a decorative village with rose-covered cottages, a quaint railway station
and a picturesque river. When 'Vin' Miniver (Richard Ney) returns from
Oxford with a newly acquired social conscience, he is indignant at the
social inequities of their 'feudal system', but one somehow knows that this
is passing youthful angst. The stoic Minivers deep in the countryside are
shown weathering the same terrors as Londoners during the Blitz. Most of
the British critics were damning, the reviewer of the *Documentary News Letter*
outraged at witnessing 'a British audience with three years of war behind
it, crying at one of the phoniest war films that has ever been made'.[49] The
vast majority of the British public, however, loved it. *Mrs Miniver* was the
top box-office film in 1942, suggesting that Hollywood's tidy middle-class
version of rural England was both entertaining and untroubling.

Ealing's *Went the Day Well?* (1942, Alberto Cavalcanti) was shot partly
on location in Buckinghamshire and contrasted with *Mrs Miniver*'s artificial studio sets. The *New Statesman* praised the film because there was 'not
a false touch, no England-my-England, or Miniveration'.[50] *Went the Day Well?*
is the story of Bramley End, which is infiltrated by Germans disguised as

Royal Engineers. Anthony Aldgate sees it as 'semi-official', on the grounds that the MOI were concerned at public complacency about invasion and because the War Office were involved in the film's production.[51] However, there were considerable delays in obtaining the equipment, and producer Michael Balcon was highly critical in general of government support of the film industry.[52] While the publicity material stated that there was less likelihood of invasion, the basic premise of the film was the resilience of the British people: 'They show us how to stand up to the trial of invasion if ever this nightmare were to become reality, and be able to emerge proud of ourselves'.[53] Furthermore, Balcon rejected one suggested title, *They Came in Khaki*, because he intended the film to focus on the villagers not the enemy.[54]

Bramley End is a far prettier village than Potter in Graham Greene's story on which the film is based, and this stresses the shocking nature of the invasion.[55] Potter's modern 'tin roofed church',[56] for example, is a drab contrast to the picturesque thirteenth-century edifice seen in the film. As in other rural films, the social hierarchy permits figures of authority to be used as points of reference, here the lady of the manor, the vicar and the squire. Mrs Fraser (Marie Lohr) is clearly a community elite figure as she accommodates several evacuees, organises billets for the recently arrived regiment, and is offended when she discovers that the vicarage has already appropriated the commanding officer. When the two German officers are entertained to dinner, the song on the wireless, 'There'll always be an England' is a reassuring reminder that the manor is a bastion of national strength. Appropriately, the final battle of Bramley End takes place in the manor house. The church is a further signifier of authority, as indeed it is in almost all 'rural' films. When the villagers are rounded up by the Germans, they are held hostage in the church, and the elderly vicar is shot dead while bravely attempting to ring the bells to alert the Home Guard.[57]

Whereas Mrs Fraser and the vicar display resourcefulness and courage, the squire, Oliver Wilsford (Leslie Banks), is the traitor in the nest, a fact revealed to the audience early on. Nora (Valerie Taylor), the vicar's daughter, who is in love with Wilsford, finally realises he is a quisling and in a brief but thrilling scene in the manor house confronts him and shoots him dead. Indeed some of the most courageous villagers are women. Apart from Nora's fierce resolve, Mrs Collins (Muriel George) contrives to throw pepper in the face of her German lodger and then bludgeons him with an axe. Cavalcanti remarked that 'people of the kindest character, such as the people in that small English village, as soon as war touches them, become abso-lutely [sic] monsters'.[58] Yet these women, though unusually aggressive for a wartime narrative, are far from monsters. Rather, they conform to the 'robustness England expected of its women',[59] and reinforce the idea of communal effort, regardless of class and gender. Sue Harper's contention that the film excludes 'sexually active females from the canon of heroism'[60] seems somewhat mean-spirited, and also trivialises the proactive roles of the two Land Army girls in the final shoot-out with the Germans. As Charles Barr argues, this remarkable rural retreat 'continuously under-mines the seductiveness of cosy English façades',[61] and is an ideal place in which to dramatise a nightmare that tests to the limit the resilience and initiative of its community.

The narrative of *Went the Day Well?* unfolds over the space of one weekend. This temporality, in which the characters experience rural life only briefly, was also used effectively in *The Halfway House* (1944, Basil Dearden) and *A Canterbury Tale* (1944, Michael Powell and Emeric Pressburger). Dearden's film uses a country inn and a Priestley-esque time inversion to enable a group of characters who have all reached an impasse in their lives to take stock and resolve their difficulties, aided by the inn's ghostly proprietors. In *A Canterbury Tale*, three troubled 'pilgrims', Alison

3. *The Halfway House* (1944, Basil Dearden), with Françoise Rosay. Canal+ Image UK.

Smith (Sheila Sim), a land girl, Bob Johnson (John Sweet), an American sergeant, and Peter Gibb (Dennis Price), an British sergeant, discover the revelatory powers of nature through Thomas Colpeper (Eric Portman), magistrate and local historian, during a weekend stay in the village of Chillingbourne. Its odd narrative about a mystery figure who throws glue on girls' hair at night baffled many critics who were otherwise captivated by its scenic qualities.[62] Although the audience are soon made aware of the identity of the 'glueman', the narrative begins to introduce a more complex set of ideas.

A Canterbury Tale was described by Powell years later as a 'crusade against materialism'[63] in its positing of urban worldliness (which the film associates with London, not Canterbury) against the spiritual values of the countryside. It has rightly been discussed in studies of wartime films as signifying heritage and history.[64] Certainly there are myriad references to the past, from Chaucer's pilgrims to the town hall's ducking stool, the bed at the Hand of Glory inn where Elizabeth I is supposed to have slept, to the crusading Colpeper Institute founded in 1886, and to Colpeper himself, his name redolent of the Elizabethan age. These motifs and the attractive surrounding countryside enable the three characters to discover within themselves a sense of heritage and history. The film includes all aspects of the traditional English village. In one comical scene the three 'detectives' ask a local for directions. It soon becomes apparent from the semi-deranged replies they receive that their chosen advisor is none other than the village idiot.

Yet A Canterbury Tale is not solely preoccupied with the past.[65] As the film's press book stated, the audience should be moved to think 'That is Britain, that is me'.[66] The self-conscious references within the narrative to Britain's glorious past suggest that without them 'the problematic present [is] unknowable'.[67] The portrait of Colpeper as a misogynistic heritage-wielding crusader is moderated by his optimism about changes in society caused by the war. Alison and Colpeper have a frank discussion during which Alison tells him that her fiancé's father, anxious to preserve the family name, disapproved of her because she worked in a department store. '"Good family", "shop girl" – rather dilapidated phrases for wartime,' Colpeper remarks. Alison sadly says, 'Not for Geoffrey's father. It would have taken an earthquake,' to which Colpeper replies, 'We're having one!' This brief engagement with the notion of social change signifies that the film does not sacrifice reality to romanticism but rather uses the countryside as a link between nostalgia and speculation about the future. Indeed the *Monthly Film Bulletin* praised the 'wide awareness of the historical background no less than the warlike background of today'.[68] The submersion in the summer-light haze of pastoral England is tempered in the last sequence by the contemporaneity of Canterbury, its levelled streets and relocated shops' signs, scaffolding-clad church towers and a cathedral made newly visible by bombing, a collective and unsentimental reminder that this is a country at war.

In Vichy France, *le retour à la terre* was the ideological basis of the Révolution Nationale. 'The earth does not lie,' Pétain proclaimed, 'it is the motherland itself. A field left fallow is a part of France that is dying.'[69] The peasant, he declared, 'has created it by his heroic patience, it is he who ensures its economic and spiritual stability'.[70] The idealisation of the peasantry and the land was not new, however. Daladier's Code de la famille, implemented in July 1939 and intended to combat the falling birth rate and stem rural decline, had also emphasised *le retour à la terre*.[71] The proliferation of rural literature in the Vichy era was merely an extension of an existing tradition: plays and novels from Daniel Halévy's *Visites aux paysans du centre* (1921) to Jean Giraudoux's *Pleins Pouvoirs* (1939) were pro-natalist and regretted the demise of solid peasant virtues. During the Vichy regime, Émile Guillamin's popular chronicle of country life *La Vie d'un simple*, originally published in 1904, was reprinted in 1943, and Henri Pourrat's Auvergnat novel *Vent de mars*, won the Prix Goncourt in 1941. Rural novels and histories were published, and earlier works were collected in anthologies or reprinted in their entirety.[72] Even the most analytical minds were moved by rural heritage. Marc Bloch wrote that while Vichy ideologues mistakenly attributed an 'ancient docility' to peasant societies, he believed that there was a great advantage in being 'rooted in the soil'.[73] Some of Pétain's rural rhetoric actually turned pre-war initiatives into legislation.

The Corporation Paysanne, established in 1940, aimed at creating *une classe paysanne*, an idea which had been promulgated by pro-syndicalists in the late 1930s.[74] Paradoxically, while Pétain desired a unified peasantry, regional prefects were directed to re-establish local customs, folklore and dialects.[75] Nevertheless, other reforms, including changes to land inheritance laws, housing improvement loans and state subsidies to halt the rural exodus outlasted the regime itself.[76] Legislation also recognised the superior resources of the peasants over urban dwellers. A law of 1941 permitted the sending of 'family parcels' from rural areas to urban relatives and friends; in 1942 alone, 13,500,000 *colis familiaux* passed through the postal system.[77] Those townspeople who had no rural connections went hungry, even with the supplement of black-market provisions.[78] By 1943, when all France was occupied, the daily ration had been reduced to 1200 calories a day, the lowest in any country in Western Europe except Italy.[79] When France was liberated, there was a general feeling among people in urban areas that the peasants were to blame for widespread malnutrition.[80] Meanwhile, Pétain's face appeared on over a million posters in public buildings endorsing the ideal family as rural smallholders, who made up 'La France eternelle'.[81]

Jean-Pierre Jeancolas argues that the cinema of the occupation valorised the provinces and vilified Paris.[82] The discourses within film of this era are more complex, however. For instance, the pastoral opening of *Le Corbeau*, where Dr Germain emerges from a farmhouse set among rolling hills, where he has been attending a childbirth case, belies the fact that this scene concerns abortion, one of the great 'evils', according to the Vichy regime. Another sequence in the script but not in the final film describes a 'very romantic image', a bonneted shepherdess sitting in lush pastures, who is revealed to be writing a letter thus: 'The stable boy is a liar'.[83] While wartime film certainly shifted from the pre-war focus on the urban working classes, the city was ever-present. Even films set in the country-side tend to disclose a dichotomous relationship with the capital and suggest an inextricable link between the two, of a longing to retain even a semblance of national solidarity in the face of searing social and political divisions. Film historians seeking elements of 'Vichy' in the cinema of 1940–44 interpret rural films as endorsements of the principles of Pétain's Révolution Nationale.[84] However, while the numerous adaptations of Pagnol's novels and plays clearly demonstrate the existence of a 'rural cinema' prior to Vichy, rural films made during Vichy also indicate a pre-occupation with the wider nation.

There were, of course, rural films that deliberately corresponded to Vichy ideology. In *Jeannou* (1943, Léon Poirier), a young woman (Michelle Alfa) living in an old village in Périgord rebels against a predictable future and goes to Paris. After becoming pregnant, she returns home, where her father consents to her marriage to a local man. The Vichyite project of the film, namely the return of the prodigal, is quite deliberate and reflects the concerns of the director, who also wrote the screenplay.[85] *Monsieur de Lourdines* (1943) has a similar theme. It was directed by Pétain's step-son Pierre de Hérain, and is based on Alphonse de Châteaubriant's novel, published in 1911. In the 1840's, Anthime (Raymond Rouleau), the son and heir to a country estate in Poitou, tires of the country and goes to Paris, where he soon squanders the family fortune. His scorn for his father's land turns to guilt as his mother becomes fatally ill after she learns of his profligacy. He returns to the countryside he formerly despised, where his remorse is twice rewarded by betrothal to a childhood friend and reconciliation with his father. The film's affirmation of *famille* and *patrie*, two key components of Vichy ideology, has been noted by film historians.[86]

Rural cinema continued to celebrate pastoral life but also suggested that Paris was culturally and psychologically significant. Marcel Pagnol's *La Fille du puisatier* was the first film to be made in Vichy after the Armistice in 1940. Shot in Provençe, its central characters belong to the *artisanat rural* typical of Pagnol's populist dramas. Patricia Amoretti (Josette Day) has been educated in a Paris convent and wears Parisian clothes, much to the pride of her father, the well-digger Pascal (Raimu). However, she meets and falls in love with Jacques Mazel (Georges Grey), the son of a bourgeois family. Following his conscription, she discovers she is pregnant, but her father's request for help from the Mazels is refused. Pascal sends Patricia to her aunt, also a 'fallen woman', to have the baby. Jacques is later reported killed in action, and the Mazel family, now acknowledging their dead son's child, seek a reconciliation. When Jacques returns alive and well, the families unite and gather round a wireless set to hear Pétain's broadcast of 17 June, suggesting that the announcement of the Armistice has overcome their differences.[87] Much of the film is not specific to Vichy ideology, however; *paysan–* bourgeois conflict and illegitimate pregnancy were pre-war themes.[88] As Evelyn Ehrlich writes, 'the film is no more Pétainist than any of Pagnol's other films, which similarly glorify the peasantry and the "petits métiers"'.[89] Nevertheless, in its celebration of *la France profonde*, the references to Paris give it a contemporaneous feel.

A more complex example of rural imagery is Jacques Becker's *Goupi Mains Rouges* (1943), an unsentimentalised and humorous portrait of peasant life. Adapted by Pierre Very from his novel,[90] it depicts an eccentric farming family in the Charente. It is set in 1920, but its array of stereo-typical motifs which epitomise urban attitudes towards the peasantry would have resonated with wartime audiences. Indeed the collaborationist newspaper *Je suis partout* found in it 'a wealth of recognisable characters'.[91] The Goupi family is hierarchical, prone to hoarding, obsessed by the farm and some treasure hidden long ago by the elder of the family, as idiosyn-cratic as the *locataires* of *L'Assassin habite au 21*. The 12-strong clan represent the trades, the professions and the history of France, and include a centenarian war veteran who seems destined to die with the secret of the 'magot' intact, a despotic female farm manager, a farmer, a carpenter,

a retired gendarme, a bistrot proprietor and an ex-colonial. The epony-
mous Mains Rouges is the descendant of a *sans culotte* who 'dipped his hands
in Marie-Antoinette's blood'.[92] The clan is divided and quarrelsome until
a murder forces them together in a unified stance, when Mes Sous insists
that 'the Goupis' business stays the Goupis' business'. The family could
therefore be seen as a microcosm of rural French society, close-knit and
patriarchal.[93]

The positive critical response towards *Goupi Mains Rouges* indicates that,
excepting Pagnol, previous *drames paysans* had been less effective. The cruel
Tisane (Germaine Kerjean), who runs the farm and doles out the wages to
the workers, was recognised by one newspaper to be 'a might brutal, as one
still finds in some areas of France'.[94] The film refers to a dark side of country
life, the sinister forest folklore, privy only to the trapper and *sorcier* Mains
Rouges (Fernand Ledoux), who prefers to live by the woods and the river
trapping animals and catching fish. His cabin walls are hung with stuffed
eagles, bats and owls, and its shelves filled with jars containing unidentifiable
small animals. This 'woodland culture' suggests that an alternative rural
romanticism is at work, one which coincides with Vichy's emphasis on
regional folklore. Although the Musée des Arts et Traditions Populaires
(ATP) was a legacy of the Popular Front,[95] Vichy supported the revival of
local culture, and by 1942 the Société du Folklore Français noted that its
membership had expanded.[96] Given his esoteric interests, Mains Rouges
proves to be the most perceptive of the characters, which is tacitly suggested
by his proximity to this other 'natural' world.

Conversely, Goupi 'Monsieur' represents the urban world. Removed as
a child from the family by his unhappy mother, he works in a Parisian
department store, the arch symbol of modernity and consumerism. He has
been invited back to the family home by his scheming father, Mes Sous
(Arthur Devère), who plans to marry him to his cousin Muguet (Blanchette
Brunoy) to ensure *remembrement*, that the land remains intact. The novel
and the film refer to the return of the prodigal son, as in both the Goupis'
anticipation of his arrival coincides with the imminent birth of a calf. Yet
he proves to be far from the urbane gentleman they were expecting. Mains
Rouges finds Monsieur easy prey for his eerie tales of local murders as
they drive to the farm, and he appears oblivious to the real reason for his
summons. In the novel he is delineated as a much more sophisticated
character. In it he is not only aware of and unperturbed by the marriage
plans, but also has a long-standing mistress in Paris, Lucette. 'There are
many such associations like that in Paris,' he tells Muguet when he finds

her reading a letter from Lucette.[97] The novel establishes a contrast between Muguet's unworldliness and Lucette's materialism which is absent from the film, thus removing the suggestion of Paris as morally delinquent. The ingenuousness of the film's Monsieur imputes a certain vulnerability to the notion of being 'Parisian'. The antithesis of the robust *paysan*, he is slender, sports a fine moustache, wears gloves and carries a cane, a dandy entirely out of place in this rough terrain. When later Mes Sous finds that he is not the owner of the *grand magasin* as they believed, but merely an employee in the tie department, he is mockingly renamed Goupi 'Cravate'.

Nevertheless, their city guest gives the Goupis a welcome status, and when the local teacher pays a call in order to reminisce about his only visit to Paris, Monsieur is brought forth as the one man who can converse with him on the subject. Monsieur delivers an elegiac satire in response to the teacher's gushing recollections of 'the Opéra … the boulevards … the Métropolitan'. The city, explains Monsieur, is the nation because it is filled with provincials. 'Paris – it's you! … the Provençaux, the Charentais, the Normands, who make Paris what it is, that's to say a bouquet in which each province is a flower!' Significantly, this dialogue is not in the novel, which mentions only that the teacher 'asked a thousand questions about the city'.[98] The suggestion that Paris is a city defined by its provincial émigrés is a potent reminder that it is not an isolated space, but embraces all France, from North to South.

Finally, despite allusions to a darker ruralism, the audience is reminded of the charm of the open countryside through Monsieur's increasing understanding of its beauty. 'How lovely your country is,' he tells Muguet. *Goupi Mains Rouges* ends in a celebration of the lush landscape, but the film has also shown its unromantic alternative as the locus of the natural world. Although the remote setting has been interpreted as typical of Vichy cinema's hermeticism,[99] Paris, though absent, is vividly evoked by dialogue which stresses its all-pervasive presence, and Monsieur embodies the vulnerability of the capital in its most difficult hour. In August 1945, *Film français* wrote that 'everyone remembers *Goupi Mains Rouges* and the pleasure we felt during the occupation in seeing a film that was also fully French'.[100] This 'fully French' film depicting a small corner of the rural Southwest also expresses an ambivalent and complex relationship with the capital which is significantly altered from that described in the original novel. Even at liberation, when Paris once again could be celebrated as the heart of the nation, rural France did not withdraw from cinema screens. As we shall see in the next chapter, it was explored with renewed vigour in literature and film.

Though much inter-war idealisation of the countryside was complemented by a critique of the town, urban Britain was also romanticised by writers and film-makers. In *English Journey* (1934), J.B. Priestley juxtaposed rural tradition and urban progress, praising the Cotswolds as the largest 'tract of the beautiful old England still unspoilt', and finding in Birmingham 'an English provincial city that has the air and dignity that a great city should have'.[101] Robert Flaherty's documentary *Industrial Britain* (1934) created an 'urban pastoralism' in his painterly shots of black chimneys, wet roofs, factories and machinery which evoked the working habitat of Britain's industrial labourers. *Coalface* (1936, Alberto Cavalcanti) showed that mining was both a socially useful and dignified endeavour. Documentary films demonstrated above all that there was a cinematic 'poetry' within urban industrial Britain that represented national strength just as effectively as its pastoral landscapes.

The war brought an added intensity to urban Britain. Continual movements of the population affected much of the countryside, as we have seen, but also its towns and cities as Britain became 'a nation of migrants'.[102] Yet with the onset of the Blitz, London became the nucleus of the nation. Although many towns and cities suffered huge devastation, notably Coventry, feature films rarely showed the provinces. Exceptionally, *A Canterbury Tale* shows Canterbury's city centre as unrecognisable, having been devastated by three heavy air-raids in mid-1942. When Alison walks along the streets, she looks at the retailers' signs, which serve as poignant reminders of where their shops had once been. Despite damage to the provinces, the perception of the Blitz was that it was very much London's ordeal. At its height, St Paul's Cathedral became the icon of national resilience when it withstood bombing on the night of 29 December 1940, apparently glowing while the City was engulfed by flames around it.[103] In *Millions Like Us* (1943), one of three key shots designed to establish the mood of the nation at war shows the silhouette of the Cathedral only just visible through the debris and smoke of a bomb-site. It portentously introduces the scene where Celia (Patricia Roc) announces that she must attend an interview for the call-up, an event which will change her life. Although St Paul's was actually used more in post-war film, London featured in many narratives, its mainline stations the departure points for people en route to a new life or an uncertain future in *In Which We Serve* (1942, Noel Coward and David Lean), *The Gentle Sex* (1943, Leslie Howard and Maurice Elvey) and *The Way Ahead* (1944, Carol Reed). Britain's history, its democratic institutions and its national heroes were on display in *The Young Mr Pitt* (1942, Carol Reed), in which

William Pitt's authority and thus the strength of the nation is rooted in Downing Street and in Parliament.

In wartime films, London was visualised as 'knowable communities',[104] in complete contrast to French films set in Paris, whose settings are almost always unrecognisable. Ealing's *The Bells Go Down* (1943, Basil Dearden) is a tribute to both the Auxiliary Fire Service and the London Fire Brigade,[105] and focuses on a small neighbourhood in the East End. Dearden's films tend to convey two themes, community and public service,[106] and *The Bells Go Down* exemplifies both. It is in many ways comparable with Humphrey Jennings's documentary-drama for the Crown Film Unit *Fires were Started,* which appeared just before Ealing's film in April 1943. Indeed both producers were keenly aware of the other's film.[107] *Fires Were Started* was unanimously praised by the critics, but it owed much of its success to its narrative, which conveyed a human element to the impressively re-constructed firefighting scenes. The strength of *The Bells Go Down* is precisely its deeper engagement with the characters which make up the community, in particular Tommy Trinder, who plays the Cockney Tommy Turk.

The film opens with a shot of Petticoat Lane market, and the narrator saying, 'In the East End they say London isn't a town, it's a group of villages. This is the story of one of those villages, a community bounded by a few streets with its own market place, its church, its shops, its police station, its fire brigade.' From this neighbourhood, a group of men volunteer as auxiliary firemen, and supervising their progress are two professional firemen, Ted Robbins (James Mason) and District Fire Officer MacFarlane (Finlay Currie). Their strict code of discipline enables the unwieldy group to emerge twelve months later as an efficient team who confidently tackle the endless fires of the Blitz. The formation of a 'people's army' from a disparate collection of individuals in *The Bells Go Down* compares with the proficient, dedicated platoon which emerges in *The Way Ahead* from an unpromising assortment of men. Whereas the conscripts of Reed's film experience combat in North Africa, the firefighting team of *The Bells Go Down* wage a war on the home front.

In wartime films, London was often represented by the East End and its inhabitants. Tommy Trinder's cockney persona was therefore a key element in the depiction of the community in *The Bells Go Down*. Although *Fires Were Started* had a protagonist, writer and AFS member William Sansom, there was clearly no substitute for a genuine actor. As the *Evening Standard* critic wrote, 'professional actors are almost always more entertaining than their real-life prototypes'.[108] Much praise had been given to the cockneys during the Blitz, and officialdom appeared to rely on their apparently un-failing spirit and optimism. *Picture Post*'s controversial cover for a special 'East End at War' issue in September 1940 showed a crying woman holding a crying child and demonstrated, according to the editorial, 'that real mixture of fatalism and perkiness which has come to be known as "Cockney"'.[109] A reader from Eire responded, commenting that 'it rests with people like the East Enders to win or lose the war'.[110] The cockney was seen as the repository of unique characteristics: a breezy wit, an intractability and a mild disrespect for authority which was tempered by good-hearted patriotism. The urban community evoked by the cockney was unique, 'a community of the poor, but of a distinctly conservative and indigenous kind'.[111] In wartime, when the nation centred on London, the cockney became both indispensable to and representative of the British character. *The Bells Go Down* uses the mildly anarchic character of Tommy Turk to demon-strate the diverse but ultimately unified nature of the community and of Britain.

Michael Balcon, Ealing's head of production, was clearly concerned that the professionalism of the London Fire Brigade was not compromised by Trinder's performance. 'To me it is absolutely essential,' he wrote to his producer, 'that parallel with the light-hearted scenes of licking the AFS into shape there should be scenes of the LFB going into action and the impression somehow given that the AFS men despite themselves are learning by precept and example how firemen should behave'.[112] Indeed Trinder's presence does make the film problematical in defining its genre, although the publicity material avoided confusion by referring to it as a 'comedy-drama'.[113] The *News Chronicle* asked whether the 'Trinder humour…lends itself to seriousness in such circumstances'. Yet as the 'wisecracking Cockney…whose sense of humour never lets him down,' as the *News Chronicle* saw him, Tommy is important if only for his fallibility.[114] While *Fires were Started* projected the epic nature of the fireman's battle, the pres-ence of less fearless characters merely underlined that 'for most people the war was lived on a less exalted level'.[115] Nevertheless the film's humorous tone makes it all the more shocking when Tommy is killed in the penulti-mate scene along with Chief MacFarlane, whom he pulls to safety seconds before. 'A magnificent pictorial moment,' wrote the *Sunday Times*.[116]

The striking aspect of the film is its use of actual footage of London on fire. In September 1940, at the height of the Blitz, the MOI ordered that panning shots 'must start from an undamaged building and must conclude on an undamaged building and [they] must not linger on damaged buildings'.[117] The images in *The Bells Go Down* reflect the subsequent relaxation of this regulation as the skylines of Britain's cities became increasingly ravaged. By 1943, it was accepted that urban devastation was a part of everyday life. Throughout the year, the *Sunday Times* published sketches of 'Bombed London', showing the destruction to churches and monuments but also the architectural treasures which were now revealed.[118] After an air-raid, the indomitable Londoners are shown carrying on with their daily tasks, and the milkman delivers to non-existent doorsteps, a familiar image of Blitz 'cheeriness'. In the final scene the camera cranes upwards through the roof of the bombed church and out to the bustling market where the traders' stalls are surrounded by piles of rubble. *The Bells Go Down* thus ends with a firm reminder of the community and its resilience. 'A picture of the people and for the people,' wrote the *Daily Mail*.[119] The aim of the film was typically Ealing in style, and it is evident from the available documentation that by focusing on a microcosm of the city Balcon wished to represent the experience of London.[120] The final shot of the market is followed by 'The End' behind which a Union Jack, Ealing's wartime motif, flutters, thus identifying the crowds with London and London with Britain.

In 1945, the community of *Waterloo Road* (Sidney Gilliat) presented another side to life on the home front, the social disruption caused by the

4. *The Bells Go Down* (1943, Basil Dearden), with Tommy Trinder. Canal+ Image UK.

war. Though the most lucrative of Launder and Gilliat's wartime films,[121] it has not received the scholarly attention that it deserves. *Waterloo Road* is interesting for its recreation of a south London locale, its exploration of female sexuality, the family, returning soldiers and references to an underworld which featured in so many post-war films. When soldier Jim Colter (John Mills) breaks camp in order to discover the truth behind rumours of his wife's infidelity,[122] his pursuit of her requires a thorough tour of Waterloo Road. Here are the comforting features of *The Bells Go Down*, the bustling street market, the friendly pub and the communal air-raid shelter. In Waterloo Road there is also a palais-de-dance, 'The Alcazar', and a seedy-looking pin-table saloon, 'The Lucky Star', which is patronised by wastrels and local thugs. The community is laid bare, exposing its respectability and its sleaziness. Unlike many wartime films, such as *Millions Like Us* and *The Way Ahead*, which necessarily embrace a cross-section of society, *Waterloo Road* focuses almost entirely on the working classes, apart from Alastair Sim, who plays the local doctor and significantly the 'detached' observer.

While *The Bells Go Down*, in keeping with war culture, used images of the community to represent the nation, *Waterloo Road*, made two years later when victory was assured, is an exploration of the neighbourhood itself. Frank Launder recalled that Val Valentine's story was inspired by an un-expected late-night stop in the air-raid shelters beneath Waterloo railway station, where he encountered a mass of people sleeping.[123] The *Times* considered that *Waterloo Road* was superior to *Millions Like Us* because 'the protagonists and their actions spring naturally from their environment and are not manoeuvred to serve a propagandist end'.[124] Other contemporary press reports perceived the film as a welcome document of London life rather than propaganda. Richard Winnington, the discriminating critic of the *News Chronicle* found the film 'a fascinating portrait of a London locality. No soft music, but the harsh rattle of trains over the viaduct, the clamour of the street market, the wailing of sirens and the crash of bombs accompany this war-time love story.'[125]

Waterloo Station, which has an economic and functional link with the community and employs several members of the Colter family, is established early on as a key point of departure for servicemen, the platforms crowded with soldiers and sailors as trains constantly arrive and depart. The scene then changes to a nearby street market milling with people, American soldiers among them, and the sound of a barrel organ as the sagacious Dr Montgomery emerges from his surgery. 'Here in London,' he says, walking along the Blitzed streets, 'the people waged a whole campaign and won it!' Then there is a flashback to the winter of 1940–41. The flashback was necessary at the time, as there had been no air-raids for a year and audiences could date a film 'within a particular three months'.[126] Nevertheless, when the film was released the 'Little Blitz' was well underway, so the regular trips to the air-raid shelters and the wail of sirens, warning of attack by V1 and V2 rockets, were once again topical. The 'campaign' however is more pertinent to audiences of 1945, who had not only survived the Blitz but also faced the lengthy process of social realignment in the post-war world.

Waterloo Road is a precursor to what Robert Murphy has called the post-war 'spiv cycle',[127] in which Ted Purvis (Stewart Granger) has avoided conscription with a fake medical certificate and devotes his time to philandering. The 'spiv' was an urban creature who by 1946 'stood for London'.[128] Purvis, flashily dressed and replete with illicitly earned cash, represents the community's 'low-life'. In his flat above 'The Lucky Star', Purvis attempts to seduce Tilly Colter while an air-raid is underway, his 'canoodling' punctuated by shots of fire engines and burning buildings outside. Suddenly, Jim Colter appears, and after a prolonged fight Purvis is beaten. *Waterloo Road* suggests that the future for which decent servicemen had sacrificed their domestic security was being compromised through the irresponsibility of a cavalier few. *Kinematograph Weekly* wrote that it was 'a warm and exuberant, if not profound slice of war-time working-class life' and, predicting the film's audience, added in typical style, 'how the masses love to see themselves'.[129] Yet London's working class, which film-makers had believed to be essential to the loyal, consensual community they had created was to be undermined by the appearance in post-war film of a semi-underworld from which the 'gangster' emerged as a central character.

The Vichy regime removed itself from the metropolis and put its ideological and political emphasis firmly on the land. The cultural status of Vichy was negligible compared to the capital, however. 'Paris,' writes Philippe Burrin, 'which had been France's center through monarchy and revolution, was dethroned by a city previously noted chiefly for its medicinal hot springs'.[130] Despite his provincial base, Pétain saw Paris as central to the Vichy regime, and mindful that Article 3 of the Armistice agreement confirmed the capital as the political centre of the country, in July 1940 he requested that he be allowed to return. However, the Germans clearly coveted their stylish new headquarters, and Ribbentrop ordered the German authorities to treat the issue 'in a dilatory fashion'.[131] While in much of Occupied France the majority of people had hardly any contact with the Germans at all, for Paris, as Sartre wrote in 1946, occupation was part of *la vie quotidienne*.[132] For four years the Germans lived among the Parisians, clearly visible yet blending in with the anonymity of city life. Paris was also marked through those who were absent, the relatives and friends who were prisoners, or had been arrested, deported or shot. Paris, as Sartre saw it, was a city of 'presence' and 'absence'.[133]

The occupiers set in motion a modernist, urban-orientated ideology which directly opposed Vichy's rural, *arrièriste* philosophy. Radio Paris presented a programme of songs, variety acts and classical concerts that, combined with frequent reminders of the benefits of working in modern Germany, offered an alternative to the 'sleepy reactionary pastoral vision of the Vichy propaganda'.[134] As most of the country's film producers were based in Paris, where both resources and studios were available, it was the most frequently chosen urban location. There was a considerable difference from pre-war cinema, however. In films made during the Popular Front era, Paris and the *banlieue* were shown as the habitats of their proletarian heroes. Even in *Pépé le Moko* (1937, Julien Duvivier), set in Algiers, Paris is still a 'desired object' and a point of reference for Pépé (Jean Gabin).[135] Conversely, films made in Paris during the occupation were notable for an absence of positive images of the working classes.[136] They disclosed neither a political positioning nor a sense of time, but favoured, as we have seen, a '*contemporain vague*' by which *policiers*, musicals, comedies, and historical and escapist dramas not only avoided direct reference to the present but also contributed to a 'cinéma d'evasion'.[137]

The already popular Georges Simenon was the most filmed author of the occupation.[138] Nine of his books were adapted, including *La Voyageur de la Toussaint* (1942, Louis Daquin) and *Cécile est morte* (1943, Maurice Tourneur), which both begin in Paris and in recognisably 'Maigret' fashion, shift to a provincial locale. There were two adaptations of Stanislas-André Steeman's detective stories featuring Inspector Wenceslaus, *Le Dernier de six* (1941, Georges Lacombe) and *L'Assassin habite au 21* (1942, Henri-Georges Clouzot), both with Parisian settings. The musical themes in *Montmartre sur seine* (1941, Georges Lacombe), starring Edith Piaf, *Mademoiselle Swing* (1941, Richard Pottier), and *Romance de Paris* (1941, Jean Boyer) were equally escapist. The historical and biographical film genre comprised 16 per cent of production during the occupation, and allowed the past glories of France to be rekindled. *La Nuit fantastique* (1941), Marcel L'Herbier's tribute to film pioneer Georges Meliès, was set in a carefully reconstructed Les Halles, where a young woman enveloped in white regularly materialises in front of a porter's eyes. Adaptations of novels which romanticised Paris abounded, from Balzac's *Duchesse de Langeais* (1941, Jacques de Baroncelli) to Eugène Sue's *Les Mystères de Paris* (1943, Jacques de Baroncelli), while Zola's *Au Bonheur des Dames* (1943, André Cayatte) celebrates the Belle Époque and the icon of urban capitalism, the department store. Yet where British films used the past to elicit clearly identifiable historical parallels in which Britain played a victorious role, French historical films, which invariably referred to Paris, were inclined to be evasive. There was thus a marked absence of films that dealt with a recognisable and contemporary Paris. Unlike the 'realist aesthetic' of British cinema, which welded documentary and fiction by using exterior shots and actuality footage, French film of the period was distinctive in its almost universal use of studio sets.

Films featuring contemporary Paris which were not categorised as musicals, detective thrillers or melodramas were rare. An exception is *Falbalas* (1944, Jacques Becker), set in the world of *haute couture*, which, writes Dominique Veillon, was 'the heart and the mirror of France'.[139] Becker, moving rapidly from *les paysans* of *Goupi Mains Rouges*, wished to make a very different film about Paris. Becker was familiar with the world of *couture*, as his mother had not only worked in a *maison* as a young woman but had opened her own establishment in Paris.[140] The *maison de couture* was of course an ambiguous setting in occupation Paris because of patronage by German officers who bought gowns for their wives. Yet *haute couture* thrived under the occupation principally because of its French clientele, which demonstrated the unabated self-indulgence of members of the bourgeoisie.[141] The *couturiers* who ministered to them claimed that they were saving the 'honour' and 'style' of Paris.[142] *Falbalas*, an expensive film with lavish gowns and rich decor, is a fantasy about a philandering *haute couturier* (Raymond Rouleau) who falls in love with a rich young woman (Micheline Presle) who resembles one of his mannequins. At the end, having ruined the lives of both the woman and her fiancé, he falls to his death with the mannequin.

There are significant touches of realism in the film that rescue it from being 'escapist'. Although the *maison* is described by Noël Burch and Geneviève Sellier as 'a true family', there is a duality in this family which makes it clear that its success is contingent on the labour of others.[143] Becker, like Jean Renoir, whom he had assisted for six years before the war, was interested in making films about ordinary workers. This concern, added to the minutiae of characterisation, reminds the audience that behind the salon's plush doors is a pool of seamstresses, their heads bent over their sewing machines. It is not an altogether harmonious atmosphere, for when one of the girls grumbles that she should be getting overtime payment, she is sharply told to go and see the patron about her complaint. The most significant sequence of the film is a rare glimpse of Paris outdoors, the near-empty grands boulevards and the employees, models and machinists riding bicycles along the streets. This is the only cinematic reference during the occupation to the ubiquitous *vélo,* widely used by petrol-rationed Parisians, bourgeois and *ouvrier* alike.

Film français, clearly unfazed by the fantasy element of the film, wrote that it was 'the visual documentation of the life of a great fashion house'.[144] As the lavish illustrations in its press book show, the producers were aiming at audiences who wanted to see fashion and glamour, and not the toil behind its creation.[145] In the post-war world, the export of *haute couture* was vital to the economic survival of France, and the US, which had developed its own fashion industry in the interim, was needed as a major customer.[146] Significantly, at liberation none of the 55 *couturiers* examined by the *comités d'épuration* were involved in *haute couture.*[147] The film's depiction of the machinists nevertheless tempers the exclusivity of this world, and suggests that for the vast majority of people *la vie quotidienne* meant hard work, not indulgence. The glimpse of the girls mounting their bicycles and riding though the streets is a reminder that the film, as Micheline Presle recalled, was made in the early summer of 1944,[148] a time of growing optimism that Paris would shortly be once again the official capital of France.

The greatest example of the imagery of Paris was *Les Enfants du paradis* (Marcel Carné, 1945), an incarnation of nineteenth-century popular theatre, the only unreserved celebration of the city in the cinema of the occupation. In 1953, Georges Sadoul wrote, '*Les Enfants du paradis* was the accomplishment of perfection for the French cinema; much more than a step forward, it was an end rather than a beginning'.[149] Indeed the production and eventual release of the film bridged the period between occupation and liberation, from August 1943, when shooting started at the Victorine Studios in Nice, to its gala premiere in Paris in March 1945. Carné appears to have deliberately slowed down the production on hearing of the Allied landings in Normandy, when the film was almost complete.[150] Ultimately this strategy guaranteed its greater impact in the context of liberation.

Despite its historical setting, or indeed because of it, the film has been scrutinised for a resistance sub-text thought to be embodied and articulated through the 'free spirit' Garance (Arletty) in her only 'enigmatic' role. Her remark, 'I adore that…freedom,' on being exonerated from stealing a pocket-watch, has been interpreted as the underlying 'resistant' message of the film. There is a more powerful suggestion however of an attachment to the city which, as discussed earlier, had often been alluded to in rural cinema. Five years later, Garance, now the mistress of Comte de Monterey, has travelled widely in Europe and even to India. She tells her ex-lover Frédérick Lemaître (Pierre Brasseur) that Scotland is beautiful but 'it's far away. Paris is the only place I love.' There is only a single allusion to the provinces, and that is one of disdain when the master criminal Lacenaire (Marcel Herrand) has murdered Comte de Monterey (Louis Salou). Advising his acolyte to escape quickly, Lacenaire explains that he must stay: 'After all, a man like myself cannot decently be expected to run the risk of being executed by a provincial hangman. Absolutely not.' Even the criminal fraternity have more standing in Paris than in the countryside.

Yet *Les Enfants du paradis* does not offer up an idealistically homogeneous world to the audience. The whole film can be read as a metaphor for a city emerging from four years of captivity in which anxieties about Paris and the nation are discernible. The Boulevard du crime is rife with murder and theft, and the Rouge Gorge inn a sordid haunt of the local 'low-life'. The theatre itself is riven with resentment. As the Funambules manager tells Lemaître, 'you cannot conceive how my theatre is torn by hatred and jealousy'. As if to transpose this danger onto the stage, Lemaître later plays Robert Macaire, a kind of 'people's villain'. Ultimately *Les Enfants du paradis* reasserts the status of Paris with all its faults, and the vitality of the crowd dominates the final impression of the film.

The focus on the capital, on the popular urban theatre and its audiences, particularly the *ouvriers* who occupy the 'gods', firmly opposes the provincially orientated ideology of Vichy, which glorified the peasantry and the countryside. Paradoxically Carné's production inverts that ethos by visualising a romanticised city, 'gilded by the nostalgic imagination of Parisians exiled in the countryside'.[151] It firmly reinstates the urban working class, which had been stripped of its positive image of Carné's pre-war films. Jill Forbes rightly argues that the film 'contributes to a nationalist project', but also suggests that it was primarily intended to 'beat the Americans at their own game'.[152] The film also offers domestic audiences a celebratory end to occupation and a timely reassertion of national self-esteem. In satisfying the psychological needs of the nation, the film is consonant with Sadoul's assessment, yet also it signifies the dramatic return of Paris as a recognisable urban space, a city which would once more provide a rich backdrop to much of the French cinema of the post-war era.[153]

British and French cinema of the wartime period is notable for its contrasts between rural and urban culture. The ways in which these images are expressed indicate the very distinct historical and political circumstances in which the films were produced. In Britain, where the emphasis was on a national 'community', the rural metaphor was used in a number of films to emphasise 'why we fight'. According to *The Lion Has Wings*, land and freedom were synonymous in the defence of Britain. An invasion of England, which was still feasible during the making of *Went the Day Well?*, was all the more shocking when inflicted on a picturesque English village, but the villagers who represent the wider nation proved more than capable of a robust defence. The hillsides of rural England, as shown in *A Canterbury Tale* and *Millions Like Us* also provided abstract settings for the contemplation, but not the resolution, of problems about the post-war world. The rural imagery of wartime film was ultimately conservative and untroubling, and as an idealised slice of British culture it confirmed the historical polarisation of town and country.

In France the countryside was a more difficult proposition for film-makers. The attention lavished on the land and the peasantry by the Vichy regime presented producers with an ideological dimension to rural representations on screen. Some film-makers openly endorsed Vichyite policies and celebrated *le retour à la terre* and its attendant anti-urban sentiments in examples like *Monsieur de Lourdines* and *Jeannou*. Cultural expressions of the city–country conflict were certainly not new, because of the historical proximity of town and country, and were topical because of the tensions between townspeople and peasantry, but rural films made in the context of the occupation had an added intensity. Rural cinema is striking for its preoccupation with Paris. In *Goupi Mains Rouges,* therefore, the apparent cultural conflict between rural Charente and Paris, as expressed in the Goupis and their city relative, permits a tacit acknowledgement of French identity, regional yet national.

During the occupation, in a captive and divided France, references to the exterior and specifically to its cultural centre, Paris, were a way of retaining some sense of unity. While Paris is implicitly present in rural films, its contemporaneity is absent in others which are actually set in the city. While British film-makers used recognisable parts of London, peopled by characters who evoked aspects of nationhood, as in *The Bells Go Down* and *Waterloo Road*, Paris merely acted as a city background, a 'blurred image' rather than a recognisable space.[154] The use of evasive genres and the prevalence of studio sets compounded that sense of unreality. The cyclists in *Falbalas* provide therefore a vivid record of Paris under the occupation. British films which referred to the past invariably centred on London and were able to articulate historical parallels. In *Young Mr Pitt*, William Pitt leads the country in a protracted but victorious defence against Napoleon's aggrandisement in an obvious analogy with Hitler's Germany. The film also contains pertinent references to France. 'Nations,' says Pitt after Napoleon's seizure of power, 'are never split by victory – only by defeat'. French historical films, which inevitably referred to Paris, a truly divided city, do not articulate notions of victory or defeat, but rather the glory of past eras. Despite the contrasts in representation in the cinema of both countries, urbanness was symbolised by their capital cities, which, as we shall see, would receive even greater emphasis in the cinema of the post-war world.

4

Countryside, City and Region in Post-war Film

The war may have altered the appearance of the British and French countryside, but the underlying ideologies had remained much the same. Propaganda had conceptualised Britain as an unchanging vista of sunny wheatfields and picturesque villages, in an all-encompassing Southern English pastoral, even though the ploughing of 27 million acres of grassland and marshes had transformed the landscape.[1] This chapter will show how post-war rural films confirmed that the rural myth belonged to wartime culture and that life in an agrarian community could be deeply unromantic. Film-makers also rediscovered the regions and rural hinterlands which had been neglected in wartime cinema, and thus sought to establish a national 'whole'. Individual national identities were re-asserted through explorations of Welsh, Scottish and Irish culture, in films that explored old, unworldly communities. However, rural cinema soon retreated to the past. Despite the critics' perception of 'costume drama' as evading contemporary realities, historical films dealt effectively with Britain's post-war rural politics. They approached questions of universal accessibility to the land and its management through a nineteenth-century perspective. Films were concerned with people, and raised questions about landowners' responsibilities to their tenant communities in an era when the notions of autocracy and democracy were sharply defined. In the context of the conflictual relationship between master and tenant, Britain's rural cinema suggested that the notion of the land as 'heritage for all', as the 1942 Scott Report proposed, was in fact deeply problematic.[2]

In France, the ideological emphasis was on the peasantry, which was promoted by Vichy as the backbone of the nation. In a country where the attachment to the land was deeply embedded in the national psyche, rural films had an added significance. Between 1945 and 1951, the French industry produced 47 rural films,[3] compared to 30 made during the occupation. Film-makers in post-war France sought, as did British film-makers, to uncover the regions. Regional films that expressed the cultural and social distinctiveness of France were critical in shoring up national identity after the divisive years of occupation. Rural film also attempted to 'realign' a severely dislocated population by showing that rural and urban were fundamentally incompatible. The rural–urban conflict was at its height in the immediate post-war years when urban populations were beleaguered by food shortages and the peasantry were regarded as 'sordid, egotistical grabbers'.[4] The provinces and the city remained linked, as they had done in films during the occupation, but the differences were more sharply etched, suggesting that urban and rural dwellers should confine themselves to their own spheres.

The city in British and French cinema of the post-war years was very much a place of the present. Film-makers visualised modern urban Britain as London, in which cameramen operating against a background of war detritus captured a contemporaneity admired by the critics for its contribution to 'realist' cinema. Urban vistas were also enjoyed by cinemagoers, who were able to watch a site of their recent history. But by mid-1947 'film noir' was projecting visions of a criminal community belonging to the urban underworld. This unpalatable aspect of city life alienated critics and even alarmed the new government, which questioned the prevalence of such adverse representations of a progressive new Britain. Yet these 'morbid burrowings'[5] were tempered by the very popular urban milieu created by Herbert Wilcox, evoking sophistication, wealth and glamour. These films threw off wartime communality in favour of the individual.

French film-makers, now free to depict urban spaces, invariably chose Paris. Paris, untouched by bombing, was now ubiquitous on screen while during the occupation its real streets had rarely been seen. Now that the occupiers had gone, the depiction of ordinary communities, obscured by history, fantasy and other escapist genres during the occupation, was now possible. Yet, as Alberto Cavalcanti wrote following a visit to Paris, 'The Parisians have throughout the occupation presented a strange mixture of strength and weakness, heroism, cupidity, treachery, resistance, apathy'.[6] Films revealed this 'strange mixture' of contradictory elements in the neighbour-hood, through portrayals of collaborators, resisters, shopkeepers and ordinary workers. Representations of Paris and its people also revealed a darker side in film noir, which suggested the underlying uncertainties of a nation still raw from the troublesome years of occupation.

In post-war Britain, the rural myth was far from obsolete. Rather than being manipulated to elicit patriotic feeling, it was invoked in response to change in the countryside, 'the eclipse of the rural world'.[7] Some rural writing reflected both nostalgia for an almost mythical past and the reality of post-war rural Britain. *Larkrise to Candleford*, Flora Thompson's trilogy of memoirs of her childhood in Victorian Oxfordshire, has been enduringly popular since its publication in 1945.[8] Mollie Panter-Downes's novel *One Fine Day*, published in 1947, juxtaposes inevitable social change with the eternal quality of the English pastoral. Its middle-class protagonist Laura surveys the detritus of the recent war, coils of barbed wire, sandbags and a bombed cottage, and realises that her 'easier sort of life has come to an end'.[9] In contrast, Angela Thirkell's lament for the rural gentry in her 'Barsetshire' novels is motivated more by resentment at the election of a Labour government than by nostalgia.[10]

The use of rural imagery in film was also changing as the land became the locus of a discourse pitting the individual against the needs of the community. Post-war films that used rural imagery demonstrated the enduring link between war and pastoralism. *Frieda* (1947, Basil Dearden), based on Ronald Millar's play,[11] begins in April 1945 when Bob Dawson (David Farrar), an RAF officer, brings home a German bride Frieda (Mai Zetterling). The residents of Denfield are immediately hostile towards her. In the middle of Frieda's painful assimilation into the community, Bob and Frieda help out on a farm, in a scene which was specially written for the film. For the first time, Frieda is shown laughing and carefree, and Bob looks happy. Freedom and tranquillity, concepts which are bound up with the English countryside, are used to suggest reconciliation and neutrality in a film which deals with British attitudes towards Germany.

The English pastoral provides the context for the main relationship in Basil Dearden's *The Captive Heart* (1946). It also tests the notion of the community against the importance of the individual. Alan Burton has analysed the film in the light of an address given in 1943 by Michael Balcon about 'realism' and 'tinsel', but does not mention that the 'tinsel' is largely dependent on an evocation of the rural myth.[12] In the film, Karel Hasek (Michael Redgrave), a Czech refugee in a prisoner-of-war camp, is compelled to begin a correspondence with Celia Mitchell (Rachel Kempson), the wife of the man whose identity he has stolen. Celia's letters evoke an intensely rural England: an idyllic hamlet with a picturesque country house, an old water pump, a Norman church and a village green. There are also armoured vehicles and evacuees at the local sweet shop. 'Everything's changed and yet nothing's changed,' she writes, 'and there's still cricket on Saturday afternoons'. This image is deeply reassuring. After a cricket match in the camp, the men come in hot and dusty, and someone wonders whether 'they're having an early spring at home'. Hasek reads out part of Celia's letter describing apple blossom, lambs, bluebells and green larch trees by the river. The men look up and listen enraptured as they are transported home. For some critics who otherwise praised the film for its expressions of communality and solidarity, visions of a clearly middle-class rural England were seen as too exclusive and individualistic. C.A. Lejeune wrote that 'this honest history' had been devalued by a 'completely phoney story'.[13] It was a box-office hit, however,[14] suggesting that for audiences, the rural myth suggesting 'home' and England had an enduring appeal.

Films also presented alternative rural imageries. Ealing's *The Loves of Joanna Godden* (Charles Frend, 1947), set in 1905 in bleak Romney Marsh juxtaposes an unromantic pastoralism with sharp contemporaneity. The film is based on Sheila Kaye Smith's novel *Joanna Godden*, published in 1921.[15] Despite the alteration to the title, the story concerns Joanna's confrontation with the reactionary agrarian community with which she finds herself competing after the death of her father. Joanna's (Googie Withers) daily struggle would have been recognisable to many post-war women who had combined paid work with running the household while their husbands were away on war service.[16] The success of *The Wicked Lady* (1945, Leslie Arliss) had confirmed that the independent woman was an appealing cinematic figure. Lady Barbara Skelton (Margaret Lockwood), bored with the landed society into which she has married, defies convention by becoming a 'highwayman', becoming in the process freed from male authority. As Lockwood's biographer writes, the character had 'touched a chord in the "new woman" emerging from the disciplines of a long war'.[17] Joanna Godden is also determined to be independent, and decides to run her father's farm single-handed. She scandalises her farming neighbours by sacking her shepherd and, against local tradition, ploughs up acres of marshland to grow fodder. 'Gentlemen, we're not farmers, we're just graziers,' she tells her colleagues at the annual farmers' dinner. But as rumbles of protest are heard around the room, she exclaims, 'it's about time that tradition about breaking up pasture was bust and I'm going to do the busting'. Later, Joanna harvests the wheat she has grown on the ploughed pastures under the disapproving gaze of the other farmers. Despite her un-conventional methods, Joanna's sheer doggedness eventually wins their respect.

The Loves of Joanna Godden defies perceived notions of the rural idyll, a defiance that is consonant with an era when National Parks were being planned to enable the public to see nature 'raw and triumphant'.[18] There are still considerable pastoral elements, notably from H.E. Bates, who co-scripted the film.[19] The score was written by Ralph Vaughan Williams, who frequently incorporated traditional folk songs into his works and who is associated with the notion of 'Englishness'.[20] Yet the pastoral setting is far from the pretty locations in wartime rural films. The opening narrative tells us that this is 'an austere land of windswept distances and scattered communities'. Romney Marsh is 'a place apart which man has slowly won, acre by acre, from the sea'. This cautionary note about man's struggle with the elements, and that nature should be respected, was not in the novel. Joanna's fiancé, Martin Trevor, drowns at Dungeness, whereas in the novel he dies from pneumonia.[21] While being more dramatic, this alteration introduces another dimension to this unromanticised pastoral, that it is a wild seaboard full of natural dangers. Indeed, the *Monthly Film Bulletin* considered that the film's main interest was not 'the loves of Joanna Godden but sheepfarming on Romney Marsh', and added that 'it is salutary for town dwellers to see something of the farmer's difficulties and tragedies and to realise that keeping sheep is not a mere Arcadian pastime'.[22] Joanna's struggle to render the land productive is admirable for its being a wilderness rather than a vista of meadows, and her gradual acceptance by the farming community emphasises her considerable stoicism.

The wartime pastoral had been that of Southern England, into which the rest of Britain tended to be absorbed. Although in *The Lion and The Unicorn* George Orwell recognised that by referring to 'England' more often than 'Britain' he may have offended Scottish and Welsh readers,[23] his writings tacitly embrace the rest of Britain. Writers like Edwin Muir, Liam O'Flaherty and Dylan Thomas argued that the war had heightened awareness of national differences, and that indigenous cultures and traditions should now be seriously revived.[24] Artistic and literary 'regionalism' attempted to challenge both the pre-eminence of London as the cultural capital and also the perception of 'middle England' as symbolising the British pastoral. By 1947, Orwell observed that England was culturally centralised. 'Not only is the whole of Britain in effect governed by London,' he wrote, 'but the sense of locality – of being, say an East Anglian or a West Countryman ... has been much weakened'.[25] Film-makers also entered into regionalism by exploring areas which had been comparatively neglected by wartime cinema. There were several reasons for this. Film crews had become more mobile, and Britain's reputation for 'realism' was greatly enhanced by the use of exterior photography. Furthermore, the success of British films like *In Which We Serve* in the US encouraged producers to make definitively 'British' films for overseas markets. Michael Balcon, for example, announced in January 1945 that Ealing would project 'the true Briton to the rest of the world' in 'films with an outdoor background, of the British scene'.[26] There was also such a shortage of studio space because of government requisitioning that by August 1946 newly formed units were being encouraged to look for 'all-location' subjects.[27] Film crews therefore travelled to lesser-known regions to make films about rural communities. *Johnny Frenchman* (1945, Charles Frend) concerned rival fishing villages in Cornwall and Brittany, *Quiet Weekend* (1946, Harold French) and *Strawberry Roan* (1945, Maurice Elvey) were set in rural hamlets in Wiltshire, and *Painted Boats* (1945, Charles Crichton) was about a barge family on the Midlands canals.

The most enduring and potent expressions of regional identity, however, were located further afield. Scotland, Ireland and Wales were appealing because they had distinct national, cultural and linguistic identities. Indeed, after the war there was an increasing concern that non-English cultures were fast disappearing, the *Sunday Times* reporting that in the remote communities of the Hebrides, Gaelic stories were being preserved on tape.[28] Two films set in Wales indicate the sense of cultural loss: *Three Weird Sisters* (1947, Daniel Birt) and *The Last Days of Dolwyn* (1949, Emlyn Williams), which partly used Welsh dialogue, showed traditional communities dislocated by change. Scotland, however, emerges as the strongest contender in the sense of producing a 'national cinema', although plans to launch the Scottish national film studios failed.[29] The Celtic hinterlands contained a shared culture in J.M. Barrie's 'kailyard' literary tradition, 'parochial, sentimental, backward-looking, small-scale, deeply religious',[30] and far more modest than Sir Walter Scott's flamboyant tartanry. *I Know Where I'm Going* (1945, Michael Powell and Emeric Pressburger), *The Brothers* (1947, David MacDonald), *Whisky Galore* (1949, Alexander Mackendrick) and *The Silver Darlings* (1947, Clarence Elder) were all made on location in the Scottish islands, and all contain elements of kailyard literature. Like *The Loves of Joanna Godden*, they insist on a respect for nature which is manifested in a deference to the sea. *The Silver Darlings*, based on Neil Gunn's novel,[31] explored the dying Hebridean herring-fishing industry. *The Brothers*, set on Skye in 1900, portrays an insular, almost primeval fishing community with a predilection for curses, brutal punishment and Puritanism. The beautiful scenery is juxtaposed with expressionistic shadows and mists, the islanders' brutish existence and whisky smuggling a dour, humourless business compared with McKendrick's *Whisky Galore*.

In contrast, *I Know Where I'm Going* contains the homely characteristics of kailyard, the romanticism of tartanry and 'faery', which evokes Celtic mythology and legend.[32] The film explored, recalled Powell, 'what's going to happen when the war is over'.[33] As in *A Canterbury Tale*, an urban outsider, here Joan Webster (Wendy Hiller) en route to the island of Kiloran to marry her older, rich fiancé, confronts a community 'rooted in older deeper values'.[34] Joan's urbanness contrasts markedly with that of Mull's inhabitants, 'dependent upon one another, feudal, democratic and totally devoid of materialism'.[35] Tartanry is represented by Rebecca Crozier (Nancy Price), an impoverished chatelaine who delights Joan with stories of the Oban games and the grand ball which follows it, but kailyard, manifested in the communality, animation and earthiness of a local ceilidh Joan attends, strikes a far deeper chord in her heart. Older cultures begin to work their magic; when she looks up at the wooden beams on her ceiling that night, a carved pagan figurehead appears to mock her, and the following day, Torquil (Roger Livesey), the local laird on leave from the navy, tells Joan a Nordic legend about a whirlpool and star-crossed lovers.

Emeric Pressburger noted that 'romantic nostalgia must give way to the reality and urgency of present and future'.[36] Therefore the film reflects public awareness of wartime profiteering[37] and adopts an anti-materialist stance. Torquil's friend Catriona (Pamela Brown) has become adept at hunting rabbits for food, and tells Joan, 'money isn't everything'. When Joan is stranded on Mull because of heavy fog, she calls her fiancé on Kiloran and tries to pay for the call with a pound note. Torquil explains that the postmistress only ever sees a pound note on pension day:

Joan: The people are very poor, I suppose?
Torquil: Not poor – they just haven't got money.
Joan: It's the same thing.
Torquil: Oh no, something quite different.

Joan, fearful of her growing attraction to Torquil, bribes Kenny (Murdo Morrison) to take her to Kiloran, but Bridie (Margot Fitzsimmons), his fiancée, confronts her. 'You that come from the city with your airs and graces and your heart of stone!' she cries. 'Why should you think that our lives don't matter at all and that yours is so important?' This final confrontation before the disastrous trip to Kiloran and her life-changing encounter with the Corryvreckan whirlpool links Joan's apparent lack of conscience firmly with her urban background.

I Know Where I'm Going, pitting tradition and unworldliness against modernism and materialism evokes the 'people's war' in its suggestion of self-reliance and discipline. 'Never,' writes Peter Hennessy of the Labour victory, 'has a Government inherited a more disciplined nation'.[38] Although the community in *I Know Where I'm Going* suffer privations – Torquil relies on the rents for Kiloran to pay for its maintenance, Rachel Crozier is servantless, and Bridie and Kenny are resigned to years of saving to get married – the islanders are self-governing and respectful to the feudal heads of the commune. They appear to adhere, without bidding, to a natural morality rooted in traditions and customs peculiar to this corner of Britain. Patrick Kirwan of the *Evening Standard* discerned its wider message of 'simplicity in place of weary sophistication' which had been evident in recent films. He believed that it would be 'hailed with relief and rapture by a public of whatever nationality'.[39] *The Scotsman* voted it 'one of the finest films yet made with a Scottish setting', and recommended it as 'a picture everyone should see'.[40] A commercial and critical success, *I Know Where I'm Going* is significant in the way that it sought to capture the continuity, tradition and benign philosophy of an old community at a time of great political and social change in Britain.

Another seam of rural cinema reflected important developments in rural politics. Conflict over the access to land has always been a defining feature of British rural politics, whereas in France the peasantry has traditionally been at the centre of rural issues. The wartime encounter between town and country raised questions about urban encroachment and rural preservation. Sir Leslie Scott's committee on Land Utilisation in Rural Areas, which reported in 1942, noted the parlous state of rural areas, and recommended improvements in housing and amenities, and controls on the 'use of the countryside by the urban public'.[41] The Town and Country Planning Act of 1947 implemented protective measures and significantly altered private-property rights by nationalising land development.[42] In April 1946, Hugh Dalton's budget allocated funds for national parks, through which he said the countryside would become 'the heritage not of a few private owners, but of all our people'.[43] Film-makers engaged with these ideas, that the countryside was to be accessible, protected and understood.

Films about country life also explored the notion of benevolent land-ownership, as seen in wartime films like *Tawny Pipit* and *Went The Day Well?* Much of the old rural hierarchy was still intact; in the midst of war, the country pursuits of the leisured classes, like foxhunting and fishing, continued much as usual.[44] After the war, writes Sadie Ward, 'there were still too many reminders of the way that the ownership and control of land maintained the division between rich and poor'.[45] Both *Spring in Park Lane* (1948, Herbert Wilcox) and *The Chiltern Hundreds* (1949, John Paddy Carstairs) show the landed gentry in a state of genteel impoverishment and giving way to the 'lower' classes. But these films were comedies. The real tensions implicit in the 'democratisation' of the land were evident in period dramas. The costume genre was treated warily by critics like Catherine de la Roche, who wrote that since the end of the war there had been 'no British films devoted to contemporary rural life'.[46] Yet costume dramas articulated contemporary anxieties and repressions, and they were very popular.[47] Rural cinema used the nineteenth century, an era when the differences between owners and tenants were more sharply defined, to great effect. Autocracy, embodied in the figure of the landowner, confronts democracy, represented by the agrarian community he oversees. *Captain Boycott* (1947, Frank Launder), *Blanche Fury* (1948, Marc Allégret) and *Jassy* (1947, Bernard Knowles) deal with the idea of autocracy and democracy, and the notion of the land being 'the heritage of all'.[48]

Captain Boycott is the story of the English landowner who has come to epitomise the notion of the absentee landlord. Like Launder and Gilliat's wartime films *Waterloo Road* and *Millions Like Us*, the film draws on the idea of communal strength over the individual. Captain Boycott's refusal to reduce his tenants' rents after a bad harvest results in his being ostracised by the community on the advice of Charles Stewart Parnell, who urges the tenants to 'shun him'. Inequality is a key theme in both *Jassy* and *Blanche Fury*, in which rural estates become subject to despotic and 'illicit' new ownership. In *Jassy*, Mordelaine is lost in a game of cards by Christopher Hatton (Dennis Price), thus dispossessing his son Barney (Dermot Walsh). In *Blanche Fury*, the true 'heir' to Clare, Philip Thorn (Stewart Granger), never owns the land legally because he is illegitimate. He is instead employed as a steward by the Furys, who have inherited the property by marriage. Barney is reduced to being a tenant farmer, but like Philip has an affinity with the land and a sense of responsibility towards the local community.

At the other end of the scale, the new landlords are represented as malevolent figures with little regard for their communities. Nick Helmar (Basil Sydney), the new owner of Mordelaine, raises the rents of the already beleaguered tenant farmers. When a deputation is sent to protest, he beats their leader Tom Woodroffe (John Laurie) to death. *Blanche Fury* depicts the Furys as equally despotic: 'Authority is not something one is given,' Simon Fury (Walter Fitzgerald) advises his son Laurence (Michael Gough), 'One takes it'. The elder Fury is indifferent to people and animals and as the film's Press Book notes, 'the country people and particularly the gypsies, regard him as an interloper'.[49] Both estates, however, are restored to their rightful owners through revenge and retribution. Blanche (Valerie Hobson), now the widow of Laurence, bears Philip's son. Jassy (Margaret Lockwood), Tom Woodroffe's daughter, contrives to marry Nick Helmar, who is later poisoned and dies. She then marries Barney, and Mordelaine is returned to benevolent hands. Both women, then, writes Raymond Durgnat, 'convey this "patrimony" to a more "democratic" character',[50] a transference of ownership in keeping with Labour politics. *Jassy* failed to convince *Picturegoer*'s reviewer, who wrote, 'We are asked to believe in a world ... where inequality was rampant'.[51] Yet underlying this and other films is the very real suggestion that the countryside as 'the heritage of all' was problematic. Collectively these complex pictures of rural life warned that nature was not to be treated lightly. Rather than the unpeopled landscape of wartime cinema, however, the countryside in post-war films was humanised, populated by self-seeking landowners on the one hand and on the other by the unjustly dispossessed, who were presented as the true inheritors of the post-war rural world.

The ideology of peasantism has been one of the enduring socio-political forces in French ruralist history. In 1949 Alfred Cobban wrote that 'France is a peasant's republic'.[52] Yet, as Henri Mendras has argued, the 1950s were characterised by great upheaval for rural France,[53] a decade which witnessed the proliferation of rural studies by anthropologists and sociologists in response to the 'urbanisation' of rural communes.[54] Meanwhile, the rural–urban relationship was under considerable strain, as at the end of the war France had been in a state of near famine,[55] which townspeople blamed on the peasants. *Agriculteurs* in Nouville, who comprised two fifths of its population, were rumoured to have created a black market by selling produce to the Germans rather than to the villagers.[56] Rural communes were rife with such stories. In 1945, a national opinion poll revealed that 53 per cent of respondents considered that of all sections of society the peasants were suffering the least.[57] The post-war ferment between the *ouvriers* and the *fermiers*, caused essentially by hunger, took years to fade. A 1949 poll, which divided the population into seven economic groups, elicited the opinion from non-peasants that the peasantry fell into categories one, two or three, while the peasants placed themselves in categories five, six or seven.[58]

The rural sector, which had been presented by Vichy as productive and unchanging, was facing great difficulties. There was a lack of modern machinery, particularly tractors, and seed for planting, while rural housing was dilapidated, with fewer than 20 per cent of homes with running water and a mere 4 per cent connected to a sewage system.[59] The agricultural economy lacked manpower after 200,000 former prisoners of war went into industry instead of returning to farm work, and the agricultural work-force fell from 7.5 to 2.5 million between 1949 and 1954.[60] Poor harvests in 1945 and 1947 necessitated imports and produced substantial increases in agricultural prices, for which urban consumers blamed the peasants. Despite these tensions, rural films suggested that the peasantry was still perceived as the cornerstone of national stability.

Farrebique (1947, Georges Rouquier) is possibly the most important rural film ever to emerge from France, 'an incomparable ethnographic document on French rustic life,' as J.G. Auriol wrote at the time.[61] Rouquier's two documentaries, *Le Tonnelier* (1942) on the art of the cooper, and *Le Charron* (1943), on the cartwright, acknowledged the revival of rural artisans due to wartime shortages, much as *A Canterbury Tale* had done in respect of the wheelwright and the wainwright. During the occupation, these tributes to rural industries were especially significant, with the small artisan being lauded by Pétainist doctrine. Rouquier later defended these 'Vichy' films on the grounds that 'we were, really no longer ourselves', and that the *artisanat* represented 'all that was essentially French'.[62] *Farrebique* was made between November 1944 and November 1945, and recorded the workings of a farm in the Massif Central, belonging to Rouquier's uncle. It epitomises Georges Duby's observation that 'the rural world is, *more than any other*, one of continuity and change'.[63] The film shows the farm through the seasons, the family sowing, harvesting crops and vines, ploughing, and tending livestock. Regional customs are included, for instance Henri, the younger son, visiting a wine cellar in Goutrens to meet his friends, where they perform a folk dance and the *patois* spoken by Old Roch is so dense it required occasional subtitles for the French audience.

In *Farrebique*, work is juxtaposed with the more fundamental elements of rural life, the passing of the seasons. Rouquier was reluctant to include any elements of progress, so as to construct an idealised, eternal rural world based on tradition and continuity. Thus family are shown living in austere conditions, as many rural people did, and much of their equipment is obsolete. They use an old-fashioned plough with oxen, Henri chops wood with an axe, and there is no tractor. Until the Monnet Plan was implemented in 1946, tractors were scarce and regional variations meant that as late as 1950 in Chanzeaux near Angers they were still uncommon.[64] Farrebique, according to pre-production notes, had neither electricity nor running water nor sanitation, features which were among the 'interesting elements in the film'.[65] In 1946, Albert Dauzat argued that it was through either 'routine or avarice' that even rich peasants continued to live in squalid conditions,[66] yet the Rouquier family have none of the obsessive rapacity of the clan in *Goupi Mains Rouges*. Whereas the Goupis are rarely seen working, the Rouquiers' life is one of unremitting toil and little leisure. Their ambitions are modest: Berthe fantasises about an electric iron, while Henri, faced with a pile of logs, daydreams of an electric chainsaw.

Rouquier's desire to make a timeless film was thwarted by the recent past. Rouquier excluded an elder son, Albert, who had returned from a prisoner-of-war camp[67] during production, so as not to have to 'deal with the present melancholy situation'.[68] Other more practical concerns could not be avoided, however. The farmhouse is deteriorating, and a harsh winter forces the question of renovation. The house and buildings need

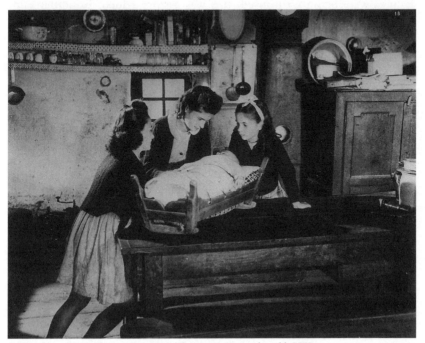

5. *Farrebique* (1947, Georges Rouquier). The continuing rural world. BIFI.

electrification, and having secured the agreement of their neighbour Fabre, who will share the lines, the cables are set up and the meter installed. Old Roch also ensures that the farm will remain intact after his death, which means buying out his unmarried sisters. At the end, Henri, now engaged to Fabre's daughter, says, 'there will always be a spring', which anticipates their life together and their future children. The settlement agreed, the old man dies content. *Farrebique* thus presents a picture of continuity and reassurance in which the past, the present and the future are in close harmony.

Farrebique proved popular with audiences, despite the much-talked-of urban hostility towards the peasantry. Notwithstanding the myths and rumours of peasant profiteering, there is little to envy in this unromantic portrait of rustic existence. But in his dreams, young Roch proudly surveys the lands before him, the result of long, hard work, 'having made his fields and knowing them just as the creator knows his creation'.[69] The life is hard, embellished only by the delights of the natural world. For urban audiences the human bond with the land and the theme of perpetual renewal would certainly have been reassuring after the uncertainty of recent years. 'It is not a film about a return to the land,' wrote *Cinémonde*, 'it is not about return at all. On the contrary, it is a step into the future.'[70] At a time when human failings were being scrutinised, this was a story which, Rouquier said, 'defied time and human passion'.[71]

For the French, the peasantry were at the core of rural life. As Lowe and Buller argue, the notion of a 'peasant society' carries with it a greater impression of distinctive and cohesive social order than does the notion of the British 'rural community'.[72] That sense of cohesion and order has always existed within diverse rural societies. 'Rural France,' wrote Marc Bloch, 'is a large and complex country whose frontiers embrace the tenacious survivals of a number of different agrarian civilisations'.[73] Indeed, one of the reasons for the failure of the Corporation Paysanne to unite the peasantry was its diversity and intra-regional rivalries.[74] The importance of regional identity to France is suggested by the re-emergence of regionalism at liberation. One of the results of the revival in late 1944 of the *peuple et culture* movement at Grenoble was Jean Vilar's theatre at Avignon, established in 1947. The theatre aimed to avoid bourgeois metropolitan theatregoers for less sophisticated regional spectators.[75]

Film directors concentrated on regional communities, which were culturally and linguistically distinct. Between 1945 and the early 1950s a range of regional novels and stories were filmed using natural exteriors. Two of Gilbert Dupé's novels were filmed, *Le Village perdu* (1947, Christian

Stengel), set in the Auvergne, and *La Ferme du pendu* (1946, Jean Dréville), in the Vendée about three farming brothers in dispute over their inheritance. Dupé's novel, Jean Dréville remarked, conveyed the Vendée peasantry as a 'vigorous and austere race'.[76] *Cinémonde* considered that the film successfully revealed the 'riches of regional folklore'.[77] The rich folkloric past of the Auvergne was depicted in *Le Village perdu*, which evokes the world of necromancy and white magic. *Sortilèges* (1945, Christian-Jacques), based on a novel by Claude Boncompain, is about a village contaminated by sorcery and superstition. Although released in the post-war period, it was shot during the occupation and evokes a similar atmosphere to *Les Visiteurs du soir*, in that two innocent lovers are caught up in a cruel and violent world. However, the village is clearly not consonant with Pétain's vision of 'natural communities', hard-working and devoted to *famille* and *patrie*. Taken as a film of the occupation or liberation, it nevertheless reveals that rural communities were perceived as being full of complexities and ambiguities.

Significantly, the notion that rural people should remain in their rural communities was articulated in several films about misguided migration to the city. In the early 1950s, Laurence Wylie noted that although parents in country areas were less suspicious of city life, 'they still dread the temptation of the city, the anonymity of a factory job where one is not one's own boss, the poor housing and living conditions and the existence of values which alienate children from their parents and their past'.[78] The reiterated theme in *Le Café du cadran*, *Faits divers à Paris* and *Sous le ciel de Paris,* of the foolhardy rustic who searches for a better life in the city only to be disappointed, was tantamount to a plea for social and geographical levelling. In 1945, the nation was already undergoing a period of flux, as men and women returned from internment, labour service in Germany and, less commonly, from deportation. The rural exodus, estimated at 100,000 per annum in the post-war years, compounded the problem.[79] Furthermore, the idea of rural–urban displacement worked in reverse. As we will see in the following chapter, several films show fugitives who commit a crime and flee Paris for the safety and anonymity of the countryside. Yet the refugees inevitably become entangled with the local communities, experience profound unease in their adopted rural environment, and leave.

Le Café du cadran (Jean Gehret, 1947) focuses on a couple from the Auvergne, a region where traditionally émigrés retained links with their native region.[80] Louise and Julien (Blanchette Brunoy and Bernard Blier) swap their country café for a more ambitious enterprise near the Paris Opéra, but Louise cannot acclimatise to city life. Julien, who is quite content at first, encourages her to change her hairstyle, which is 'all right for the countryside' but not suitable for Paris, but she soon attracts an urbane musician charmed by her rural naïveté. Julien meanwhile becomes reluctantly involved in a betting racket set up by the previous owner. When they realise that their lives are in complete disarray, they decide to give up the café and return to the Auvergne. A film 'whose primordial quality is its simplicity', according to *Film français*,[81] *Le Café du cadran* posits the city as eternally seductive but fundamentally unstable, while the countryside remains constant and is clearly where these migrants truly belong.

In *Faits divers à Paris* (1949, Dmitri Kirsanov) and *Sous le ciel de Paris* (1950, Julien Duvivier), migration proves fatal for two young women bored with country living. *Faits divers à Paris* is a melancholy picture of disappointment and desperation. Raymonde (Denise Fontaine) leaves her peasant family and her fiancé François (Olivier François) to work in a Paris café. On arrival, a young thief, William (Roger Legris), steals her handbag with all her money. She goes to the café, where she finds that not only is she to be treated as a servant but the patron tries to seduce her. Raymonde leaves the café, and William, who has followed her, offers her accommodation in a cheap hotel. Unbeknown to her, the rooms are used by prostitutes, and William and the proprietress are engaged in various illegal dealings. Raymonde is befriended by William, who is in reality marginalised and lonely. Hearing that François has married, Raymonde marries William. But when she discovers her handbag hidden in their bedroom, she realises how he makes his frugal living, and she commits suicide. A heartbroken William accompanies her body back to her native village, where she is buried in the small churchyard.

Faits divers à Paris is a low-budget and little known film, but the story is very effectively conveyed. The shots of François ploughing and harvesting stress the dignity of work, as *Farrebique* had three years earlier. Raymonde's parents are far from the image of the prosperous peasants of popular myth and, as in *Farrebique*, their austere mode of living has little glamour. The future to Raymonde appears routine and dull. Yet her contact with the city is shown to be improvident and dangerous, and the exciting life she fondly imagined is illusory. At home, François's life is not easy. At first, he is seen ploughing rock-hard soil on an icy day, yet he is also shown liberated by his surroundings and through self-sufficiency. The film makes it clear that the peasant is born to this life and the town dwellers to theirs, and is quite explicit in its suggestion that any deviation is ill-advised.

One of five stories in *Sous le ciel de Paris* (1951), written and directed by Julien Duviver, is another cautionary tale. Within the framework of a big-budget production,[82] the evocation of a similar theme appears significant, especially as it was distributed overseas. Yet it is also a celebration of Paris made by a director of international standing.[83] The press book sent to British exhibitors includes several typically 'Parisian' shots, including the Eiffel Tower and the bridges of the Seine from the rooftops near the Sainte Chapelle.[84] The film starts like a travelogue, journeying across the recognisable Parisian skyline, following 'the flow of the Seine', from an old woman in the Rue Mouffetard begging for a few francs to feed her cats, to a fashion shoot at the Palais de Chaillot featuring Dior's 'new look' gowns. Paris is shown as a city of enormous variation, but for people unaccustomed to it, it can be dangerous. Denise Lambert (Brigitte Auber) arrives at the Gare de Lyon. 'Now she isn't a commuter...she's a provincial,' remarks the omnipresent narrator.[85] Denise, impressed with all she sees about her, arrives at the tiny apartment of her friend Marie-Thérèse (Christiane Lénier) and unpacks, her lace blouse denoting the 'slight "backwardness" underlying the provincial'. Denise is warned that Paris is very different from Saint Raphaël, but she is confident that she will find work and fit in. But one night on a deserted street behind the Sacré Coeur, a psychopath, the focus of another story, attacks Denise and kills her. The inclusion of this tragic tale in a film which purported to represent Paris signifies the persistence and potency of the idea of rural and urban incompatibility. Like *Faits divers à Paris* and *Le Café du cadran,* the film suggests that the rural and urban worlds are strongly linked but culturally entirely separate.

There were, however, humorous versions of this theme. André Berthomieu directed a trilogy of films between 1946 and 1948 featuring Bourvil, who was invariably cast as un *paysan naïf* lured to the sinful city. The idea of the rustic being drawn towards exterior forces was extended in *Jour de fête* (1949, Jacques Tati), one of the most popular comedies of the era. Tati plays a rural postman, François, who is roused from his slow-moving existence by witnessing the wonders of modern technology in the shape of a film about the US postal system. Seeing that trains and planes are used to deliver American mail, he sets off at high speed on his own mode of transport, a bicycle, his gangly figure pedalling madly round the commune delivering letters. Finally, beaten, he decides to join in the harvest instead. At a time when American culture seemed to be 'invading' France,[86] rejection of efficiency and speed in favour of the old, steady, rural traditions seems highly significant.

Significantly, in *Le Beau Serge* (1958, Claude Chabrol), acknowledged as the first *nouvelle vague* ('new wave') film, all the familiar motifs are well in place, but the film is tinged with a great sense of loss. François, a student in Paris, returns to his home village after an absence. He is concerned to see his best friend Serge drunk in the village square, and discovers that his wife is expecting their second child and fears that it will be a 'mongol', as their first is. Serge sees that François has become 'bookish' and bourgeois, and has the accompanying morals. The villagers lead a harsh existence. When the children come out of school, Serge tells François that some of them walk for miles in the snow to get there. The dejected priest says his congregation is dwindling rapidly, and his attempts to set up a youth club have folded in three months. When Marie, the local 'tart', is raped by the man she thought was her father, Serge dismisses it saying 'it's only natural'. *Le Beau Serge* is a deeply pessimistic view of the peasantry; they succumb to alcoholism; incest is tolerated; morals are disintegrating due to the abandonment of religion. To François, this has become an unrecognisable world. Yet it has an upbeat ending when Serge's wife bears a normal baby and his face lights up with joy. As the realist aesthetic of the young creators of the *nouvelle vague* was contingent on urban imagery, the rural themes of *Le Beau Serge* demonstrate the everlasting fascination with the countryside.

Urban France had been devastated by wartime bombing. Twenty-five per cent of all the buildings in France had been destroyed and nearly half the railway tracks.[87] Almost every town of over 100,000 had been seriously damaged, and some, like Caen and Le Havre in the vulnerable North, razed to the ground. Five million people, an eighth of the population, were homeless.[88] The numerous monographs published between 1945 and 1949 on the effects of the war on urban areas reflected the nationwide impact of bomb damage.[89] Yet post-war urban France has been curiously neglected in Georges Duby's otherwise comprehensive history, although the section on the occupation and liberation years in his parallel history, of rural France is considerable.[90] Despite various studies of urban France in the 1950s, this subsequent lack of interest would suggest that French rural history has a far greater significance in national cultural history as a whole.

Unlike rural cinema, that consciously travelled to the regions, urban cinema focused on Paris, which was almost the only identifiable city. While other cities were ravaged by bombs, Paris remained intact, and the songs of Maurice Chevalier, Edith Piaf and Yves Montand revived the culture of *le petit peuple* of pre-war days.[91] Film-makers too celebrated the city after four years of films in which there had hardly been a recognisable Parisian street. They too recaptured a pre-war milieu which had fascinated novelists, songwriters, film-makers and photographers, a world belonging to *le petit peuple*, from shopkeepers to artisans to figures from the underworld.[92] A range of films, among them *Les Portes de la nuit* (1946, Marcel Carné) and *Antoine et Antoinette* (1947, Jacques Becker), brought *le petit peuple* sharply up to date in post-liberation Paris. In both communities, where decent working people share problems, there is an anti-social presence who is challenged by communal good. In Carné's film the hero identifies a collaborator, the traitor of the community who is eventually eradicated, a target of cinematic *épuration* in effect. Becker's film also identifies an unpopular urban figure, the power-wielding shopkeeper whose attempts at seduction are ultimately thwarted. Yet other films also showed that the notion of community in postwar Paris was problematic. *Impasse des deux anges* (1948, Maurice Tourneur) shows an isolated individual deprived of family and community ties. As we shall see, in this and other films, community and its concomitants, belonging and sharing, are also presented as phenomena of the past.

Les Portes de la nuit was originally an expensive vehicle for Jean Gabin and Marlene Dietrich.[93] After their withdrawal, the film shifted focus from personalities to Paris itself.[94] It opens with an aerial shot of the city and a narrator's voice announcing 'the sad winter following the magnificent summer of the liberation'. The camera then closes in on a *quartier populaire* near the Barbès Rouchechouart metro, where the narrative unfolds over 24 hours. In Carné's pre-war films, like *Le Jour se lève* (1939), the design of the *milieu ouvrier* was an important part of the cinematic aesthetic. In *Portes de la nuit*, the metro, streets, shops, the bistro and an apartment building were meticulously constructed by Alexandre Trauner, the designer of *Les Enfants du paradis*. The artificial-looking decor presents a planned and detached version of 'reality' that assists in conveying distasteful themes: disloyalty and duplicity that threaten the equilibrium of the community. The suggestion is that while Paris has been restored to the French, and the occupiers are no longer in residence, there are still enemies within who needed rooting out.

Les Portes de la nuit has been criticised for a fatalism which 'does not sit comfortably with the new times of jazz and modernity',[95] yet the unpleasant realities of the occupation, collaboration and denunciation are ultimately more acceptable if they are presented as consequences of fate. The main reason Marlene Dietrich gave for withdrawing from the film was its evocation 'of regrettable attitudes from the occupation which…will constitute bad propaganda abroad'.[96] This is one of the strongest impressions left by the film, of a community whose recent past is very much on the surface. Diego (Yves Montand) has returned from travelling abroad after a period in the Resistance, knowing that in the area is the man who betrayed his friend Raymond (Raymond Bussières) to the Gestapo. The bistro Chez Germaine, where Diego and his friends go to celebrate, operates under the black market, and they dine well. The restaurant is an accepted part of community life, which is stressed by its wide patronage and its impeccable facade of loyalty to the Allies. Army officers' caps hang on the hat-stand, and the walls are covered with photographs of De Gaulle, Churchill and Stalin. Guy Sénéchal (Serge Reggiani) is a regular patron who, it is later revealed, swiftly changed allegiance from the Milice to the Allies on liberation. He is now feted as a local hero, his murky past well hidden. His father (Saturnin Fabre), the proprietor of the slum-like boarding house in which the Lécuyer family lives, is also a former collaborator. When Diego confronts Guy with his treachery, the 'collabo' cannot bear the guilt of his treachery. In the film's most striking scene at the end, Guy walks, eyes blazing, onto a railway track in front of an oncoming train.

Les Portes de la nuit received mixed reviews. It was the first film made by Carné since *Les Enfants du paradis*, and was keenly awaited. In *L'Écran français*, Georges Altman wrote that *Les Portes de la nuit* was 'a new and violent view of a Paris weakened by privations [and] rotten with the black market'. The expressionistic images, fatalistic dialogue and Diego's retribution on Guy suggested 'the misery of the slums, the triumphant return of exploiters of the poor, the shame of double-dealing and of corruption'.[97] This was not an optimistic impression of post-liberation Paris, but a Paris 'far from that of which we used to dream'.[98] In 1953, Georges Sadoul admitted that these elements were recognisable in 'contemporary life', but considered that Diego's claim that the only danger was travelling the world was inappropriate given that Paris 'had so recently been bristling with barricades'.[99] Critics were alienated more by the film's preoccupation with fate as the agent of events than by the 'regrettable attitudes' of which Dietrich had complained. The hero is a victim of destiny rather than being part of a morally charged Resistance community. Indeed, the spectre of destiny (Jean Vilar), personified by a tramp who stalks the protagonists, evoked Carné's pre-war films, which had been suffused with a sense of entrapment and moody fatalism.

While for French critics such pessimism was not consonant with a newly liberated and self-governing France, British critics considered its significance as a record of post-liberation Paris. Although Dilys Powell was disappointed with the film as a whole, she urged an understanding of the context in which it was produced. 'For an English audience,' she wrote, 'it is not easy to fall into the mood in which such a film was made; one should perhaps not hastily condemn its febrile melodrama'.[100] C.A. Lejeune perceptively concluded that despite the 'commonplace ideas' about destiny, the film evinced 'the malaise in the city, the uneasiness, the willingness to surrender to chance and mood'.[101] *Les Portes de la nuit* was commercially 'an unmitigated disaster'.[102] It was, however, mentioned in a survey taken in 1948, in which respondents listed their favourite films of 1946–47. Of the 45 per cent of people who cited French films, *Les Portes de la nuit* was ranked tenth.[103] The idea of destiny dominating events was for audiences a way of denying culpability for the activities which had caused and continued to cause suspicion and conflict in their communities. The 'poetic realist' mode enabled Carné to approach the difficult task of depicting a community which was divided by the legacy of the recent past.

The political conditions of the occupation and its ideological divisions had meant that cinematic expressions of community had not been explicit, but rather metaphorical within a variety of genres. The liberation era, however, permitted the depiction of present-day community life in a state of harmony and co-operation. *Antoine et Antoinette* shows a contemporary working-class neighbourhood. The film was shot in the Paris streets, which gives it a bright, open aspect, although, as in *Les Portes de la nuit*, fate intervenes. Briefly, it concerns a young working couple, the Moulins (Claire Maffei and Roger Pigaut), whose lives are bouleversés by the discovery that they have won the lottery. On going to cash the ticket, Antoine finds that it has gone, and the rest of the film revolves around his frantic search for it. Another important part of the narrative concerns the local 'villain', the all-powerful Monsieur Roland (Noël Roquevert), a grocer. He has designs on Antoinette, endearing himself by selling her superior vegetables and giving her presents of scarce delicacies. Monsieur Roland is deeply unpopular, a character who would have had resonances with audiences, as during the occupation shopkeepers had enjoyed considerable power in local communities. 'You have an immense role. Fill it with authority,' proclaimed one official poster.[104] The importance of food was considerable; even in the very cold winter of 1946, respondents to the national opinion poll prioritised food over heating.[105] Contemporary attitudes to these minor potentates were encapsulated in a novel, *Au Bon Beurre*, published in 1952,[106] in which Charles-Hubert Poissonard, proprietor of the 'Bon Beurre' *crémerie* is depicted as a petty tyrant who swindles both his customers and his peasant suppliers during the occupation. In *Antoine et Antoinette*, Roland is eventually foiled, and he is but a minor irritant in everyday life. The strength of the community, which was so absent in films during the occupation, is in its solidarity. Indeed, despite a lavish poster which stressed the more exclusive Parisian landmarks, the film actually shows a humanised cityscape, its inhabitants surviving by *débrouillard*, 'making do' and good neighbourliness, in a slice of working-class life absent in film during the occupation.

Urban spaces were not always carefree environments. Communities had been destabilised by those missing or displaced by the occupation, some of whom never returned. The proliferation of film noirs, incorporating murder mysteries, gangster dramas and *policiers* and characterised by urban landscapes, expressed myriad underlying tensions about life in post-war France. The film noir, focusing on alienation and isolation, has been attributed to a post-war malaise, and was a feature of French, British and American cinema of the post-war years.[107] Yet the term 'film noir' was coined by French film critics in 1947. It emerged from the *série noire*, popular American detective fiction that was published by Marcel Duhamel from 1945.[108] These films, some of which will be discussed in chapter 5, focus on groups and characters who often find themselves alone and victims of hostile forces.

In *Impasse des deux anges*, the landscape of the past is entirely different to the reality, as Marianne and Jean (Simone Signoret and Paul Meurisse) discover. After the war, they revisit what had been a charming hotel on a picturesque backstreet to discover that the Impasse (a street in Paris) is dirty and deserted and the hotel in ruins. The only sign of life is a young girl, Anne-Marie (Danielle Delorme), alone and living beyond a broken gate in the wall. Just behind them, she explains, is a 'no-man's land', an abandoned building site which is now a market where she sells 'luxury' goods to willing customers. This bleak landscape, in which a parentless girl scrapes an illegal living projects an unpalatable dimension to urban life. 'This place,' notes the script, 'gives the impression of dépaysement',[109] and indeed the sense of isolation and hopelessness emanating from this microcosm of the city places it outside mainstream society. Marianne, a famous musical actress living in a bourgeois area, tells Anne-Marie, metaphorically her younger self, that she had good luck which enabled her to escape poverty. In a juxtaposition of vitality and despondency, wealth and poverty, symbolised in the 'no-man's land' and Marianne's exclusive neighbourhood, *Impasse des deux anges* expresses the varied and often disturbing imagery of the urban world. While

British cinema experienced its own urban noir phase, its projection of alienation and marginalisation did not contain the painful underlying elements
which characterises the French film noir of the immediate post-war years.

In Britain, urban destruction had also occurred on a national level.
200,000 houses had been destroyed, and twice that number rendered
uninhabitable.[110] Bombing had flattened three-and-a-half million London
homes and razed a third of the City. St Paul's Cathedral, which had appeared
invincible at the height of the Blitz, now stood at the centre of an immense
demolition site, and had become 'the country's chief war memorial'.[111] Out
of eight million people in Greater London, at least 40 per cent had left
their neighbourhoods for a time during the war.[112] Sir Patrick Abercrombie
was recruited by the government to devise a plan for Greater London, and
his report was published in 1944. His emphasis was on humanising the
metropolis, by separating industry and commerce from residential areas,[113]
whereby each locality would have a human centre. In the documentary *Proud
City* (1945, Ralph Keene), Abercrombie explains that the 'spirit of the old
village communities has survived', and that 'the old local loyalties are still
there'. The Greater London Plan effectively espoused the ideal of the 'urban
pastoral' that documentary maker Humphrey Jennings had successfully
conveyed as part of the national heritage. Indeed film-makers of the post-
war period appear committed to the notion of modern as urban.

The film-makers' vision of community was synonymous with urban,
metropolitan Britain, but mostly it remained a London-based view, not least
because London reflected the reality of its recent past. One *Picturegoer* reader
had had his sensitivities heightened by two British and American films set
in London: 'The comparison between the authentic background of *Waterloo
Road* and the frightful synthetic background of *None But the Lonely* Heart
prompts this letter'.[114] The critics, always supportive of authenticity, were
equally enthusiastic about films like *Waterloo Road* and *Hue and Cry*, which
they saw as capturing the atmosphere of London communities. Dilys
Powell of the *Sunday Times* believed that during the period immediately
after the war, London became a film-set in its own right:

> It must be about three years since the British cinema made the startling
> discovery that the streets of London were a perfect setting for the film of
> action…with a growing emphasis on background, not at the expense of, but
> in relation to, character…the shifty and the natty, the sober, the savage, the
> ironic, the cosy could only belong to that jungle of streets with their steam of
> fried fish, their hoarse voices, their flapping leaves of dirty newspapers and
> their bleak bomb-clearings.[115]

During the filming of *Passport to Pimlico* in July 1948 on a Lambeth bomb-site, *Kinematograph Weekly* reported that 'the story of this film, whimsical though it may be, could not have been possible but for the village life of our London inner suburbs'.[116] The popular image of post-war London is indeed enshrined in Ealing films like Charles Crichton's *Hue and Cry* (1947) and *The Lavender Hill Mob* (1951), and Henry Cornelius's *Passport to Pimlico* (1949). Reviewing *The Lavender Hill Mob*, C.A. Lejeune wrote that Ealing's London was not the 'visitor's London, but an older, more indigenous London: city streets, docks, inner suburbs, school crossings, faded crescents'.[117] In 1952, Michael Balcon attributed Ealing's predilection for London-based subjects to a special affinity with the capital and an aptitude for 'local' subjects: 'If you do well locally, you do well nationally,' he explained, 'and I believe that the indigenous film is the truly international film. This, I suggest is the reason for our success with stories of London and Londoners – we know the heart and the mind of the people.'[118]

Ealing's output, then, seems linked to a specific conceptualisation of the 'British character', but it encompassed a range of genres from dramas like *It Always Rains on Sunday* (1947, Robert Hamer) to comedies like *Passport to Pimlico*. *It Always Rains on Sunday*, which shows that a communal existence can be stifling and constraining, contrasts sharply with the chummy congeniality of *Passport to Pimlico*. Other studios focused on the capital in terms of small communities, of which *Waterloo Road* (1945, Sidney Gilliat) had been the prototype. Art director Alex Vetchinsky had spent hours visiting *Waterloo Road*'s shops and pubs to create an authentic set.[119] On its release, the *Daily Mail*'s critic concluded, 'It lives, it moves, it is London in wartime', setting the tone for most of the reviews. *London Belongs to Me* (1948) was another Gilliat film, an adaptation of Norman Collins's 'Dickensian' bestseller[120] about the residents of a Kennington boarding house who campaign to free one of the tenants who has been charged with murder. The novel and the film are set in 1939, but its theme clearly recalls the wartime community spirit of *Waterloo Road*. *London Belongs to Me* caught the claustrophobia and loneliness of the boarding-house environment, which Patrick Hamilton captures in his novel *The Slaves of Solitude*.[121] It also used London's most dramatic features. The straggling procession of petitioners who walk to Whitehall over Westminster Bridge in the pouring rain is a memorable image. After the war, when the streets of London still resonated with their own recent history, film units increasingly left the studios to harness that contemporaneity.

London was the city of the future. As the *Observer* noted, the Germans had 'blasted away mess as well as loveliness', and the capital now enjoyed 'unobstructed views, the remodelling of old glories and shaping of new ones – what a chance for the young Londoner!'[122] *Hue and Cry* is the story of some East End youngsters led by Joe Kirby (Harry Fowler) who discover that a gang of local villains are using a boy's paper to pass secret messages. Scriptwriter T.E.B. Clarke recalled that the original idea was one spectacular scene conjured up by producer Henry Cornelius in which 'hundreds of boys took virtual possession of London for a few glorious hours'.[123] *Hue and Cry* moves from Covent Garden market, where Joe works, to Kingsway and Battersea, to an expanse of wasteland near St Paul's and the wharves of the docklands that the youngsters use as their playground. The dramatic finale is staged near Wapping, where they charge down a huge flight of steps to confront the villains, St Paul's looming large in the background.

The overall effect is of an energetic adventure round London's landmarks, juxtaposing images of surviving buildings with bombed ruins. To many Londoners in 1947, a film in which buildings seemed to possess a triumphant resilience confirmed that the city had weathered a considerable storm which merited recording. C.A. Lejeune wrote of the 'rubble … mercifully transformed by the clatter and play of children,' and concluded, 'I have never seen a picture that gave a more vivid impression of London as a great city of buildings and wharves, skylines and pavements, roar and silence and changing light'.[124] Furthermore, the victory was enabled by the resourceful 'cockney', a staple of wartime film who was enjoying an 'Indian summer' in popular culture.[125] The vibrant presence of the boys undertaking a deed for the good of the community conveys great optimism, and the final routing of the villains in a desolate docklands setting is a timely metaphor for a more significant recent victory.

Hue and Cry is almost entirely an outdoors film. Conversely, *It Always Rains on Sunday* returns repeatedly to the interior domestic space in which Rose Sandigate (Googie Withers) conducts her life. Tommy Swann (John McCallum), an ex-lover, escapes from Dartmoor and seeks refuge in Bethnal Green by hiding in Rose's Anderson shelter. Her efforts to help him reveal the claustrophobia, routine and predictability of her existence. As Pierre Sorlin argues, the film delineates the East End by setting up oppositions between the bustle and noise of Petticoat Lane, redolent with new sights and sounds, and the repeated return to the silent, still Coronet Grove.[126] To Rose, its silence and monotony becomes stifling and constraining, a far cry from the cosy, close-knit neighbourhoods of wartime film. The bright, outdoor landscapes

6. *Hue and Cry* (1947, Charles Crichton). Canal+ Image UK.

of Googie Withers's previous film, The *Loves of Joanna Godden*, contrasts with the darkly lit interiors of *It Always Rains on Sunday*, and the protagonists' lifestyles are interestingly polarised. As Rose's story unfolds indoors, outside Bethnal Green, a community of particular vitality,[127] is evoked. From Petticoat Lane market, the shops, the pub, the amusement arcade, the youth club, the local dance hall, the camera repeatedly returns to Coronet Grove. Charles Barr argues that the 'clutter of intersecting lives and cameo performances in this teeming East End environment is a distraction from the main drama'.[128] Yet these elements animate the film by juxtaposing an internalised stifling home existence with a larger bustling and vibrant community beyond.

The depiction of 'spivery' in *It Always Rains on Sunday* caused some critics to question the kind of interpretation of working-class London that the film was presenting. In post-war London, the spiv was a modern reality and part of popular mythology,[129] but the antithesis of the warm-hearted cockney. *Monthly Film Bulletin*'s review of *It Always Rains on Sunday* evoked nostalgia for this benevolent figure: 'It is perhaps a pity that thousands of honest cheerful citizens of Bethnal Green could not have had a stronger representation, but for those who like serious portrayal of a section – a very minor section – of East End life it can be recommended'.[130] C.A. Lejeune also missed the lovable Eastenders, accusing it of neglecting the 'merriment and kindliness and beauty' of the East End.[131] Arthur Vesselo of *Sight and Sound* judiciously decided, however, that the film's communal conviviality redeemed its unsavoury subject matter: 'to object to a picture of Bethnal Green because it includes aspects of low life and dwells on some of them,' he wrote, 'seems to be pushing the argument too far'.[132] The skilful portrait of a community at large had in effect negated the concentration on individual wrongdoers.

A number of post-war films drew criticism for dwelling too much on the underworld, a phenomenon which had not featured in wartime cinema, as it would have undermined the notion of consensus. The underworld revealed rather unpleasant aspects of the community. Identifiable by their pessimism and their depictions of 'urban sleaze',[133] Britain's film noirs proliferated. *They Made Me a Fugitive* (1947, Alberto Cavalcanti) was one of the first which dealt with the urban underworld, in company with a range of others, including *Appointment with Crime* (John Harlow, 1946), *No Orchids for Miss Blandish* (St John Legh Clowes, 1948) and *Brighton Rock* (John Boulting, 1948), which also demonstrated the existence of a provincial gangland. The publicity for *They Made Me a Fugitive* capitalised on the enthusiasm of the press for crime reporting[134] and adopted the style of newspaper head-lines: 'Soho Gang Hides Escaped Convict Killer' in '*The Daily Record*' and 'London Gang War' in '*The Sun*'. All these films were assured of good audiences, given the recent results of the Bernstein Questionnaire in April 1947, which revealed that crime films were the third most popular genre.[135]

These representations of modern urban Britain were, however, anathema to the idea of the 'new Jerusalem'. In June 1948, a few months after *Brighton Rock* was released, there was an outburst in Parliament. At a time when spivs and gangsters were synonymous with London, *Brighton Rock* was outspoken in its suggestion of a provincial underworld. When the scenario was submitted to the British Board of Film Censors for approval, the censor concluded by stating, 'It is questionable that Brighton Town Council may not appreciate having this unpleasant and sinister tale located in their holiday resort'.[136] Indeed the film provoked a flurry of letters to local newspapers, despite the opening 'disclaimer' that, as in Graham Greene's novel, the story was set in 'the years between the two wars'. *Good Time Girl* (1948, David Macdonald), about juvenile delinquency, and *No Orchids for Miss Blandish*, based on James Hadley Chase's 1939 sensational thriller, seemed to be the final straw for one member of the Cabinet. During a debate on the new Films Bill, the President of the Board of Trade, Harold Wilson, spoke out in the House:

7. *It Always Rains on Sunday* (1947, Robert Hamer), with Googie Withers. Canal+ Image UK.

> We are getting tired of some of the gangster, sadistic and psychological films of which we seem to have so many, of diseased minds, schizophrenia, amnesia and diseases which occupy so much of our screen time. I should like to see more films which genuinely show our way of life...I should like to see the screen writers go up to the North of England, Scotland, Wales and the rest of the country, and to all parts of London which are not so frequently portrayed in our films.[137]

British cinema, it appeared, was determined that Britain would not be shown in a good light. Films about the underworld did not evoke the community spirit which had dominated wartime production, but the exploits of the anti-social individual.

Another critic of *Good Time Girl* had already demonstrated, however, that the public responded to another quite different interpretation of the city, the glamorous and wealthy West End. In December 1947, Herbert Wilcox was urging producers to make 'open pictures, happy unclouded pictures … mass entertainment for mass audiences'.[138] In austerity Britain, Wilcox's 'style' was extremely successful, helped by the fact that his wife Anna Neagle was something of a national icon because of her portrayals of Queen Victoria and Nell Gwyn. Neagle's films are mostly set in London, which indicates the centralisation of cultural representations of 'Britishness'.[139] Partnered by the debonair and charming Michael Wilding in four of the five films in the 'Mayfair' cycle, Neagle appealed to post-war audiences weary of rationing and queuing. The second film in the series, *Piccadilly Incident*, won the Daily Mail National Film Award for best film of 1946.[140] The Courtneys of Curzon Street, a family saga from the Boer War to the Second World War, in which an Irish maid marries a baronet, was the top box-office film of 1947.[141] C.A. Lejeune wrote that it was 'tosh of the highest order but if my livelihood depended on [getting] the right film into the average cinema this is one I wouldn't dare to miss'.[142] Its successor, *Spring in Park Lane* (1948), was an altogether more jocular film in which Wilding, as the impoverished Lord Richard, disguises himself as a butler and meets upper-class Judy (Neagle).

The popularity of *Spring in Park Lane* owed much to the fact that it shows an exclusive world. It opens on busy Park Lane, filled with buses and cars, lined with fountains and statues, where modern flats are juxtaposed with opulent mansions. The audience is taken into one of these grand houses and the world within. Like Angela Thirkell's novels, the country gentry are impoverished and crumbling, and Richard's family have resigned themselves to tolerating the squatters who have infiltrated their castle. But the urban aristocrats are thriving, and Neagle and Wilding perform some stylish dancing routines. 'Chromium plated below stairs romantic comedy drama,' concluded *Kinematograph Weekly*, 'cunningly and comfortably located in London's Mayfair. Excellent popular booking.'[143] This entirely innocuous fairy tale was far from the sleazy dens of Soho. Indeed, on seeing *They Made Me a Fugitive* released the same month, the *News of the World* critic longed for 'the simple sentimentalities of *The Courtneys of Curzon Street*'.[144] Images of glamorous upper-class London, a complete fantasy for most audiences, represented a comfortable respite from modern urban living, and had the same sense of escapism in 1940s Britain that the 'screwball' comedies of the 1930s had provided for moviegoers in depression America. Moreover, the Wilcox–Neagle version of London life, without a suggestion of class conflict, had, according to *Kinematograph Weekly*, 'captured the affection and esteem of practically all classes of audiences'.[145] The patrician Mayfair milieu was conspicuous, however, in its exclusivity and its privileging of individual pleasures over than the wider good of the community. But in post-war Britain, the popularity of these films symbolised the need for a little self-indulgence, which was something of a luxury compared to the social responsibility urged on the cinemagoing public of the war years.

During the post-war years, British films of rural life revealed that the countryside had even greater depths than the rural idyll of wartime cinema. *The Captive Heart* indicated that the pastoral was synonymous with wartime, while *The Loves of Joanna Godden* proved that the countryside was also an austere, forbidding place. For a time, film-makers freed from the constraints of wartime production explored more distant regional communities to enhance the realism of their films through location filming. The Celtic hinterlands, however, which possessed specific identities and cultures far removed from the materialistic and consumer-driven metropolis, had a special intensity. The Celtic community was contrasted with English urban bureaucracy and modernity in films like *I Know Where I'm Going* and *Whisky Galore*. On a more fundamental level, films about country life explored the concept of patriarchy and community in the era of town and country planning, with its new emphasis on people and the land being accessible to all. Democratic 'natural' leaders of the community challenged the despotic masters of *Captain Boycott*, *Blanche Fury* and *Jassy*, but their uneven success in assuming the reigns of benevolent power indicated the persistence of the old rural hierarchies.

In France, post-war cinema consciously incorporated a regional element. Films with rural settings increased as part of the reconstruction of a national identity, which was based not on uniformity but on cultural variation. *Farrebique*, which effectively acquitted the peasantry of charges of greed, was popular with audiences, and film-industry spokesmen sensed in it essentially 'French' qualities. The continuation and endurance of a 'regional' cinema indicates the importance of the peasantry as a cultural symbol to the French. For rural people, the city was portrayed as a place of iniquity and danger. The message in *Faits divers à Paris* and *Sous le ciel de Paris* was unequivocal, to resist the temptation to migrate. It was equally the case that urban-dwellers did not belong in the countryside, even, as in *Le Beau Serge*, those who were born there. In effect, cinema was restoring and relocating the population in communities and environments appropriate to their cultural origins. For the inhabitants of Paris, the city was unique. The legacy of occupation was much in evidence: collaboration and profiteering were present in *Les Portes de la nuit* and *Antoine and Antoinette*. Yet, also in these two quite different films fate plays an inordinately important role in the narrative. Becker's film showed ordinary working people settling down to life again with a helping hand from the lottery. In *Les Portes de la nuit*, destiny's control over individual lives seems incongruous in a newly liberated city, while the resolution of the conflicts within the community seems by no means final. The plethora of film noirs evoke the anxiety, uncertainty and moral disillusionment of living in post-war urban France, a country with a troubled recent past.

British post-war 'realist' cinema concentrated on urban working-class communities in films like *It Always Rains on Sunday, London Belongs to Me* and *Passport to Pimlico*. The response to critical demand for realism had also involved the depiction of the unpleasant realities about crime in every community. Film noirs and thrillers were audacious and surprising, and, as Geoff Brown argues, 'began to recognise the part that sex and violence play in urban life, began to delve beneath the characteristic British restraint'.[146] The nefarious networks of the underworld contradicted the caring, consensual community of wartime cinema. Gangland appeared to be almost synonymous with London, but the controversy over *Brighton Rock* indicated that for once the focus on crime on a local level had stepped outside the boundaries of a London-based national cinema. The anonymity of the capital, even in films that showed well drawn and identifiable communities, was for critics and others a slightly more comfortable milieu in which to explore the inner workings of the underworld. However, by 1950, the director of Brighton Rock was depicting a city under a far greater threat from an outside enemy. In *Seven Days to Noon*, London is once again evacuated, but this time the advancing enemy is atomic power. However, between 1945 and 1949 audiences also needed a break from the everyday worries of austerity Britain. Herbert Wilcox's 'Mayfair' confections, which peeped into milieux far from the gangster-ridden East End and Soho, were the most popular films of all. These pictures were the moral antithesis of the un-materialistic and unworldly communes of the Celtic fringe in their privileging of the individual over the community. The wholesome and integrated communities of British wartime cinema had given way to more contradictory and diverse portrayals in the post-war world.

5

Cinema of the Return:
Acceptance and Alienation

The return of service personnel, prisoners of war and deportees was central to the social, economic and political reconstruction of both Britain and France. In May 1945, Britain awaited the return of four-and-a-half million servicemen and half a million women. 'The sense of collective relief,' writes Peter Hennessy, 'the lifting of six years' worth of millions of individual anxieties ... can only be guessed at, not measured'.[1] The rhetoric of 'never again' was audible, a guarantee that the veterans of this war would share in a new society. Britain was to be founded on the principles enshrined in the most publicised and popular document of the war, the 1942 Beveridge Report. Even Conservatives, who did not share the public's enthusiasm, felt bound to defer to it.[2] Although Mass Observation reported that four fifths of servicemen did not believe wholeheartedly in any party,[3] by 1945 the armed forces were being identified by the left-wing press as the natural beneficiaries of a socialist government. In July the *Daily Mirror* ran an emotive campaign urging women to vote 'on behalf of the men who won the victory for you'.[4] The Labour Party was duly elected, and Britain's wartime servicemen and women were successfully demobilised by the end of 1946.

Those who had forged a sense of community in such films as *In Which We Serve* and *The Way Ahead* were now 'demobbed' and de-glamorised. Those actors and technicians absent from the industry were also returning. In *Picturegoer* in July 1945, actor Derek Farr paid tribute to those who had 'made British production possible', and asked of the 300 actors who were in the services, prisoners of war or war workers, 'What is to become of them?'[5] Occasionally actors were given roles which reflected their own experiences in the services. As a Captain in the Grenadier Guards, Derek Bond was taken prisoner in 1944 near Florence, and spent the rest of the war in a prisoner-of-war camp outside Munich. When cast in his first film as an officer in the prisoner-of-war drama *The Captive Heart*, he was, reported *Picturegoer*, 'thoroughly at home in the part'.[6]

In the event, film-makers unearthed a rich seam of material in the readjustment difficulties experienced by all manner of people. In Angus Calder's words, 'the fear of death was departing; the fear of life was returning'.[7] Advice tended to involve re-creating wartime camaraderie, showing an awareness of the value of the community-based existence in the services. The British Legion proposed that 'mixing-in' would ensure that the serviceman would feel 'a full member of the civilian community'.[8] The BBC's programme *Civvy Street* bluntly stated that in rejoining the civilian world of the banker, the accountant and the engineer, the ex-serviceman clad in bowler hat rather than uniform was 'once more that nonentity, a civilian, and profoundly bored'.[9] While officialdom and the public had limited patience with those finding readjustment difficult, film-makers were unhesitant about addressing those anxieties. As ex-servicemen came to terms with the fact that their old life of comradeship had vanished, films explored, with a sympathetic eye, the difficulties in their relationship with the community. As time passed, the ex-serviceman was portrayed as cynical, world-weary and alienated. He descended from an existence where responsibility towards others was critical to a life in which self-seeking individualism predominated. By the end of the decade, the ex-serviceman had become almost stereotypical in his villainy.

Civilians uprooted by the exigencies of war were also shown at odds with the community, where the notions of acceptance and belonging were sharply defined. In 1944, Mass Observation had evidence that 'the purpose-fulness of war, the sense of common cause and effort for an end beyond self and employer, has captured very many minds and is one of the things which people most dread losing when the war is over'.[10] The community on the screen was no longer the warm-hearted collective which beckoned the spectator to join. The town of Denfield in *Frieda*, which Robert remembers as a 'pleasant, peaceful spot', has an ugly insularity that compels its residents to ostracise his German bride. Yet several years later, in *The Franchise Affair*, the community is hostile to any stranger. By the late 1940s, when advocates of communal life like J.B. Priestley were disillusioned, the notion of the benevolent community seemed to be long past.

In France, *les absents* were not the victorious heroes that Britain awaited, but the casualties of the occupation, over 940,000 prisoners of war and

750,000 workers in the Service de Travail Obligatoire (STO) in Germany.[11] Concentration-camp survivors comprising *résistants* and political and racial *déportés*, who had numbered 138,853, were now only 40,190. Only 2.7 per cent of the racial *déportés* had survived.[12] In total the *rapatriés* comprised over 4.5 per cent of the French population. Almost every family had had to cope without at least one man for part or all of the occupation.[13] The liberation of France represented far more than just a territorial deliverance from the occupiers, the return of loved ones and a resumption of normal life. France was a nation in turmoil through its recent history, a hasty and ignominious military defeat which led to an 'accommodation' with the occupiers,[14] and the fact of collaboration. Of these divisive years, *les absents* knew very little.

Rapatriés faced innumerable difficulties. The deeply ambivalent attitude towards them is indicated by the lengthy period between liberation in August 1944 and *Retour à la vie* (1949, Henri-Georges Clouzot, Georges Lampin, André Cayette and Jean Dréville), the first film about returning *prisonniers de guerre* and *déportés*. In 1945, the perception of the *prisonniers de guerre* who formed the majority of *les absents* was confused and contradictory. Vichy had placed the prison camp at the heart of its communitarian ideal, an organic community, disciplined, obedient, loyal and classless, its interns the future sons of a regenerated France, as Pétain wrote in a prisoner-of-war magazine, 'the true cement of French unity'.[15] Imprisonment, according to the Vichy propaganda machine, resembled a sojourn in a summer camp, to which François Ambrière alluded in his novel, *Les Grand vacances*.[16] However, in 1945 General de Gaulle's founding myth of the post-liberation period was contingent on a united France, whose citizens had stood together in resisting the enemy. Crucial to the 'Gaullist resistancialist myth'[17] was the collective sacrifice of *les absents*.

The *politique* of the Ministère de Prisonniers, Déportés et Rapatriés (MPDR) was to unify *les absents*, whether *prisonniers*, forced labourers or racial or political *déportés*. One poster proclaimed, 'They are united. Do not divide them,'[18] a slogan which suggested a natural unity, regardless of category, but implying that they were divided in the public mind. As we shall see, the public classified the *rapatriés* in terms of degrees of suffering. They were marginalised by the government, which desired that for the good of national solidarity they be forgotten. The late appearance of *Retour à la vie* indicates that *le retour* was not only a highly emotive and painful issue but also that it had not been prioritised in shoring up national identity. Subsequent depictions of *rapatriés* were rare, although, as we shall see, *Le Diable au corps* (1947, Claude Autant-Lara) was provocative about the absent soldier. The problems of the *prisonnier de guerre* became subsumed into a range of films that express a general malaise in French society. The powerful themes which emerge from these films – betrayal, revenge, guilt and alienation – suggest that they functioned cathartically within the process of national recovery.

Historians of the British forces during the Second World War have so far tended to focus on the effects of the conflict on the combatants, rather than the complex repercussions of its aftermath.[19] The psychological effects of the deaths of 326,000 members of the armed forces[20] were felt not only by their families but also by the communities to which they belonged: platoon, aircrew or ship's company. At the outbreak of war, their individualism was quickly subordinated to their new-found status as 'expendable units'.[21] The strain of physical combat was compounded by the proliferation of rumours about faithless wives,[22] notably after the arrival of American servicemen in Britain in early 1942.[23] In response, commanding officers occasionally wrote to wayward spouses upbraiding them for being unpatriotic.[24] In the war 'at the sharp end,' writes John Ellis, 'possibly the only effective check on the inevitable breakdown of individual resilience was the support of the men in one's immediate ambit ... a fierce and enduring commitment of men one to another'.[25] Thus while repatriation restored servicemen to their families, it broke other unique ties. Army psychiatrist Lieutenant-Colonel T.F. Main argued that demobilisation was potentially destabilising and 'likely to lead to a loosening of the bonds of mutual effort and of the larger group loyalties which sprang up in the period of mutual danger'.[26] Significantly, the Ministry of Labour's recruitment campaign for miners in 1947 appealed to wartime camaraderie: 'There's comradeship in the mining community such as there was in the services'.[27] Yet by then demobilised men, assimilated or not, were left to their own devices. Films then began to depict the ex-serviceman as missing both the purpose of the war and the fellowship of service life. Once a vital constituent of a team in *In Which We Serve* and *The Way Ahead*, the former hero was now portrayed as an isolated and ambivalent individual at odds with society.

J.B. Priestley's novel *Three Men in New Suits* (1945)[28] reflects his enthusiasm towards a government committed to 'community' over 'private interests'.[29] Each fictional returnee is invested with a deep humanity gained from his wartime service, which contrasts with the selfishness and lack of compassion they encounter in civilian life. Priestley's innate optimism returns at the end of the novel when the spirit of community triumphs as the men for whom war has been a formative experience come to realise that they have the ability 'to create a new life' by working together.[30] Yet the village still harbours the unpalatable elements which made the men's homecoming a culture shock. By 1949, Priestley, in common with other idealists, was disheartened by the persistence of those elements. He believed that there was an apathy caused by lack of leadership, an 'infection' which had spread down to the 'ex-Service lads'.[31] His script for Henry Cass's film *Last Holiday* (1950) reveals his growing cynicism about the 'deserving' ex-serviceman. At an expensive seaside hotel, a police officer arrives in pursuit of Squadron Leader Derek Rockingham (Brian Worth), a currency smuggler. When Rockingham is reminded of his 'first class war record' he dismisses it, saying that it meant very little when he was looking for a job. Rockingham's subsequent departure separates him from the residents, who unite to run the hotel when the staff go on strike and experience 'the common joy of finding something useful to do'.[32] While Priestley supports the notion that there is still mutual satisfaction in pulling together, the disgraced Rockingham will not be a part of this benevolent community.

Even before the war had ended, *Waterloo Road* (1945, Sidney Gilliat) engaged with the idea of creating a just and equitable society. It suggested that the average 'Tommy' deserved to live in a community based on the values for which he had fought. Jim Colter (John Mills) absconds from camp when he hears that his wife has been seen out with the local 'spiv' Ted Purvis (Stewart Granger). Doctor Montgomery (Alistair Sim) tells Jim, 'You make the sacrifices, you fellows in the services. You don't want the Ted Purvises of this world to reap the benefits when it's all over.' Significantly, the critics were universally enthusiastic over Colter's successful scrap with Purvis. *Kinematograph Weekly*, ever-vigilant of audience tastes, concluded that 'it will please the crowd all right'[33] and *Picturegoer* that it was a 'homeric' fight, with 'real guts and a lot of satisfaction in it'.[34] The public also related to Purvis's routing. A respondent to an audience survey wrote, 'here was a "Ted Purvis" just like the one you had met ... you went out of the cinema immensely cheered by the fact that the soldier had fought a great fight, and won, and that the rotter had really got his just deserts'.[35] This response suggests relief that a hard-working London neighbourhood which has survived the Blitz, has been well rid of an undeserving parasite.

The number of post-war films depicting unsettled misfits seems to corroborate Mass Observation's warning that while individual difficulties may be slight, the 'aggregate total of restless and unsettled people will present a problem'.[36] In Ealing's *Dead of Night* (1945), a compendium of ghost stories, the war is present in a metaphorical sense. The men in each story reject reality and society, representing wartime culture, retreating instead into a 'private world of doubts and fears', representing civilian life.[37] In 'The Haunted Mirror' (Robert Hamer), Peter (Ralph Michael) is tormented by the reflection in an antique mirror of a room in which a gruesome murder took place the century before. The reflection obsesses him to the point of insanity, and he tries to strangle his wife Joan (Googie Withers). Peter is not an ex-serviceman, but Ralph Michael usually played 'everyman' heroes, as in Ealing's *San Demetrio-London* (1943, Charles Frend) and *For Those in Peril* (1944, Charles Crichton), but in *Dead of Night* he finds himself without those bonds of companionship. As Charles Barr writes, it 'demobs and disorientates the Ralph Michael character and puts him into a life of unreality'.[38] Joan smashes the mirror and ends the nightmare, but the conflicts and inadequacies the vision have summoned up in Peter's mind have been abated rather than fully extinguished.

A number of other films deal directly with ex-servicemen who are plagued by severe uncertainties and doubts. Significantly, British cinema had no equivalent to *The Best Years of Our Lives* (1946) by American director William Wyler, a moving, perceptive film about the return of three demobilised men to their home town, for whom family, community and the American way of life prove to be the agents of recovery. It clearly struck a chord with British audiences, as it was the top box-office film of 1948.[39] British films like *Great Day* (Lance Comfort, 1945), *They Made Me a Fugitive* (Alberto Cavalcanti, 1947) and *Cage of Gold* (1950, Basil Dearden) are less sure about the benevolence of the community, and belong to a larger group identified by Andrew Spicer as indicative of a 'profound social dislocation and a crisis of masculine identity'.[40] The ex-servicemen in these three films become embroiled in criminal activities, descending from the heights of patriotic heroism into an abyss of self-indulgence. These characterisations, however, become less sympathetic by the end of the 1940s. *Great Day* is about a veteran of the First World War who steals a ten-shilling note. He is anguished by his act, and is dealt with gently. In contrast, *Cage of Gold* portrays an ex-RAF officer as an unredeemed rogue who cares little for the people around him and dies as a result of his fecklessness.

Great Day is based on a play by Lesley Storm about a rural Women's Institute preparing for a visit from Mrs Roosevelt.[41] It was released in April 1945, only three days after the death of President Roosevelt. Its stress on communal effort clearly comes too late to constitute propaganda, argues Neil Rattigan, so it must be 'a recognition of the people's contribution to the people's war, and indeed a celebration of the community which the war engendered'.[42] While the film certainly celebrates community, the changes to the original play provide further insights as to its meaning. In the play, the character of Major Ellis, a World War One veteran, is marginal, and when he does appear he is a misogynistic bully, deriding the Institute as a 'dreary female conspiracy'.[43] In the film, the part of Ellis is greatly enhanced, undoubtedly because Eric Portman played the role, but also because it addresses post-war adjustment at a time when demobilisation and its attendant difficulties were imminent.

Ellis's solitary plight contrasts with the communality of the Women's Institute. Rejected for the Home Guard through ill-health, his frustration that he cannot contribute has led him to feel excluded from village life. In a scene not in the play, Ellis explains his feeling of entrapment to his daughter Meg (Sheila Sim) as they sit watching a hawk soaring above them. This scene recalls one in *A Canterbury Tale* in which Thomas Colpeper and Alison Smith, also played by Portman and Sim, talk privately on a hill.[44] The spiritual intensity of Colpeper is there in John Ellis, but while the Pilgrims Way encapsulates for Colpeper England's heritage and beauty, Denley imprisons Ellis, its close-knit community emphasising his conspicuously redundant presence. In the play, Ellis's successful suicide effectively dismisses an unloved and unpleasant character, whereas in the film Ellis is redeemed by Meg, who saves him with reassurance and understanding, suggesting that veterans deserve to be understood.

The fall from grace of ex-RAF officers Clem Morgan (Trevor Howard) in *They Made Me A Fugitive* and Bill Glennon (David Farrar) in *Cage of Gold* is far more dramatic. There had been a heroic mystique about the airforce since the Battle of Britain in August 1940. In one of his most memorable speeches, Churchill spoke about the debt owed to 'the few', while pilot Richard Hillary, who embodied the courageous airman, described his experiences as one of 'the few', being shot down, horrifically burned and 'patched up' by surgeon Archibald McIndoe.[45] Squadron Leader John Pudney's poem 'Johnny-in-the-clouds', used in Anthony Asquith's film *The Way to the Stars* (1945) became almost as famous as Rupert Brooke's 'The Soldier'.[46] In the film, 'Toddy' (Rosamund John), owner of 'The Red Lion' where the flyers congregate in the evenings, is unrepentant that she married an airman (Michael Redgrave) who was subsequently killed. Her conviction would have been deeply reassuring at a critical time when many women were coming to terms with losing their loved ones. Significantly, *The Way to the Stars* was voted best film of the war by 500,000 readers of the *Daily Mail* in April 1946 at a time when war films were actually far less popular.[47]

Given the exalted status of the airman, Morgan's and Glennon's decision to get into 'rackets' appears to be the result of complete disillusionment. Their entry into underworld communities, Morgan into the London gangland, Glennon into international currency smuggling, excludes them from the mainstream 'purposeful' community of work, home and family. Morgan spends his time in Soho bars on the verge of alcoholism, a disease that afflicted some ex-servicemen who missed the 'convivial camaraderie' of the services.[48] Through sheer boredom he joins a gang of black-marketeers, but he balks at the idea of smuggling narcotics and is framed by the gang-leader 'Narcy' (Griffith Jones) for murder. Morgan escapes from prison and finds refuge at an isolated house. Bitterly, he explains to his hostess that he merely continued doing 'what the country put me in a uniform to do', a line which the British Board of Film Censors objected to, noting that 'it is not likely to help recruiting and is a disparagement of H.M.'s forces'.[49] Both the *News Chronicle* and *Picturegoer* were unmoved by Morgan's feeling of exploitation and abandonment.[50] *Sight and Sound,* however, discerned a mood of 'post-war depression and spiritual confusion', and Morgan himself personified 'decent humanity ... demoralised by war and unfitted for peace'.[51] Morgan shows his residual morality in refusing to handle cocaine, and although he is arrested there is clearly the possibility of redemption through a sympathetic policeman and a young woman who promises to wait for him. With luck, then, he will return to society and enjoy family life. Not so for Bill Glennon in *Cage of Gold,* who threatens the cornerstone of community and nation, the family.

By 1949, rebuilding the family, which had been disrupted by the war, was a pressing issue.[52] At the peak of the conflict, two-and-a-half million husbands were separated from their families and most of the quarter of a million men posted abroad did not see home for at least five years.[53] The separation took its toll on some marriages, and there was a huge rise in divorces from 9970 in 1939 to 24,847 in 1947.[54] The report of the Royal Commission on Population published in 1949 concluded that women's war work had been a contributory factor in the decline in the population, and recommended incentives to make motherhood more attractive.[55] *Cage of Gold,* made in 1950, is therefore propitious in that the heroine is pressurised to choose between two men to safeguard her family. Bill Glennon is the antithesis of Alan Kearn (James Donald), a dull but worthy doctor torn between working for his father's practice in the NHS and Harley Street. Indeed Glennon opts for an 'international' existence which completely detaches him from British concerns. As he complains to former lover Judy (Jean Simmons), 'When your only trade is shooting down aeroplanes, you have to make it the best way you can'. Attractive and apparently affluent, he charms his way back into Judy's life, but being unremittingly caddish he deserts her on their wedding night although she is pregnant. Judy later marries Kearn, who has chosen the NHS. A few years later, Glennon returns to disrupt their happy family. By making the 'right' choice, Judy has 'returned' to marriage and motherhood while the socially irresponsible Glennon, who is shot dead, has been thoroughly expunged. Thus the community has been neatly restored to a condition of equilibrium.

The ill-used serviceman was an enduring character. In *Room at the Top* (1959, Jack Clayton), the story of Joe Lampton's (Laurence Harvey) rise to 'the top', the legacy of Joe's experience as a prisoner of war is given more emphasis than in John Braine's novel.[56] Arriving in the prosperous town of Warnley to start a promising job in local government, Joe tells his new colleague Charles that he is relieved to be shaking off grimy, working-class Dufton. 'When I was a POW,' he says, 'at least there was…a limit to the time you served, but Dufton…that seemed like a lifetime sentence'. Setting his sights on Susan Brown, the daughter of a wealthy mill owner, he meets her boyfriend Jack Wales, a former Squadron Leader. 'Sergeant Observer eh?' says Wales, and to Joe's enquiring look adds, 'I can always tell'. In the novel, Wales is a harmless, rather comic character endowed with 'a big RAF moustache' and 'an amiable, rugged face',[57] a far cry from the supercilious snob on screen who calls Joe 'Sergeant' at every opportunity, consequently fuelling Joe's determination to reach 'the top'. In Basil Dearden's *League of Gentlemen* (1960), the seven 'flawed' and impecunious ex-army officers assembled by Colonel Hyde (Jack Hawkins) for a daring bank robbery are initially enticed by the prospect of money which will offer some relief from their present entrapment. Yet as Tim O. Sullivan writes, it is more the possibility of recapturing 'the old camaraderie, self-respect and unity of purpose' which is absent in their civilian existence.[58]

The civilian population had also experienced fear and danger. The majority of lives had been disrupted,[59] and an estimated four million people had been involved in three waves of evacuation. The 'Blitz' had made one-and-a-half million people homeless and had prompted migration to the outer suburbs, breaking up neighbourhoods on a large and sometimes permanent scale.[60] Many wartime communities had seen a constant ebb and flow of people, including those disgorged by neighbouring airbases and army camps. As Patrick Hamilton observed in his novel *The Slaves of Solitude*, 'The war seemed to have conjured into being, from nowhere, magically, a huge population of its own – one which flowed into and filled every channel and crevice of the country – the towns, the villages, the streets, the trains, the buses, the shops, the hotels, the inns, the restaurants, the movies'.[61] Hamilton suggests that his boarding-house refugees will not easily find peace after the war.

The same rootlessness is evoked in films where the residents of seedy boarding houses, shabby rooms and run-down hotels, are isolated and disillusioned. The urban squalor of these establishments not only compounds the outsider status of the people who inhabit them but contrasts with the cheery conviviality of wartime pubs and hotels, which enhances the camaraderie within. The chumminess of the Red Lion in *The Way to the Stars*, where airmen and residents enjoy a nightly sing-song, is a world away from the anonymity of the lodging house in *It Always Rains on Sunday* (1947), where a dozen homeless men sleep. *The October Man* (1947, Roy Baker) is one of several films of this period to feature an obsessed protagonist. Jim Ackland (John Mills), recovering from a year in hospital following his involvement in a fatal accident, moves to the Brockhurst Common Hotel in the London suburbs and is alarmed by the proximity of the residents. His room seems like a prison cell where he is tormented by intrusive sounds, a space where the idea of 'a trustworthy and unified community' does not exist.[62] In *London Belongs to Me* (1948, Sidney Gilliat), the parsimonious Mrs Vizzard (Joyce Carey)[63] presides over her seedy lodging house in Kennington, a sanctuary for a fake medium and a young murderer. In *Train of Events* (1949, Sidney Cole, Basil Dearden and Charles Crichton), two outsiders, an orphan of the Blitz and a German deserter, are expelled from their temporary refuge, a dingy room in a tatty London boarding house. The rootless English girl and the displaced German are simply too marginalised ever to be assimilated into British society.

The influx of European and American servicemen certainly made an impression on the British people. The 'GIs' had more impact on the British population than any other nationality,[64] and were depicted in positive terms in films like *Waterloo Road* and *The Way to the Stars*. After the war, however, they were not always popular. In *Train of Events*, Jim Hardcastle (Jack Warner) grumbles when his daughter Doris (Susan Shaw) arranges to meet a former GI boyfriend who is visiting London, 'I suppose you'll be chewing gum again and calling me "Pop"'. After the Americans had returned home in 1945, film-makers were more preoccupied with Europeans. In *Frieda* (1947, Basil Dearden) based on Ronald Millar's successful play,[65] the audience is invited to consider a problematic outsider, the German bride of an English officer. In 1945–46, German women married to servicemen were arriving in Britain. While some marriages failed because of anti-German feeling in Britain, others were very successful.[66] An emotive publicity campaign was mounted, the press book emphasising that the film was 'delving into a great controversy of our time'.[67] Advertisements asked, 'Would You Take Frieda into Your Home?', a question to which various 'members of the public' gave their answers.[68] Cinema managers were encouraged to assemble local 'juries' to debate the question and to interview resident German girls to ask about how they had been received.[69] 'Journey's end,' Bob tells Frieda, after days of arduous travelling. Yet this is merely the beginning of myriad difficulties ahead of them.

Frieda has been interpreted in two ways. Charles Barr argues that the conflicts which are 'seething just below the rational humanist surface' are articulated primarily through Bob (David Farrar).[70] Apparently exterior problems are the reflections of his own repressed fears, which he projects onto Frieda in the form of unconsciously 'sadistic' behaviour: he fails to 'smooth the way' for her arrival; leaving his teaching post increases her guilt, and he brings her into awkward public situations, notably his MP aunt Nell's speech about German culpability.[71] Charlotte Brundson's and Rachel Moseley's reading of the film centres on Frieda's femininity, which 'demobilises' fixed notions of national identity into an acceptable post-war 'norm'.[72] As *Frieda* becomes assimilated into the community, her conspicuously 'German' appearance, braided hair, brogues and leather coat disappear, and she becomes femininised and 'English'. The film, however, is about Bob and Frieda, and Denfield.

Bob's disorientation is anticipated by the film's exciting opening, in which the wedding ceremony is conducted in the shell of a Polish church amid exploding bombs. The scene is lit in a 'noirish' style which is juxtaposed with images of Denfield, which though it appears as a bright, pleasant market town, seems in comparison inexplicably bland. At home and relieved of his RAF uniform he seems emasculated and de-glamorised. 'I'm not very sure of myself,' he tells the Headmaster, and after he resigns his brother Tony (Tony Jackson) says, 'You don't look so good in civvies Robert,' to which he replies 'I don't feel so good either'. Indeed Ricky (Albert Lieven), Frieda's Nazi brother who appears near the end of the film, can be read as Bob's other 'warped' self, committed to war and incapable of functioning in the civilian world.

Meanwhile all Denfield's prejudices are mustered against Frieda. A builder whose son was killed at Ardennes refuses to carry out repairs on the Dawsons' house; groups of women stare and gossip loudly when Frieda and Judy (Glynis Johns) go to the town hall to register Frieda for a ration book; there are absentees in Bob's class at school and a note is passed round likening Frieda to a 'werewolf'. Edith (Gladys Henson), the Dawsons' loyal maid, complains that the whole town is acting 'as if we've got the plague or something'. Yet by Christmas 1945 Mrs Dawson (Barbara Everest) tells her sister Nell (Flora Robson), 'Oh, Frieda's one of us now'. But when Ricky materialises, Bob and the whole community erupt with repressed violence, proving how very tenuous their acceptance of Frieda has been. Barr notes that Denfield's strength is its 'closeness',[73] yet the tortuous route Frieda undergoes to be accepted indicates that community 'closeness' can be a hostile force, and indeed is only brought about, just as for Elsa in *Retour à la vie*, after her attempted suicide. When a Mass Observer attended a screening of

8. *Frieda* (1947, Basil Dearden), with David Farrar and Mai Zetterling. Canal+ Image UK.

Frieda, he noted that 'there was clapping when the aunt said in the car that all Germans were bad'.[74] Nell recognises the community's natural tolerance towards strangers, but she believes it is ill-considered, 'our strength and our weakness'. The threat Frieda represents lies beyond the scope of the film itself, a fear that Frieda may be a 'Nazi "werewolf" in sheep's clothing, contaminating the very blood of the next generation'.[75] In *Frieda*, a darker 'other' world of the film noir is summoned up and seemingly quashed.

The film noir is primarily associated with a male protagonist who is tormented by a crime (though he is often innocent), and consequently feels excluded from the community. *Frieda,* whose heroine feels culpable for the crimes of Germany, shows that such unease was not gender-specific. Rose Sandigate in *It Always Rains on Sunday* is alienated from her own neighbourhood by helping her fugitive ex-lover, but she is safely returned to it after his arrest. *The Franchise Affair* (1951, Lawrence Huntington), based on Josephine Tey's novel,[76] focuses on the social alienation of women, demonstrating the persistence of the notion of the prejudiced community. Marion Sharpe (Dulcie Gray) and her mother, who are newcomers to rural Milford, a town much like *Frieda*'s Denfield, are completely ostracised by the locals, who believe that they have abducted a local girl. A local solicitor, Robert Blair (Michael Denison), acts for them and soon finds that Milford, 'such a quiet dignified little place' according to his aunt, has become riven with suspicion and hatred. His only allies are the two men who run the local garage, both ex-servicemen who experience in the operation the sense of purpose they had known in the war. When the girl is proved to be a liar, the Sharpes are vindicated. While the novel merely describes Marion Sharpe's sympathy for the girl's mother, who she says now 'has nothing. Just a desolation,'[77] the film shows her doting and duped aunt standing alone outside the court, condemned to the same marginalisation suffered by the Sharpes.

This portrait of an ambivalent and far-from-benign community differs from other films, especially the Ealing comedies. Yet these films evoke and reiterate the wartime community, in which there is indeed a 'return' to privations but also the camaraderie that war instilled. The community most nostalgic for the war is in *Passport to Pimlico* (1949, Henry Cornelius). Miramont Place in Pimlico, populated, as in Ealing's wartime films, by a cross-section of society, is discovered to be part of ancient Burgundy, and the residents declare independence from Britain. Briefly, they revel in freedom from restrictions, but when Whitehall imposes frontier controls, Miramont Place is under siege. All the wartime motifs appear – evacuation, rationing and communal meals – while residents like Arthur Pemberton (Stanley Holloway) joyfully dust off their ARP helmets. Significantly, Henry Cornelius wrote in *Kinematograph Weekly* a few months after the film's release that 'not in any sphere of life in Britain today does there seem to be a common purposeful emotion which could be compared to wartime'.[78] Beneath the whimsy, the idea that community spirit and the desire for success and freedom can be reconciled is being tested. As Charles Barr argues, the sadness at the end is not the distribution of ration books, but the proof of the extent of the polarisation 'between recreated past and threatening future'.[79]

As Britain entered the 1950s, retrospective appeals to wartime communality continued. *The Happy Family* (1952, Muriel Box) again conjures up the notion of siege against outsiders. Its background was the Festival of Britain, 'as much the creation of nervousness as of confidence'.[80] Nervousness is suggested by an evocation of Churchillian doggedness rather than the security of Attlee's 'New Jerusalem'. The Lords, who run a small shop on the South Bank, protest against its demolition so that an access road to the Festival's exhibition site can be built, and barricade themselves in. The Lords are resisting not just the road but the Festival itself, an event intended to celebrate Britain's recovery from the war. The Festival was, as Michael Frayn saw it, the last great manifestation of the 'Herbivores', before Churchill and his 'Carnivores' assumed power.[81] The Lords represent the last bastion of the wartime community; in their self-imposed rationing and their rabbit called Winston, their espousal of Churchill's Britain is undoubted.

A poster of a naked man emerging from a barbed-wire fence with the caption 'Retour à la France, Retour à la vie' encapsulates the main event of 1945.[82] *Retour à la vie* was made in 1949, the first film to be made on the subject of deportation and imprisonment. The considerable gap between the liberation in August 1944 and its making, during which there was a plethora of 'resistance' films, indicates that the return of France's absent population was a troublesome issue. At the end of 1944, the 'Semaine de l'absent' organised by the Ministère de Prisonniers, Déportés et Rapatriés (MPDR), reminded the nation of its missing population and of the government's commitment to the moral readjustment of the *rapatriés*. The greatest proportion of *rapatriés* were *prisonniers de guerre*, who were held responsible for the military defeat and four years of occupation, repression and hardship. In the 'hierarchy of suffering' which emerged in the public consciousness after liberation, *prisonniers* were at the bottom.[83] Nevertheless, film-makers found it easier to deal with their return and readjustment than that of the *déportés*.

Of those who began arriving in April 1945 from Nazi concentration camps, the few Jewish survivors were simply assimilated into the 'undifferentiated mass of déportés'.[84] Significantly, the prologue of *Retour à la vie* only refers to 'prisonniers militaires' and 'déportés politiques'. The response of the authorities to the *rapatriés* was ambivalent from the outset. The higher 'status' of *déportés* is indicated by the fact that they were provided with greater financial and welfare assistance than *prisonniers* had received.[85] On the one hand, an emotional de Gaulle made a great show of greeting the first women *déportées* from Ravensbruck at the Gare de l'Est while a band played 'La Marseillaise'.[86] On the other, *prisonniers*, whose solidarity was evident in the increased membership of the Fédération Nationale de Prisonniers de Guerre,[87] were perceived as politically destabilising, an official memorandum from the MPDR noting that they could become 'stakes in an internal political struggle'.[88] *Les Lettres françaises* however, argued that these 'exiled brothers…had a right before all others to speak in the France of tomorrow'.[89] Despite demands for a postponement until May, when repatriation would be complete, the municipal elections were held in April, although *déportés* and *prisonniers de guerre* were being included on lists of electoral candidates whether they had returned or not.[90] In their absence, women, who represented 53 per cent of the electorate had voted for the first time and were urged to do so on behalf of *les absents*.[91] 'How righteous their indignation will be,' exclaimed the Socialist Party, 'if through carelessness or ignorance you have contributed to the ruination of their hopes'.[92] However, female enfranchisement emphasised the sense of exclusion felt by *les absents*, and compounded the difficulties of some in readjusting.

Charles de Gaulle's mission was to consolidate the 'Nation' and the 'Resistance' into an all-embracing heroism with which he tried to smother the unwelcome 'cult of veteranism'.[93] Victims described their own diverse experiences in over 100 works published between 1945 and 1947.[94] According to J.M. Guillon, the historiography of 'resistance' writing began with an exultant phase that lasted until 1951.[95] The film industry also concentrated on celebrating France as a community of *résistants* rather than dissecting recent history. Of the 11 war films made between liberation and the end of 1945, eight had Resistance themes.[96] As the director of the Cinématographie française, Michel Fourré-Cormeray wrote that films should let other countries know 'of the sacrifices and the heroism of our people'.[97] Resistance films, which had all but disappeared by 1948, engaged with the idea of common purpose, which had been absent in films during the occupation. Audiences could watch and identify with their compatriots as they engaged in resistance activities on screen.

Until 1949, the sporadic references to *rapatriés* in film tacitly confirmed their problematic status in society. As we saw in chapter 4, in *Farrebique* (1947) director Georges Rouquier excluded Albert, who had just returned from a prisoner-of-war camp, because his appearance would have subverted the portrait of tradition and continuity Rouquier sought to achieve. On the other hand, in *Nuit sans fin* (1947, Jacques Séverac), the returning soldier, although he has done national service in North Africa rather than fought the war with Germany, is welcomed by a celebration involving the whole community. While *prisonniers de guerre* did not merit the attention of film-makers until *Retour à la vie*, the response to *The Captive Heart* (1946, Basil Dearden), which reached French cinemas in August 1947, is significant. Its story of four years spent by British prisoners in a German camp had a vicarious appeal at a time when there was no equivalent film in France. 'These men,' concluded *Cinémonde*, 'deserve to have their film'.[98] During the occupation, Maurice Chevalier had entertained internees in a camp where he had been imprisoned during the First World War, and his songs, urging them to 'have faith in the future', were broadcast to other camps.[99] Yet the sense of comradeship which Chevalier and other singers inspired, and the solidarity and *esprit de corps* which Vichy propaganda so assiduously promoted, were values found in post-war films about *résistants*, not *prisonniers*.

The controversy which raged over *Le Diable au corps* (1947, Claude Autant-Lara) indicates the sensitivity about absent soldiers and their importance to the country. Based on Raymond Radiguet's acclaimed novel,[100] set during the First World War, the story concerns a love affair between a boy of 17, François (Gérard Philipe), and a young woman, Marthe (Micheline Presle), whose husband is fighting in the trenches. Marthe becomes pregnant, but just as the Armistice is being celebrated and her husband returns, she dies in childbirth. Radiguet wrote that for François and many boys like him, the war merely represented 'four years of a great holiday'.[101] Indeed in the film Marthe and François are 'liberated' by war and able to behave in a manner which would have been unthinkable during peacetime. François abrogates his responsibility to his family by lying to his parents, and Marthe neglects her wifely duties, encapsulated in the moment when she tears up a letter from her husband. The producer, Paul Graetz, demanded that one piece of dialogue be cut. François has just read Marthe a sonnet by Rimbaud, 'Le Dormeur du val', describing a dead soldier:

Marthe: I am definitely not made for war.
François: No-one is.
Marthe: But everyone is in the war.
François: Not us.[102]

The scene was excised, but the film still provoked much controversy. At the premiere in Bordeaux, the audience whistled and protested throughout,[103] and the municipal council declared it 'shocking, scabrous and painful'.[104] In a highly publicised incident at the Brussels Film Festival in 1947, the French ambassador walked out of the screening, exclaiming 'the film is a scandal'.[105] The crucial point was that the betrayed man was a soldier 'fighting at the front for his country',[106] even though Marthe is ultimately 'punished' by her death as the war ends, thereby relegating her transgressive behaviour to the past.[107] Veterans were disturbed by the film. The mayor of Vannes banned it under pressure from associations of *anciens combatants* and family organisations.[108] *Le Diable au corps* was nevertheless considered an important film, because it was entered for the Cannes Film Festival in 1947. The melee of responses the film drew from various quarters was largely due to the fact that it cast aspersions on the army as one of the nation's fundamental institutions at a time when reasserting the national community was vital.

The sensitive subject of *rapatriés* was not dealt with directly until 1949 in *Retour à la vie*, directed by Henri-Georges Clouzot, Georges Lampin, André Cayatte and Jean Dréville. It is not mentioned by either Susan Hayward or Alan Williams in their books,[109] yet it is the only major film of the period to address *le retour*. Four of the sketches are about returning *prisonniers de guerre* while one deals with deportation, which was still something of a taboo subject. Indeed, after the initial welcome given to *déportés*, their return was 'the event most quickly effaced from the memory'.[110] In the published script of *Les Portes de la nuit* (1946, Marcel Carné), Diego and Raymond mention Buchenwald and Dachau, but the conversation is not in the film.[111] Indeed the censor, the Commission de contrôle, which previewed *Retour à la vie* does not mention the sketch about the *déportée* and describes it as a film about *prisonniers de guerre*.[112] The official silence about *déportés raciaux* is reflected in the prologue, which refers only to military prisoners and political deportees.

Le Retour de Tante Emma (André Cayatte) concerns the homecoming of Emma (Mme de Revinksy) from Dachau. She lies dying in a darkened room, her silence contrasting with the loud arguing of her nephews outside. In her absence, Gaston (Bernard Blier) has forged her signature on a document in order to obtain a legacy, but now requires another signature. His children, he tells her, are suffering 'like you, the sufferings of hell'. Long past caring, Emma agrees to sign, her selflessness emphasised by the fact that Charles and Gaston quarrel again while she does so. Charles de Gaulle's mission to reunite France was predicated on the idea that the victims of Nazism had all suffered equally, which was contradicted by the arrival of emaciated concentration-camp survivors at the reception centre at the Hotel Lutétia in Paris in April 1945.[113] In an effort to cover up the truth about the camps, letters from interns to their families describing conditions were retained by the *contrôle postale*.[114] The sight of the victims themselves could not be prevented, however, so their conspicuous striped 'pyjamas' were quickly banned from official ceremonies.[115] Emma is similarly inconspicuous, a shadow of her former self, silent and barely visible. The suggestion that Gaston's children have suffered in equal measure to Emma, and that Gaston has profited from her absence, would have been deeply uncomfortable for French audiences.

Le Retour d'Antoine (Georges Lampin) is a lighter episode about a former prisoner Antoine (François Périer) who returns to his job as a barman in a Paris hotel to find that it has been requisitioned by the American Women's Army Corps (WAC). Having no parents, no family and no commitments, he tells his friend and fellow barman that 'it's easy coming back'. However, when he begins night duty the handsome Antoine is soon pursued by two flirtatious WACs. In a fit of pique, the captain transfers him onto the day shift, but Antoine successfully maintains his dignity compared to the empty-headed and silly WACs. While making Antoine a disruptive influence on a supposedly disciplined community of women, it is also a wry comment on the American Allies who had liberated the city, despite de Gaulle's insistence that France had liberated itself.

Le Retour de Jean (Henri-Georges Clouzot) deals with the darker aspects of the human psyche. Jean (Louis Jouvet), an ex-prisoner of war living in Paris shortly before the Allied invasion, is traumatised by the past and deeply embittered. His bad humour is exacerbated by pain from a wounded leg which requires regular morphine injections. The *locataires* of the boarding house where he lives are a motley collection of war refugees and loners who disgust Jean with their clamour to listen to war bulletins on the radio. 'Enough of these prisoners,' he cries. 'Enough of the radio. Enough of you all!' He rejects any attempts at intimacy, and repulses the attentions of a woman lodger, saying 'I'm finished with women'. Yet when Jean finds an escaped German prisoner in his room who is badly wounded, he immediately relates to him. Discovering that the fugitive is a former SS torturer, Jean feels compelled to find out what motivated the man to perpetrate such evil deeds. The German explains that as a youth after the last war, his life was disordered and chaotic, but Nazism changed everything. 'I felt a member of that body,' he says, 'I gave myself to it entirely'. Like Bob in *Frieda*, faced with the fanatic Nazi Ricky, the German's presence unleashes Jean's repressions and fears. The truth is that Jean is now as marginalised as the SS officer had been. Half fascinated, half repelled, he listens to the fugitive justifying himself and defending his 'duty'. The prisoner also provokes powerful emotions in the local community. Crowds of people are seen and heard baying for his blood, and have to be restrained by the police. The 'people's anger,' as Yves Farge called the *épuration* of collaborators, is here deflected onto the official foe.[116] Still conscious of a link with the German as a fellow escapee, Jean injects him with morphine to ease his painful death.

Le Retour de René (Jean Dréville) is an optimistic tale, although Dréville also satirises the arbitrary nature of the *comités d'épuration* by whom he was twice censured in 1945 for making films for Continental.[117] Preparations for welcoming René Martin (Noël-Noël), the one-hundred-and-fifty-thousandth *prisonnier*, a mistake as it turns out, are overshadowed by references to *comités*. A government delegate tells an official that his *comité d'épuration* is judging cleaning staff at the Propagandstaffel (Propaganda Office) and the Majestic Hotel. Asked about a recent judgement, the delegate says that the suspect was acquitted. 'You're joking,' replies the official. 'But she was a terrible collaborator!' 'Yes,' says that the delegate, 'but apparently she was in the Resistance'. Immediately, then, the audience are told that the *comités* are alarmingly capricious and ready to condemn or discharge on an almost whimsical level. This scene is also a wry comment on the attempt to label almost the whole of France as a community of resisters.

René is presented as an example of the town's loyalty to *les absents*, but returning home he discovers that his wife has left him, and that a refugee family is living in his apartment. He is assailed everywhere by strange sights and unfamiliar people. In a bar filled with American and British soldiers he is amazed to hear a young *trafiquant* in a bar boasting about his lucrative 'business'. After a destabilising period, all ends well and René is befriended by the friendly refugee widow and her two children, a 'surro-gate' family with which Vichy propaganda had consoled *prisonniers de guerre* during their captivity.[118] While this ex-prisoner of war experiences a fairly unproblematic rehabilitation, Dréville's targets are essentially the bureaucrats who not only mete out rough justice in the name of the people but create and preserve a facade of loyalty to *les absents*.

Le Retour de Louis, also by Jean Dréville is remarkably similar to the British film *Frieda*, made two years earlier. Dréville might have seen and been inspired by *Frieda*,[119] although Louis (Serge Reggiani) and Elsa (Anne Campion) were based on a real couple who lived in his village. Unlike Bob and Frieda, Louis and Elsa are mutually in love. Their romance, indicated by soft-focus shots and whispered exchanges, gives an alternative emphasis to the story, which does not venture into the territory of collective responsibility with which Frieda is concerned. Yet Elsa encounters the same hostility from the community when she arrives to live on Louis's family farm. Although essentially kind, his mother is reluctant to embrace Elsa at the station because 'everyone is watching'. Elsa, like Frieda has come from a country 'in ruins', and both her parents are dead, yet her tragic circumstances do little to assuage the ill-will of the villagers. A rock is thrown through the farmhouse window during their first meal, and Louis's sister, whose husband was tortured and is now an invalid, is unreservedly hostile towards her.

The lack of engagement in *Le Retour de Louis* with the wider issue of post-war relations with Germany which dominates *Frieda* indicates how very differently it was perceived by the respective writers/directors. The Germans

9. *Retour à la vie* (1949, Henri-Georges Clouzot, Georges Lampin, André Cayatte and Jean Dréville). *Le Retour de Jean*, with Louis Jouvet. BIFI.

were obviously in greater proximity to the French during the occupation simply because of their presence in towns and villages. Furthermore, three quarters of a million French people went to work in Germany under the Service de travail obligatoire (STO), a subject of controversy even now because of disagreements over the extent to which they were actually 'forced' workers.[120] Whereas Frieda becomes problematic for Bob and fuels his inner angst, the 'problem' of Elsa is projected onto the community, from where there comes an 'official' response. The pathetic-looking deputation of two veterans who arrive at the farm with the mayor, who reads out a list of local men shot by the Germans, appears more like a token complaint than a concerted protest, and they soon slope off back to the village. But when the mayor saves Elsa's life, albeit an obviously far less romantic rescue than that of Frieda by Bob, it is extremely significant. As the community's representative, the mayor's act symbolises the communal nature of the atonement. As Joseph Daniel writes, the story 'uncaps' the likely disapproval of the average French person by showing the audience that such disapproval is entirely unjustified.[121] When the villagers appear delighted at Elsa's rescue, their sudden benevolence is unconvincing to say the least, but it provides a satisfactory resolution to an issue which is clearly still very raw.

Not unexpectedly, *Retour à la vie* elicited a mixed response. The Ministère de la Population was concerned that the film projected the 'painful impression' that the return of *prisonniers* was filled only with bitterness.[122] The Commission de contrôle passed it for exhibition, but on the whole it was badly received by critics concerned that none of the sketches showed what they considered a 'normal' return. The critic of *L'Écran français* emerged from the screening 'with a feeling of uneasiness and a sort of shame and disgust'.[123] However, *Cinématographie française* concluded that it would interest 'all classes of the public', and in particular *déportés* and *prisonniers de guerre* who had lived through such experiences.[124] On being shown in Britain in April 1950, reviewers were impressed with its verisimilitude. The *Sunday Times* wrote that 'the whole piece reflects the post-liberation mood with an accuracy which I have found in no other French film'.[125] The *Observer* found in it 'an extraordinary plea for tolerance'.[126] Whatever insights the film offered into the experience of returning, it would be several years before that subject was addressed once more.[127]

In this context it is worth considering the response in September 1947 to the re-release of *Le Corbeau* (1943, Henri-Georges Clouzot), which had been banned as 'anti-French' at liberation. Its re-appearance on screen provoked an interesting response from *Film français*: 'It is a strange and powerful work whose tragic worth and bitterness shows the profound pessimism on the part of its creators'.[128] Although the onus is on the film-makers for such an interpretation, this comment acknowledges the fact that the occupation was a time of moral turpitude. *Le Corbeau*'s Dr Germain is isolated through creeping suspicion, which is compounded by his outsider status. Male alienation due to war was powerfully articulated in the novel *D'Entre les morts* (1956),[129] on which Hitchcock's masterful study of masculine angst *Vertigo* (1958) was based. The novel's protagonist, Roger Flavière, is alienated not through vertigo but through rejection from the army, making him feel 'doomed to be an outcast'.[130] He fails to prevent his friend's wife from committing suicide, and spends four years exiled in North Africa. He returns to Paris at liberation an alcoholic and obsessed by the past: 'While the other survivors of the war were busy gathering together their bits and pieces, re-building their homes, renewing their friendships ... he had nothing but ashes to poke'.[131] Flavière's path to self-destruction is a perfect metaphor for the painful business of readjustment to post-war life.

The films discussed so far indicate just some of the tensions present in post-liberation France surrounding the return of *prisonniers de guerre* and *déportés*. France also had a huge number of civilian refugees, an estimated 2.4 million people uprooted by *l'exode*, 5 million left homeless and 200,000 displaced foreigners from 17 different countries,[132] for whom the MPDR was responsible.[133] Films not directly concerned with *le retour* raised fundamental questions about this state of flux, about alienation and acceptance, exclusion and inclusion, themes which de Gaulle was eager to bury in his bid to reassert the national community. The film noir, a key style in British and American post-war cinema, had an added bitterness in France, where the term was coined by film critics in 1947 to denote a certain type of crime fiction.[134] In 1948, Gavin Lambert wrote about 'The New Pessimism' which had emerged through the 'disturbed and uncertain conditions of the last few years'.[135] In *Quai des Orfèvres* (1947) Henri-Georges Clouzot's first since being reinstated into the profession,[136] because an innocent character is arrested but does not protest, there is a sense in which culpability must be assumed by somebody. The unwillingness to defend oneself has been identified as a trait in films of this period,[137] and in *Quai des Orfèvres* the hasty acknowledgement of guilt suggests that it is already present. Guilt, disillusionment, betrayal and revenge suffuse *Les Portes de la nuit*, *Un Revenant* (1946, Christian-Jaque), *La Fille du diable* (1946, Henri Decoin) and *Panique* (1947, Julien Duvivier), all of which interpret social realignment in particularly bleak terms.

Revenge in *Les Portes de la nuit* and *Un Revenant* is cathartic for the two protagonists, who have suffered past betrayals. In *Les Portes de la nuit*, it is a time of reckoning for Diego (Yves Montand) when he returns to find that the hero of his *quartier* is none other than the *milicien* who denounced him and his fellow *résistant*. They are both avenged as the collaborator kills himself, but the price paid for revenge is too high, and Diego faces a lonely future, having lost the woman he loves. *Un Revenant* evokes a different kind of bitterness about the past. Jean-Jacques Sauvage (Louis Jouvet) returns to his native Lyons after twenty years and discovers that a youthful 'accident' was actually an attempt on his life by a bourgeois family, fearful that his forthcoming marriage would allow him access into their business. Sauvage dupes his former fiancée Madeleine (Gaby Morlay), now the wife one of the conspirators and unaware of the conspiracy, into leaving her husband, but he abandons her at the last minute. Given the inclusion of *Un Revenant* at the Cannes Film Festival in 1946, where three of the five other films had resistance themes, it should be interpreted as a contemporary drama, indeed an allegory about the return of *les absents*. Gaby Morlay's screen persona before and during Vichy exuded self-sacrifice and stoicism, and in *Le Voile bleu* (1941, Jean Stelli), her portrayal of a woman widowed in the Great War who devotes herself to rearing other people's children symbolised the suffering of France.[138] Metaphorically, then, she must still suffer in *Un Revenant* in the wake of another more divisive war. Noël Burch and Geneviève Sellier thus argue that Sauvage is avenging all soldiers by blaming women for four years safely at home while men were away risking their lives.[139] Sauvage's caustic detachment, contrasting with Madeleine's warm optimism, suggests an inner emptiness and disenchantment with human nature.

As in British cinema, the notion of the outsider, particularly the fugitive who impacts on the community, is a recurring theme. The arrival of fugitives in *Nuit sans fin* and *La Fille du diable* reveal disconcerting traits within the community. In *Nuit sans fin*, Olivier (André Valmy) flees Paris after accidentally killing someone. He finds work at a farm, but soon arouses the enmity of the young men in the village. When a body is found, a group led by the postman elects to hunt him down. This sequence demonstrates urban–rural antagonism, but the self-styled vigilantes are reminders of community *épurateurs,* who in 1944 carried out over eight thousand 'exécutions sauvages' in towns and villages all over France.[140] In *La Fille du diable*, Saget (Pierre Fresnay) flees Paris after robbing a bank. Having assumed the identity of the wealthy and long-lost nephew of a local shopkeeper, he is feted by the residents of the man's home town. Two people discover the truth, a seemingly affable doctor who blackmails Saget into funding community enterprises, and Isabelle (Andrée Clément), an orphan known locally as the 'devil's daughter' who admires Saget's exploits. In Saget and Isabelle, adult alienation is juxtaposed with juvenile delinquency as Isabelle's gang smashes the windows of bourgeois houses. This reflects the concern about the increase in juvenile crime after the liberation, which was partly attributed to the fact that a generation of children had grown up during the 'unhealthy atmosphere' of the occupation.[141] Isabelle is disillusioned at seeing Saget's 'good works', and denounces him, but shoots herself when he is arrested. 'The tone in general,' wrote *Cinémonde*, 'is not without some resemblance to *Le Corbeau*'.[142] Indeed on the first day of filming, Pierre Fresnay, the lead in *Le Corbeau*, was met by a hostile deputation of *résistants,* who proceeded to read out a list of comrades who had been shot,[143] echoing the sequence in *Le Retour de Louis*. This 'return' has had a double benefit to the village, in providing a new TB clinic and ridding the town of a disturbing, anti-social youth. Yet it is also a story of betrayal and guilt, two unpalatable but unavoidable themes in post-liberation France.

The notion of being an outsider in the community was most powerfully conveyed, however, by Julien Duvivier's *Panique*, based on George Simenon's novel *Les Fiançailles de M. Hire* (1933).[144] Duvivier had spent the war years in Hollywood, and *Panique*, his first French film, was keenly anticipated.[145] Monsieur Hire (Michel Simon) is Jewish, a solitary, eccentric man who is regarded with deep suspicion by his neighbours. When a local woman is murdered, he is immediately suspected, and the culprits contrive to plant the victim's handbag in his apartment. Eventually, he is harried out onto the streets by an angry mob, takes refuge at the top of a nearby building where, watched by the crowd, he loses his footing and falls to his death. The film's evocation of revenge and duplicity were recurring themes during this period, yet the savagery of the 'lynch' sequence had particular resonances with the recent past. The critical response indicates considerable discomfort with the film's *dénouement*. *Film français* noted that 'the crowd scenes and the fierce portrait of cruel people is deeply agitating'.[146] *L'Écran français*'s critic was indignant at the implication of 'collective sadism'. 'I refuse to believe,' he wrote, 'that amongst the good people who populate the *arrondissements* of Paris, there would not be some who would protest at the murder of a solitary man'.[147] *Opéra* was unconvinced by the synopsis, which explained that 'M. Hire dies chiefly the victim of the stupidity and cruelty of man'.[148] 'M. Hire,' countered Jean Fayard, 'dies chiefly the victim of the cruelty of Spaak [the screenwriter] and Duvivier'.[149] This defence of the crowd appears rather forced, given that *épuration* had taken the form of a witch-hunt in some regions. Its 'carnivalesque' nature has been seen as evoking a world of licensed violence, of euphoria, excess and finally closure,[150] which *Panique* strongly suggests.

None of the critics mention Hire's Jewishness, which gives a sinister dimension to the crowd's motivation. As we have seen, of all the *rapatriés*, the Jewish victims of the camps were the fewest in number. As Peter Lagrou points out, the success of racial deportation depended on pre-existing antisemitic policies,[151] which permitted 76,000 Jews to disappear into the camps. For the few survivors, Vichy's virulent antisemitism was not easily forgotten.[152] It had certainly not disappeared with the discovery of the Nazi genocide in 1945, as repatriation officials in Toulouse noted that the 'intrigues' of repatriated Jews might provoke a 'new crisis of antisemitism', and resolved to halt their militancy.[153] The deep roots of antisemitism in France seemed to persist in some areas. In 1949, researchers found in a small town which had been temporarily occupied by German troops that of all 'foreigners', the Jews were the group for whom the residents had least sympathy.[154] In this context, Monsieur Hire appears even more a hapless victim of existing prejudices, and as the ultimate outsider a tragic figure of the recent past.

British and French cinema adopted rather different strategies in depicting the return of their absent populations after the war. In Britain, there was little hesitation about including the returning serviceman on the screen. It would have been an easy task to portray the returnees as homecoming heroes, robust and confident and full of tales of derring-do in the wake of victory. Yet films like *Great Day* and *The Captive Heart* instead showed the ex-serviceman and prisoners of war as vulnerable, ill-at-ease with the present and nervous about the future. As if in anticipation of difficulties ahead, at the end of 1945 the demobbed Peter in *Dead of Night*, hero of Ealing's wartime communities, is shown paranoid and disorientated. When demobilisation was past, the public grew tired with the maladjusted ex-soldier or airman. Claims that 'we're all in the front line now' provoked Captain Quintin Hogg MP to refute the implication that there had been 'any comparable degree of sacrifice or hardship between those who worked in civvy street and those who underwent the rigours of life in the field'.[155] Nevertheless, film-makers' depictions appeared to shift as public sympathy waned, and the redemptive ending of *They Made Me a Fugitive* gave way to the damaged 'hero' of *Cage of Gold*.

Civilians, many of whom had been disturbed and unsettled by the war, also returned. Masculine anxiety was indeed critical to the popular film noirs which continued until the early 1950s. At a time when Britain had an influx of European refugees, audiences were asked to consider the ultimate outsider, Frieda, testing the validity of the benign community which wartime film-makers had espoused. Underneath Denfield's acceptance of Frieda lies the extant prejudices of an ambivalent and uncertain population. Suspicion of outsiders was proved to be an innate and enduring facet of community life. *The Franchise Affair* was released during the last few months of the Labour government, and depicted a small town where strangers were immediately thought culpable of a crime. As a character in *Three Men in New Suits* remarks, 'What men remember now is what divides them, not what unites them'.[156] It seemed that the wartime community spirit no longer existed, and could only be recalled though nostalgic stories of siege and civilian battles. 'We are revolutionaries,' wrote J.B. Priestley in 1949, 'who have not swept anything away'.[157] *Passport to Pimlico* showed the 'deep compulsion to dream of consensus'[158] in reclaiming wartime solidarity, but it also exposed underlying conflicts between the recognisable past and the uncertain future.

Le retour was the central event of 1945 in France, and was essential to the rebuilding of a profoundly fractured nation. The official response was to welcome, resettle and merge *les absents* into the 'mass of French people who had been behind the Resistance'.[159] The *rapatriés* were a problematic issue, *prisonniers de guerre* evoking a humiliating period in the recent past and *déportés* a more diverse group who elicited more complex responses. The sufferings of all *rapatriés* were ultimately smothered because they subverted the founding myth of post-war France, though memories of deportation were sustained by the hundreds of associations which emerged after the war. Film-makers' trepidation was demonstrated by the release four years after *le retour* of *Retour à la vie*, yet even then this singular film did not refer to the 2000 Jewish *déportés* whose return to France had been equally unremarked.

Prisonniers de guerre were less controversial, but in *Retour à la vie* they are depicted as victims of their circumstances, rather than the heroes of the hour. Appearing during a plethora of resistance films, *Le Diable au corps*, albeit a story of another war, reminded audiences of the absent soldier. The protest from veterans is explicit in its condemnation of a wife's infidelity, but is conflated with a more significant audience response, a profound discomfort at the undermining of a national institution during a time when national identity had to be rebuilt. Reclaiming the past became an obsession, whether motivated by revenge or guilt. The outsider, Albert Camus wrote, was 'wandering on the fringe, on the outskirts of life'.[160] In *La Fille du diable*, Saget is falsely idolised and duly punished, in *Nuit sans fin* Olivier is killed, in *Un Revenant Sauvage* is alone and bitter. Yet the 'crowd' which represented ordinary French people, was also culpable. The *épuration* perpetrated by the locals in *Nuit sans fin* and *Panique* on the unwelcome outsiders indicates lingering uncertainties. De Gaulle's France, however, had to be seen as a whole. 'The time for tears is over,' he said, 'the time of glory is returned'.[161] Films of the post-war period showed that the return of *rapatriés* and civilians to normality seemed to be a return not to a glorious nation, as de Gaulle envisaged it, but to one governed by suspicion and uncertainty.

6

Women in Britain: 'Returned' or Renewed?

Much of the research carried out on gender in British post-war cinema suggests that women were shown in a rather regressive light. Since the early 1980s, female representation in films of the 1940s and 1950s has been identified in fairly simplistic terms as moving from 'the dignified woman of the 1940s, with her tailored suit and upper-class accent' to 'the pouting young blonde of the 1950s'.[1] Recently, women's cinema of the 1950s has been characterised as constituting 'conformity and deviance', in which women are in polarised spheres; either 'returned' to their traditional milieu in the home, or displaced onto 'other' spaces in which they behave in transgressive fashion.[2] Some films have been interpreted as presenting their female protagonists with clear choices between the two spheres, a situation which has been seen as emblematic of the choices faced by British women.[3] It has also been argued that Gainsborough's 'historical' melodramas of the 1940s not only allowed glamour-starved female audiences to indulge in narratives foregrounding lavishly costumed, bejewelled, feisty heroines, but also that as a genre they conveyed and reflected women's true interests and desires extremely successfully.[4] Ealing, on the other hand, has been condemned by Sue Harper as offering two 'horrid alternatives to the female audience...virginity or respectable conjugality'.[5] Christine Geraghty believes, however, that Ealing's view of marriage is more nuanced.[6]

It is not the intention of this chapter to become embroiled in current debates about the extent to which films acknowledged and represented the shifts in women's position in society. Rather, given the vital significance of female participation in the wartime community in its various permutations, it will examine the dynamics of women's relationship with the community in the post-war context. It will examine how women were perceived as members of peacetime society in relation to their families, their husbands, their children, and of course to each other. What part were they expected to play now that the war was over, or was it simply a matter of 'returning' women to pre-war modes of living? This chapter will attempt to answer these questions and those which were left unspoken by focusing on some of the key issues affecting women: work, marriage, children, divorce and sexuality, and the ways in which these areas were represented in film.

That women's lives were disrupted by war is not in any doubt. Of 130,000 civilians killed or badly wounded, 48 per cent were women.[7] The war introduced the majority of the female population to new experiences: employment in munitions and aircraft factories, on farms, in civil defence, or as one of 467,000 members of the auxiliary armed forces.[8] Married women often had to cope with childcare, housework and part-time or full-time work, and for those 4.5 million whose husbands were on active service, managing the household alone. Women formed a large proportion of the 60 million changes of address during the war.[9] Some endured separation from their evacuated children, while others in 'safe' areas received the children of strangers into their own homes.

Employment is pivotal to the debate about women and social change. Of 22 interviews analysed by Penny Summerfield with women from all classes who had worked in a range of wartime occupations, 20 reported that the war had changed them in some respect merely through liberation from the marital or parental home.[10] As Monica Dickens wrote, 'It seemed that women, having been surplus for twenty years were suddenly wanted in a hundred different places at once'.[11] Between 1939 and 1945, 7.5 million women worked in the auxiliary armed services, civil defence or in industry.[12] By 1943, the peak year for female mobilisation, women represented 39 per cent of the total occupied population, compared with less than 30 per cent in 1931[13] and double the figure for the First World War. Most upper and middle-class girls opted to join the services, but a few who balked at the alternatives worked in industry. By 1943, engineering, aircraft and ship-building employed 1,635,000, the largest proportion of working women.[14] 'Well groomed young ladies,' writes Angus Calder, 'whose idea of Hell was a Factory ... worked machines beside girls from the Rhondda whose physique was an eloquent indictment of the years of depression'.[15] In *Millions Like Us* (1943, Frank Launder and Sidney Gilliat) this meeting of opposites is conveyed through Jennifer and Annie. Settling into the factory hostel, upper-class Jennifer is horrified to see her room-mate Annie hopping into bed without removing her underwear, while Annie stares open-mouthed at Jennifer, her face smothered with vanishing cream and surrounded by a collection of designer clothes.

Even willing workers reported difficulties in being taken seriously in the early days of the war. Elaine Burton wrote to the *News Chronicle* complaining that she had been rejected from numerous jobs and the paper received such a large response from similarly disgruntled women that she was given a regular column to air women's issues.[16] Women's magazines, on the other hand, stressed women's ability to combine domestic duties with war work. *Woman's Own* negotiated the difficult path between efficiency and femininity in its editorials and fiction to its predominately lower-middle-class readership. A 1942 cover entitled 'I am doing everything I can', illustrating a woman at home gathering newspapers for recycling and at work busy at her factory machine, was emblematic of the magazine's wartime appeal.[17] Though the Ministry of Information were slow to realise the propaganda potential of the women's press, by 1941 government spending constituted a vital source of advertising revenue.[18] While articles became increasingly military in tone, stressing the 'battle on the home front', women's magazines, with their tips on cooking with rations and coping with shortages, reminded women that they were not alone.[19]

Any qualms about employing women rapidly dissipated in 1940 when two million were needed in industry to replace some of the 19 per cent of the male population in the services.[20] In March 1941, the Registration for Employment Order required all women between 19 and 40 to register at their local employment exchange as to their availability for work.[21] The following autumn, the age limit for registration was increased to 45, and in 1943 to 50.[22] The most dramatic moment came in December 1941 when the government introduced military conscription by the National Service (No 2) Act, by which women were directed into the armed services, civil defence or industry. By March 1942, all single women between 20 and 31 were liable to conscription.[23] Those with dependants, the wives of men in the services and others unable to work were labelled, in a derogatory fashion, 'immobile women'.[24] Servicemen's wives were exempt, the prevailing opinion being that their husbands needed their wives at home when they returned on leave.[25] In *In Which We Serve*, (1942, Noel Coward and David Lean), Kath, wife of Chief Petty Officer Walter Hardy, rebukes her mother for repeatedly urging her to evacuate their Plymouth home. When Kath is fatally wounded during the Plymouth Blitz, she murmurs to the stretcher-bearer, 'Tell Walter I didn't want to leave the house'. Until 1942, the loving wife at home was still the dominant image, and represented even to the feminist Vera Brittain the 'cornerstone of that family unity which is the moral foundation of English life'.[26] But home-based wives were not always biddable creatures, and one of the common grievances was about service-men's pay. Indeed one of the reasons behind *The Way Ahead* (1944, Carol Reed) was, according to War Office records, a 'lack of a proper spirit of patriotism among some sections of the female population'.[27] The film shows the soldiers' wives in a supportive network, drinking tea and discussing letters recently received from their husbands. Life was to change dramatically, however, both in a real sense and on screen as the recruitment of 'mobile women' challenged existing notions about women and work.

The Lamp Still Burns (1943, Maurice Elvey) was based on Monica Dickens's humorous book *One Pair of Feet*, about her training as a nurse during the war, although its serious tone resonates more with Elisabeth Sadler's memoir *Sleep and Cease Crying*, a vivid, often harrowing account of nursing injured civilians and servicemen.[28] In *The Lamp Still Burns*, architect Hilary Clark (Rosamund John) designs a medical room for factory-owner Larry Rains (Stewart Granger), but notes with irritation that he 'looked at me as if he thought a woman's place was the home'. In order to 'show him', she abandons her successful practice and chooses instead one of the most traditional female professions. On the face of it, then, a retrogressive step in which the film subscribes to the wartime ethos of community and social responsibility. Sue Harper argues that it is about 'obedience, sacrifice and reform – obedience to the authorities, sacrifice of a woman's will and a reformed social order stripped bare of desire'.[29] However, this neglects the fact that the film supports the idea of married nurses, which the demands of the profession prohibit. The impossibility of career and marriage is exemplified in two scenes, one where Hilary's colleague Christine resigns on her engagement, despite her promotion. The other is when Matron tells Hilary about the necessity for difficult decisions while glancing wistfully at an old photograph of someone obviously from her past. Clearly the satisfaction of nursing does not always compensate for individual needs and desires.

Hilary's individualism, however, is dominant throughout. At the end, summoned before the hospital board on a disciplinary matter, she seizes the opportunity to expose the unfairness of having to renounce 'the right to a home and children of my own'. In reality, in order to recruit more nurses, who were in short supply even before the war, one of the revised conditions of service in the Ministry of Health's campaign in 1945 was the acceptance of married nurses.[30] Rains falls in love with Hilary, declaring that he will fight for reforms and that she will 'have a job and a home', a reassuring note to men that women will be home-makers as well as workers.[31] This recognition of combining career and motherhood signifies a shift towards the 'individualist' narratives of post-war films. Interestingly, *The Feminine Touch* (1956, Pat Jackson), about some disillusioned trainee nurses who are inspired anew by a compassionate Matron, follows one nurse more closely than the others, but the film has much in common with *The Way Ahead* or *The Gentle Sex*, in which individuals merge into a committed whole.

At the beginning of the war, volunteers to the auxiliary services had mainly been young middle- and upper-class women seeking 'adventure',[32] but by 1943 they came from all classes.[33] The services were hierarchical in terms of appeal, as were all types of employment. When waiting to register, Celia in *Millions Like Us* daydreams in turn of the WAAFS, the WRNS, the ATS, the Land Army and nursing, and of being 'courted' by glamorous men. The services as a whole, though, were not popular with men: when Mass Observation asked soldiers, 'Would you like your wife to join?, 32 per cent replied 'certainly not', 16 per cent 'wouldn't like it' and 36 per cent said they would prevent it.[34] The ATS, the biggest of the women's services, with 198,000 members, elicited a complex response from both men and women. It compromised notions of femininity because of the 'manly' uniform, yet it also had a reputation for sexual immorality. Indeed *Millions Like Us* suggests this when Celia's flirtatious sister, who always has a man in tow, joins the ATS. Yet the ATS was closest to the front line and suffered the highest casualties:[35] 355 dead, 94 missing and 24 taken prisoner. Its 93rd Searchlight Regiment, which used radar to locate enemy aircraft at night was the only such unit in the world.[36] While early publicity suggested the inferior status of the ATS, by 1941 a recruitment leaflet stated that 'the army invites you into its ranks because it has been proved that women and girls can do some of the most important activities as well as men'.[37]

Of all the services, it was the most democratic. An application to the WAAF from 16 Bahamians in 1942 had caused near panic until they were discovered to be white Bermudians, but 30 black West Indian women were readily accepted into the ATS in 1943.[38] Furthermore, the recruitment of 18-year-old Princess Elizabeth that year gave the ATS the royal seal of approval. Indeed, while *The Gentle Sex*, released the same year, includes in its community of new ATS recruits the obligatory 'good-time girl', the most significant role is given to the quasi-royal Anne, a Colonel's daughter, who confers complete respectability on the service. As Rosamund John recalled, 'Until that film, many people didn't realise that women were working on gun sites and driving lorries'.[39] *The Gentle Sex* effectively demonstrated the seven recruits carrying out their duties with, according to the *Sunday Times*, 'naturalness and courage and an agreeable lack of heroics'.[40]

The other auxiliary services, being smaller, received comparatively meagre attention on screen, though the occasional 'Wren' appeared, which suggests that they were held in highest esteem. In the only post-war film to deal directly with female demobilisation, *Perfect Strangers* (Alexander Korda), released in September 1945, Deborah Kerr's character is a Wren. Unusually, she is lower-middle class, although, as we shall see, part of her 'transformation' involves adopting middle-class sophistication. Wrens were often either members of or married into the aristocracy. In Gainsborough's *The Man in Grey* (Leslie Arliss, 1943), the present-day prologue shows Lady Clarissa Rohan (Phyllis Calvert) meeting the handsome Peter Rokeby (Stewart Granger) at an auction when she is on leave. Whereas Regency Clarissa is the hapless victim of her brutal husband, Wren Clarissa is the model of modern womanhood, independent and free to marry for love.

Wrens in post-war films with wartime settings tended to be stoic and competent. These films also indicate a definite shift from wartime narratives in which the idea of community predominates to those which question the purpose of the war and its effects on personal relationships. In *Piccadilly Incident* (1946, Herbert Wilcox), Diana Fraser (Anna Neagle) meets baronet Alan Pearson (Michael Wilding) during an air-raid, they fall in love and marry days before she is posted to the Far East. Her ship is torpedoed and Diana is marooned on a desert island, where for three years she loyally fends off the advances of a lusty Canadian sailor. When she eventually returns to England, she finds that Alan has remarried and has a son, but she is willing to sacrifice her happiness for him. In the rather unsettling ending, however, a judge concludes that Alan's son is still illegitimate in the eyes of the law. Julie Hallam (Virginia McKenna) in *The Cruel Sea* (Charles Frend, 1953) has a mature professionalism which helps her to be both rational and compassionate towards the man she loves. Similarly, in *Appointment in London* (1952, Philip Leacock) war-weary flyer Dirk Bogarde is soothed by his friendship with Wren Dinah Sheridan, and in *The Gift Horse* (1952, Compton Bennett), June, newly married to a naval lieutenant, knows that his next posting is highly dangerous yet says nothing as they whisper their goodbyes.

The sense of equality in the services emanates from personal recollections. 'I went into the services a snob,' one upper-middle-class woman commented, 'and came out a human being'.[41] The notion of cross-class understanding also worked in reverse as a working-class Wren noted, 'They might have a bit more money than I have but they're no better than me, because I've proved to myself that I can do these things and I can hold my own with people'.[42] Some women found that demobilisation was a wrench. A former Sergeant Major in the ATS remarked that 'I missed the companionship as well as the authority. If I'd [sic] hadn't been in the army, I'd never have the confidence that I have now.'[43] Although the bonds of fellowship were clearly strong, and in some cases enduring, in women's wartime organisations, scant attention was paid to them by film-makers, who perceived the issue as purely male. Despite the existence of half a million servicewoman, there was a dearth of films on the subject, a noteworthy exception being *Perfect Strangers*.

Perfect Strangers in effect supports the idea of 'transformation' brought about by war, proposed by, among others, Richard Titmuss, Arthur Marwick and Alva Myrdal and Viola Klein.[44] The film focuses on a couple reunited after three years' separation, during which they have served in the Royal Navy and the WRNS. In 1940, Robert Wilson (Robert Donat), a down-trodden clerk with a delicate stomach, is conscripted into the Navy. There he metamorphoses into 'Bob', a strapping, confident, handsome officer. The frumpy Cathie (Deborah Kerr), whose husband takes a dim view of women who work, wear make-up or smoke, is introduced, with the help of worldly wise Dizzy (Glynis Johns), to not only lipstick and the 'permanent', but camaraderie, excitement and 'rejuvenation via the Wrens'.[45] In one scene, Cathie is shown delivering a vital message to her Commanding Officer by motor-boat across a dangerous stretch of seaway and then being praised by him for her bravery. Meanwhile, Robert is shipwrecked and hospitalised in Tunis, where he becomes attracted to Elena, a nurse. When Richard, Dizzy's cousin, confesses that he is in love with Cathie, she is tempted and realises that 'I'm two persons and I used to be one'. Immersed in their new lives, Robert and Cathie begin to dread their reunion, and so when their leaves coincide in 1943, both decide to ask for a divorce.

When they eventually meet in a pub, both are startled to see their poised and glamorous spouses. Robert is taken aback at Cathie's request for a pink gin. The initially hesitant meeting escalates into a squabble over past habits. Cathie complains that Robert was 'a bit of an old maid', while he exclaims, 'I detested Clacton on Sea', where they had not only spent their honeymoon in 1936 but every subsequent summer. Yet Cathie reveals that her transformation has gone much deeper than mere looks and a penchant for alcohol. When Cathie discovers that Robert called her 'simple, uncomplicated, quiet, dependable,' she retorts, 'I've run myself for the past three years with complete efficiency. I've worked with just as good brains as yours and held my own with them – and had nothing but respect and courtesy wherever I went.' Robert, having met the competent Elena, has indeed recognised that woman's place is not necessarily in the home, and says so to Cathie, who argues that 'it always will ... but not our sort of home'. Later, Robert petulantly criticises her appearance, saying that she looks like a 'blonde golliwog', suggesting that he is losing the battle.

Finally, however, a reconciliation is effected in their flat, and it is the prospect of a common goal which draws them together. Robert finds Cathie looking out at her favourite view of London, now devastated by bombing. 'Poor old London,' murmurs Robert. Cathie agrees, saying that 'It'll take years and years'. Suddenly their individual differences seem to dissipate, and Robert says, 'Well, what does that matter? We're young.' It is the beginning of not only a new relationship for them, but also their participation in the rebuilding of London and the greater nation. As Sue Harper argues, as far as marriage is concerned it 'is about the demolition of the "wall" of old-style marriage and the wide blue expanse that opens up beyond'.[46] The *Monthly Film Bulletin*'s conclusion that it 'assumes that all that is needed for marital happiness and success in life is physical well-being and glamour'[47] does the film an injustice. As a result of their experiences, which have required them to take more responsibility than they had within their own restricted lives, this couple are deeply committed to the future. Cathie is no longer the victim of Robert's 'passive-aggressive' nature but an equal partner in a companionate marriage. Their marriage in effect has been given a second chance through their mutual 'transformation'.

Approximately 55 per cent of men in the services were married, and for many couples the war meant separation for long periods.[48] Other difficulties were experienced by couples who had married quickly and regretted doing so soon afterwards.[49] In 1939 and 1940 there was a sharp rise in marriages per 1000 of the population, and overall between 1940 and 1945 there was a substantial increase in the numbers of marriages compared to the previous six years.[50] Of the hasty wartime weddings in *In Which We Serve*, *Millions Like Us* and *Piccadilly Incident*, only the first survives the duration, the other two curtailed by death and separation. Although films made during the war are matter-of-fact about the deaths of husbands and fiancées, such as *Millions Like Us* and *The Gentle Sex*, in which Celia and Ann are bereaved and face an uncertain future, both women are shown being compensated by the companionship of colleagues.

Films made towards the end of the war are much more optimistic about marriage, whereas in reality the groom's departure and potentially lengthy absence sometimes resulted in infidelity. As *Woman*'s agony aunt, 'Evelyn Home', remarks, 'women were vulnerable to men other than their husbands'.[51] A former munitions worker, briefly married before her husband's posting overseas, recalled that her affair was the outcome of working long hours and being 'desperate for some outlet'.[52] In *Waterloo Road*, Tilly's 'drifting' towards Ted Purvis is handled sympathetically and is attributed to loneliness and the fact that her husband is unwilling to have children during the war. Dr Montgomery advises Jim that in denying women their natural desires 'their repressed and rebellious nature runs amok in a big way'. However, all ends well, and in the last scene we see her contentedly rocking a pram. While she is tempted by another (unsuitable) man, she is never actually unfaithful, and her role beyond the scope of the film is certain, as a loyal wife and loving mother once her natural, and by implication more important, desires have been met. Significantly, the critics were sympathetic towards Tilly: 'loyal and attractive but war weary' wrote *Kinematograph Weekly*, while the *News Chronicle* pronounced her 'warm and solid and refreshingly unrefined'.[53]

References to true infidelity were mainly confined to post-war films. In *Train of Events* (1949), Philip (Peter Finch), a demobbed actor, discovers his promiscuous wife waiting for him one night in his digs. Defending herself, she tells him, 'after all, you were away a long time,' to which he replies, 'So were a lot of other men. Their wives didn't look on themselves as war-free widows.' When she tries to seduce him, he strangles her in a fit of anger and disgust. Cuckolded husband Lieutenant Morell (Denholm Elliott) in *The Cruel Sea* is deserted by his actress wife on the last night of his leave, claiming a dinner engagement with a business contact. When the man phones, Morell hears himself described as 'that damn fool husband of yours', and he is deeply humiliated. Both these films reflect the grim realities of wartime separation, but it would have been anathema during wartime to suggest that a wife of a serviceman would be anything other than loyal and faithful.

Once husbands started to return, problems did arise, especially for those who had been married only a short time. 'When he came out it was very, very difficult to get to know him again,' recalled one serviceman's wife.[54] In April 1945, a *Picture Post* description of the reunion of one couple who had been married only 18 months when the husband was posted overseas indicated their unease.[55] Women's magazines explored similar problems in fiction and in letters pages.[56] Indeed fictional accounts of marital difficulties were extraordinarily enduring. In 1951, *Woman's Own* published a story entitled 'She Married a Stranger', which tells of a woman who qualified as a GP while her husband was in Africa during the war. He is missing the army and wants to return to Africa, which would mean abandoning her career in the new NHS. In the end, she agrees, 'if it meant I'd be the wife Jake wanted'.[57] Six years earlier, a plethora of articles and pamphlets appeared advising women how to cope with signs of stress in their spouses, from 'silence and depression to tears, violence and compulsive drinking'.[58] Even that bastion of tradition, the BBC acknowledged in 'Civvy Street' in March 1946 that the greatest problem for men was facing reality. 'The girl-wife has become has grown-up, and perhaps become "tough" from factory life,' declared its presenter. 'The housewife and mother, becoming a huntress for food, has given up glamour for a time-saving turban and stout-soled shoes.'[59] The answer lay in understanding the wife's situation during the husband's absence.

A film that explored this subject was *The Years Between* (1946, Compton Bennett), which, in contrast to *Perfect Strangers*, is about an upper-class couple and is set in an idyllic village. The film was based on Daphne du Maurier's semi-autobiographical play, written in 1943 while she awaited her husband's return from active service.[60] Diana's (Valerie Hobson) husband Colonel Michael Wentworth (Michael Redgrave), an MP, is reported killed in action. In the play Diana quickly resolves to stand in his place, yet in the film she is completely devastated by his death and argues that 'Michael wouldn't like it'. However, Muriel Box's screenplay by no means neglects the feminist perspective, and the emotional intensity of Diana's near-nervous-breakdown is matched by her later determination to run for Parliament. She plunges energetically into women's issues, such as day nurseries and canteens. When she is asked to base her maiden speech on the party debate on education, Diana abandons her notes and describes instead its relevance to 'Mrs Smith', mother of two evacuated children, munitions worker and part-time fire-watcher. 'As she's been doing a man's work,' she concludes, 'she doesn't see why she shouldn't have a man's pay packet at the end of the week'. The equal-pay issue was a radical inclusion, for it was hotly debated at the end of the war because of the common practice by employers of avoiding paying women the 'rate for the job', but it was never implemented, partly due to the findings of the 1945 Royal Commission.[61] The Commissioners were in favour of equal pay for teachers and civil servants, but not in commerce, or in industry, where 'Mrs Smith' would have been employed.[62] None of Diana's parliamentary activities are in the play, however, apart from one speech about salvage made in Scene 2, which is heard off-stage from a garden.[63] Indeed the film gives Diana a much more prominent role in serving the public and the country.

When her 'dead' husband unexpectedly returns from a prisoner-of-war camp, Diana's personal life has also changed, as she is on the point of marrying again. His dismay at finding she has a career reflects the contemporary anxieties serving men had about their wives. 'I don't want a wife who's forever making speeches and being Madam Chairman on committees,' Michael explodes. 'I'm not the only one either, there are thousands like me, millions of fellows who...want to come back to the life they knew and the wife they love.' Diana defers to him and agrees to give up the seat and devote herself to the marriage. But her self-sacrifice is not matched by her husband's, who in fact was working underground and faked his own death to ensure secrecy. While expecting women, then, to prioritise home and family above their own desires, masculine loyalty is such that wife and family are subordinate. In the play, Michael discovers Diana's relationship with Richard and accepts an offer of working in Europe on reconstruction, in a sense abandoning his family once again. Diana is moved by his beliefs and assures him that 'When you come home again, I'll be different...I promise you'.[64] In the film, the couple decide to part after Diana reproaches Michael, saying, 'you didn't love me enough to tell me what you were doing'. But Diana's childhood Nanny (Flora Robson) intervenes, reminding them that Churchill said, 'nations must have faith in one another to find peace,' and they should understand one another. The last shot is of the Wentworths on opposite sides of the House of Commons. Diana has clearly won a seat on her own merits, which suggests their independent but equal status. Interestingly the *Monthly Film Bulletin* considered the ending 'rather unsatisfying, for the break-up of the marriage is really the only solution'.[65] Women, however, may well have found it satisfying in that the 'understanding' to which Nanny refers is conditional on Diana's maintaining her career, which is just as important as her personal life. Furthermore, given her professional status, her commitment to post-war reconstruction has great potential.

Female MPs were exceptional, but in general the issue of working married women was a controversial issue. Many men, for instance, considered a working wife as a wartime expedient. Although Harold Smith considers that on the whole 'wives considered wartime conditions exceptional and…reverted to the relationships which they had established prior to the conflict', it has been argued that the notion that the entire female population longed to return to the home was largely engineered by the press and policy-makers.[67] Analysing the various wartime investigations carried out by employers, Myrdal and Klein conclude that the proportion of those who wished to remain at work, particularly among older women, was 'astonishingly high'.[68] This is confirmed by the fact that though there was a slow but steady rise in female employment, from 29.8 per cent of the employed population in 1931 to 30.8 per cent in 1951 and 33.5 per cent by 1960, the most dramatic figures relate to married women.[69] In 1931, only 16 per cent of working women were married, but this had risen to 43 per cent by 1943.[70] Although there was a decline in 1947 to 40 per cent, the proportion rose again to 43 per cent in 1951 and 48 per cent by 1955.[71] Government policy was confusing to say the least, particularly with regard to childcare provision. There had been 72,000 child nursery places in 1944,[72] but by 1947 700 nurseries had been closed, creating added difficulties for women with pre-school children.[73]

In June of the same year, however, a labour shortage during the export drive necessitated a vigorous recruitment campaign for women workers by the Ministry of Labour, one poster declaring, 'Women, please lend your support a little longer: let's work together for prosperity'. Although the Minister, George Isaacs, was hesitant about encouraging women with young children to work, the government circumvented this problem by persuading employers to offer more flexible hours. In a Central Office of Information film entitled *Women Must Work* (1947), married as well as single women were targeted, and assured that crèches would be available.[74] The desperation for workers in the mills and textile factories of Lancashire and Yorkshire resulted in nurseries being opened, though, as in wartime, this was a temporary policy.[75] These policies that vacillated between restoring the family and the purely economic need for women to produce exports were deeply contradictory.

In the professions, by the end of the war there were 7198 female doctors and 549 dentists, compared with 2580 and 82 respectively in 1928, while the numbers of solicitors, barristers, accountants and architects increased from a handful pre-war to several hundred afterwards.[76] In the few post-war films featuring career women, the protagonists are invariably unmarried, such as those played by Flora Robson: an MP in *Frieda*, a magistrate in *Good Time Girl* (1948, David MacDonald) and a nurse in *No Time for Tears* (1957, Cyril Frankel). Female participation in some professions appeared to need explanation, however obliquely. In *I Believe in You* (1952, Basil Dearden), Matty (Celia Johnson) is a far more experienced probation officer than new recruit ex-colonial Henry Phipps (Cecil Parker). Indeed Matty articulates the philosophy behind the film in reassuring the work-shy Norma (Joan Collins), 'I believe in you,' and expertly communicates with her mainly working-class charges. Matty advises the unwittingly patronising, upper-class Phipps to 'meet them on their own level'. In a personal aside, Matty begins to tell Phipps that she became a probation officer in 1943, having previously driven ambulances, but she ends the conversation abruptly. The inference is that in 1943 she lost somebody she cared for inspiring her to join the probation service. While the women she deals with are on the margins of the community, Matty's own authority within it has been achieved through sacrificing her own desires.[77]

Medical dramas became particularly popular in the 1950s. Nursing represented an unproblematic shift from the supportive, caring roles women were given in wartime films as gender roles were rigidly prescribed; women were nurses and men were doctors. In *Life in Her Hands* (Philip Leacock, 1951), a grief-stricken widow is comforted through saving lives as a nurse. *No Time for Tears* is set in a children's hospital, where Anna Neagle's Matron constantly defers to the superior authority of Dr Seagrove (Anthony Quayle). The establishment of the NHS in 1948 created greater career opportunities for women, but how did films suggest they coped with its demands in addition to their natural roles as wives and mothers? *The Feminine Touch* stresses the vocational side of nursing, but also takes up the issue of married nurses, which clearly had not been resolved since *The Lamp Still Burns*. During the first days of training, a student nurse points out the fact that marriage would end their careers, 'a crazy rule, isn't it?' When the feisty Pat disappears for the whole night with a doctor, Matron (Diana Wynyard) reprimands her for her 'indiscretion', but Pat explains that they were recently married. Matron immediately says that real love is a privilege and cites a case of a 'friend', patently herself, who had stayed to qualify while her fiancé went overseas, a decision she bitterly regretted as he died shortly after she had qualified. Trainee nurse Susan (Belinda Lee) is nevertheless inspired to follow her fiancé to Canada. Marriage and romantic love is thus being posited as more important than devotion to duty and the community.

It is rare to find female doctors on screen. Joy (Muriel Pavlow) in *Doctor in Charge* (1957, Gerald Thomas) is training to be a doctor, although the examiner advises her that 'doctoring and lipstick don't mix together'. Within a comedy this observation can be lightly dismissed, but dramas are more suggestive, an excellent example being *White Corridors* (1951, Pat Jackson). Among the troubled staff at provincial Yeoman's Hospital is lovelorn nurse Dolly Clark (Moira Lister), who feels betrayed by irresponsible young doctor Dick Groom (Jack Watling) when she discovers that he is engaged to a rich man's daughter. Enraged, she confronts him, saying, 'I suppose you think I'm just a career girl,' an oddly disparaging phrase suggesting that a career is an inferior alternative to marriage and family. Dolly exacts her revenge when Groom fails to diagnose a cerebral abscess on a patient and she tells Groom's father, the chief surgeon. Dolly is summoned before Matron, but angered by her reprimand mutters accusingly, 'Frustrated old spinsters'. In a few poignant seconds, Matron, visibly shaken by the truth behind Dolly's outburst, quickly composes herself to receive her next visitor. Again then, there is a brief suggestion that a woman has found solace in her vocation.

The crux of the narrative lies with Sophie Dean (Googie Withers) and her fiancé, Dr Neil Marriner (James Donald), a dedicated research pathologist who, at considerable personal risk, is researching penicillin-resistant infections. Sophie, herself a gifted doctor who identified the cerebral abscess and saved the patient, has applied for a job in London. Neil, who understands and respects Sophie, feels that he cannot stand in her way. Sophie assures him that 'I'm not a careerist ... [but] I'd like to do some good in the world if I can'. When young Tommy is brought in with an injured hand and fails to respond to penicillin, Neil attempts to find a successful antibiotic, but in doing so accidentally infects himself. Tommy dies, but Neil recovers after Sophie decides to risk her career by injecting him with an experimental drug he has been working on. As Pat Jackson remarked, his work on documentaries like *Western Approaches* (1943) informed the way the film's drama is conveyed.[78] It has no musical score, but relies instead on the high standard of acting and restrained but sensitive direction. As a result, Sophie and Neil are presented as an authentic modern couple, whose respect for each other's careers equals their mutual love. Moreover, at a time when a number of films appeared about vulnerable children, *White Corridors* is bravely unsentimental about the boy's death, although Jackson recalled that J. Arthur Rank disapproved of the ending.[79]

In general, women were rarely seen as authority figures. Muriel Box noted that women police officers were conspicuously absent in *The Blue Lamp* (1950), and her film *Street Corner* (1953) attempted to redress the balance. 'It was about time women had a chance to show what they did,' she recalled, 'and the film was specifically designed to show their work'.[80] Box's comment about her career, that it was 'Terribly difficult ... they were prejudiced against you from the very start',[81] was symptomatic of attitudes towards women who were determined upon forging a career. The history of women police, for instance, has been described as one of 'apathy and prejudice', although the Second World War saw a significant expansion of women in the force.[82] In 1939, the number of women police officers accounted for less than 0.4 per cent of the force, but ten years later, numbers had quadrupled, and women were admitted into the Police Federation.[83] In 1930, the Home Office recommended that women police be assigned to cases involving 'women or children reported missing, found ill, destitute or homeless, or in immoral surroundings'.[84] In *Street Corner*, the officers are seen dealing with these prescribed areas: a woman accused of child neglect, a young mother caught for shoplifting, and an army deserter who is also a bigamist. There are two derogatory references in *Street Corner* to 'coppers in skirts', both from women, one from the deserter and the other from the local 'tart', complaining that being moved on by women is 'bad for business'. Indeed, while researching the film Muriel Box discovered that a prostitute would deem it 'insulting' to be arrested by a female officer.[85] These characters distrust women patrolling the streets, and articulate their contempt in terms of what they perceive as the officers' lack of femininity. There is much emphasis placed on the appearance of women police officers in the film, which to the present day is attributed to their low status within the force.[86]

Promotion beyond sergeant for women was uncommon. In 1955, for instance, in Newcastle-upon-Tyne there was only one female Chief Inspector amongst a force of 500 officers.[87] On screen, women of higher rank are invariably shown as unfeminine, for example the lumpen Miss Jones in *I Believe in You*. In the detective thriller *Sapphire* (1957, Basil Dearden), when Superintendent Hazard needs to discover the provenance of a red taffeta petticoat, he consults Sergeant Cook, whose 'butch' appearance does not bode well. 'What do you make of that?' he asks. 'I wouldn't know *what* to make of it sir,' she replies, adding, 'It certainly isn't built for durability'. The best-known unfeminine sergeant was played by Joyce Grenfell as Ruby Gates in two of Launder and Gilliat's St Trinian's films. Her wistful question to her long-term fiancé, 'Sammy, could it be wedding bells?' in *The Belles of St Trinians* (1954) is rewarded not by nuptials but, in *Blue Murder at St Trinians* (1957), promotion to sergeant. After 14 years of engagement, Ruby seems destined to remain in unhappy spinsterhood.

In 1948, Catherine de la Roche was disappointed at so few films exploring the 'fundamental changes' between men and women.[88] Certainly the most significant consequence of women's wartime employment was that their expectations were different not only about their roles in the workplace, but about marriage and of their lives in general. Women were beginning to think of marriage as a relationship rather than just an institution; the companionate marriage was emerging.[89] But contrary to de la Roche's bleak pronouncement, some films had shown the occasionally insurmountable difficulties in marriage, as in *The Years Between* and *Perfect Strangers*. In *The Years Between*, which de le Roche does mention as exceptional, the fact that Michael and Diana take up positions on opposite sides of the House is suggestive not only of their political differences but also of the continuing tensions within their marriage. In the period drama *Blanche Fury* (1947, Marc Allégret), when Laurence Fury (Michael Gough) demands that Blanche (Valerie Hobson) come down and entertain his friends late at night, she retorts angrily, 'I have no intention, Laurence, contrary to the fashion of the times, of being ordered around by my husband!' This dialogue is not in the original novel,[90] and its addition indicates that post-war realities were being incorporated into costume dramas.

Neither did films attempt to cast a rosy glow over the institution of marriage. Indeed *Picturegoer* was at pains to refute the suggestion by no less than the Archbishop of York that one of the reasons for the increase in divorce was 'the sentimental and glamorous picture of marriage presented by the cinemas, followed by disillusionment in real life'.[91] *Picturegoer* listed British films which showed that marriage was subject to strains and stresses, and at worst deeply unhappy: *The Man in Grey*, *Waterloo Road*, *The Wicked Lady*, *Perfect Strangers* and *Brief Encounter*. The conclusion was that while American films might glamorise marriage, British films certainly did not.[92] In *Brief Encounter* (1945, David Lean), Laura renounces her chance of life with Alec, but we know that she will always love him. Other films which are critical of marriage include *They Were Sisters* (1945, Arthur Crabtree), in which, to the despair of her siblings, the gentle Charlotte (Dulcie Gray) is so crushed by her manipulative and bullying husband Geoffrey (James Mason) that she is driven to suicide. Similarly, the indecisive Mary in Lean's *The Passionate Friends* (1948) sacrifices her true love for her pragmatic and rather passionless husband. In *The Net* (1952, Anthony Asquith), a loyal wife, loved but neglected by her scientist husband is flattered by the attentions of his colleague, but her rejection of him is rewarded by her husband's 'emotional' return.

The Loves of Joanna Godden (1947, Charles Frend) tests the veracity of de la Roche's contention. The film can be seen as a companion piece to *It*

Always Rains on Sunday (Robert Hamer) released the same year. Both produced at Ealing, which, under the leadership of Michael Balcon, has been charged with a 'profound misogyny',[93] they nevertheless feature strong female characters. Both films are based on novels. Sheila Kaye Smith's *Joanna Godden* is about a woman farmer in the Romney Marshes in 1905, while Arthur La Bern's pre-war setting has been updated to post-war Bethnal Green and is about a housewife, Rose Sandigate.[94] The two films have markedly different settings, with much of *The Loves of Joanna Godden* shot outdoors and Rose's milieu in *It Always Rains on Sunday* mostly interior. They present oppositional spheres for post-war women in environmental and spatial terms, city and countryside and work and home: Joanna independently running a farm; Rose, dependent and tied to her kitchen. Yet both women behave in an individualistic fashion within their social parameters. The protagonists in the two films are played by Googie Withers, an actress with a striking appearance and powerful persona. 'I loved those meaty parts,' she recalled of her 1940s roles. 'I didn't want, and never played, the "genteel" parts, the English rose type.'[95] Withers's co-star in both films was John McCallum, whom she married in January 1948.[96] As we saw earlier, Rose and Joanna have difficult relationships with the community, Joanna

10. *The Loves of Joanna Godden* (1947, Charles Frend), with Googie Withers and John McCallum. Canal+ Image UK.

because she defies convention when she takes over her father's sheep farm, Rose because she is shielding her fugitive ex-lover.

Joanna refuses long-term fiancé Arthur Alce (McCallum) because he assumes that Little Beynham will be 'our farm'. 'I'll run the farm myself,' she retorts. The corresponding scene in the novel describes only Joanna's indignation at the local solicitor's suggestion that she employs a bailiff to manage the farm.[97] Joanna's rejection of Arthur in the film emphasises her belief that she has choices other than marriage. Her flaunting of traditional methods draws disapproval from the local farming community, and she suffers a major setback when her new 'looker's' attempts to cross-breed results in the deaths of many animals. Arthur comments angrily, 'It's all very well being a woman farmer so long as you don't stop being a woman – and that's what you've done'. This attack on her lack of femininity prompts Joanna to respond to the advances of her neighbour, Martin Trevor, and they marry. Meanwhile Arthur marries Joanna's flirtatious younger sister Ellen (Jean Kent). Neither of these marriages succeeds, however. Martin drowns, and the unscrupulous Ellen absconds with Martin's father, where- upon Joanna and Arthur are finally thrown together.

The film is dismissed by Sue Aspinall as demonstrating that 'even self-sufficient women cannot manage without men'.[98] Yet it is clear from the end of the film that Joanna and Arthur will enjoy a companionate marriage, a partnership on equal terms rather than the meek capitulation Aspinall suggests. Googie Withers clearly perceived its radical stance, commenting in 1990 that 'it was an interesting film which pre-dated the feminist movement'.[99] Furthermore, critics felt that the romantic aspects inherent in the new title were irrelevant. C.A. Lejeune considered that it suggested 'a series of "hot amours"', which was 'tasteless, misleading and a lot of bunk'.[100] Dilys Powell of the *Sunday Times* was at a loss to find what the synopsis, 'thoughtfully provided', mentioned as Joanna's attraction for her 'looker'.[101] Certainly, the ending sees the couple united, but the momentum of the narrative has been Joanna's admirable stand against the inflexibility of the farming community, which clearly resonates with women's wartime independence.

In general, the representation of women is more nuanced than Sue Aspinall would have us believe. The 'pouting young blonde'[102] she refers to is Diana Dors, who took advantage of her voluptuous figure in a number of films, but eschewed glamour in arguably her greatest role, as murderess Mary Hilton in the harrowing *Yield to the Night* (1957, J. Lee Thompson). *Genevieve* (Henry Cornelius, 1953), which for some epitomises the idea of 'classic' British 1950s cinema, features highly independent women and 'the model of a modern marriage'.[103] Kay Kendall, who is identified by Geraghty along with Virginia McKenna as a new kind of female star,[104] is sophisticated, sexually experienced and respectable. Although Geraghty contends that the film's conclusion effectively abandons the women's autonomy in favour of allying with their partners,[105] the film celebrates Kendall's impromptu trumpet-playing and Dinah Sheridan's cavalier attitude towards housekeeping.

Woman in a Dressing Gown (1957, J. Lee Thompson) presents quite another view of marriage. Like *It Always Rains on Sunday*, the female protagonist is largely confined to the house. Jim Preston (Anthony Quayle) is fond of his slatternly yet loyal and good-hearted wife Amy (Yvonne Mitchell), but is having a love affair with Georgie (Sylvia Syms), a young secretary at his office who is pressing him to leave Amy. When Ted Willis, the author of the original television play, adapted it for the big screen he developed the extramarital affair.[106] Therefore the audience is privy to intimate scenes and whispered exchanges, in contrast to Jim's domestic conversations, which are conducted through a barrage of loud 'easy listening' music. Though the two women appear to offer Jim quite different options, youth against middle age, efficiency against chaos, the polarisation between them is actually minimal. When Jim visits Georgie in her tidy flat at the beginning of the film, she dons an apron to cook him Sunday lunch, and we view them through a barred window, the camera then moving down to rest on a rain-drenched brick wall. Firstly, the mise-en-scène here suggests as much 'entrapment' as we witness in Amy's daily disorganised routine. Indeed, it echoes a later scene in which Jim puts his intoxicated wife to bed and the couple are shot from behind the bars of their bedstead, as it were inexorably 'imprisoned' together. Also, as John Hill argues, the effect of the earlier scene is to disrupt our identification with Jim and Georgie, revealing the emptiness in the relationship between the two.[107] Georgie, efficient, self-assured, and at first seemingly oblivious to the devastation she is causing, is not particularly sympathetic. Towards the end, Amy asks Georgie, 'couldn't you … somehow, have found the strength to leave him alone?' which very much echoes the editorials in *Woman* and *Woman's Own* of the time, which placed the onus on the 'other woman' to curtail extramarital affairs. Monica Dickens, a regular contributor to *Woman's Own,* advised 'leave the Married Men Alone!' and cautioned that where there was the danger of an affair, 'it is up to the girl to stop it'.[108] Amy and Jim's 17-year-old son Brian, the moral arbiter in the situation, identifies Georgie as the wrongdoer, saying,

'What kind of woman could do this to my mother, to our family?' Despite her shambolic ways, then, Amy is presented as a virtuous figure.

Amy's tragi-comic attempts to redeem her marriage shift from pitiable to rather dignified. When she invites Georgie home to 'talk like civilised people', her well-laid plans are soon in tatters: her newly set hair ruined by a sudden downpour, the zip on her 'special' dress broken through her efforts to squeeze into it, and a few calming nips at some whisky bought for the occasion sending her into a drunken stupor. Jim and Georgie thus arrive to find Amy dishevelled and hungover. Georgie's presence forces Amy and Jim to examine their marriage for the first time. Utterly devoted to her husband and son, Amy tells Georgie that 'it takes twenty years to build up a home, and you can break it up in five minutes'. Those shared years seem to give her strength, and she tells Georgie the unromantic facts about the man she is taking on: the snoring, the rheumatism, the phobia about sunshine and his habit of smothering food in 'whole dollops of sauce'. Then she adds, in surely the film's most poignant lines, 'You know a thousand things about him. I know a million. That's what marriage means. To know a man inside out and still love him.'

Kinematograph Weekly believed that it 'will shatter many a housewife's complacency and cause a few husbands to take stock of themselves'.[109] Indeed both Jim and Amy become aware of how much she has sacrificed. Faced with being alone, she exclaims 'I don't need you anymore...I can find a job,' and more pointedly, 'Maybe this is the best thing that could happen to me. For years I haven't thought of myself, only of you.' Jim's guilt at Amy's helplessness ultimately forces him to abandon Georgie, but there is also a suggestion that the earnestness behind Amy's semi-desperate stab at independence has jolted him into reassessing her as a person. In any case, the film ends on a pro-marriage note when Jim confesses to Georgie that 'it's been too long between Amy and me'. The intensity and complexity of the characters as they dissect their relationships make it one of the most insightful domestic dramas of the era, having, as *Sight and Sound* remarked, 'a special prominence in the contemporary British cinema'.[110] *Woman in a Dressing Gown* demonstrates that British films could effectively explore the travails between married people and the paralysing minutiae of domestic life.

A vital part of post-war social policy concerned the family. The lowest recorded birth rate in 1941[111] prompted a Royal Commission on Population to be set up in 1945. As fears of depopulation had largely dissipated by the time the report was published in 1949, the focus shifted to stabilising family life.[112] The Commission's recommendations included provisions to

11. *Woman in a Dressing Gown* (1957, J. Lee Thompson), with Yvonne Mitchell and Anthony Quayle. Canal+ Image UK.

make motherhood more attractive through increased family allowances, nurseries, playgrounds and advice on pregnancy and contraception.[113] Motherhood came under scrutiny, and one of the most important ideas to emerge was that maternal deprivation, such as that caused by wartime evacuation, could lead to delinquency, as promulgated by the influential child psychologist John Bowlby in the early 1950s.[114] Women's magazines readily engaged with these debates. While established periodicals like *Woman*, *Everywoman* and even *Good Housekeeping* introduced innovations, such as special pages for teenagers, the main emphasis was, as in pre-war days, family life and domesticity.[115] These efforts to preserve the sanctity of the family were reflected in *Woman's Own* and *Woman*, in which the family was seen as central to a woman's world.[116] Protection of the family also dominated matters concerning adultery and infidelity, particularly in the letters pages. The advice given by *Woman*'s Mary Grant to those contemplating divorce, that having children was a panacea for even the most unhappy marriages now seems shockingly simplistic. One woman who wrote that her year-long marriage was 'not a success' and she had fallen in love with another man, was advised to 'stop seeing the man in question, settle down and raise a family'.[117]

In this context, the representation of women as mothers was an important element in film, and as Christine Geraghty notes, 'Children are everywhere in post-war British cinema'.[118] It is clear from some films, for instance, that being both a mother and being sexually fulfilled are incompatible, even contradictory, an example being *Madonna of the Seven Moons* (1944, Arthur Crabtree), where pious wife and mother Maddelena's sexuality exists in her schizophrenic 'other self', the fiery, passionate (and childless) Rosanna. Two post-war films in which the motivation for adultery is partly attributed to kindly but dull husbands demonstrate the incompatibility of sexual satisfaction and successful motherhood. In *Brief Encounter,* for instance, Laura's anguish over Alec is intensified by the fact that she has two children. Returning home late after their first tryst, she is guilt-ridden on finding that her son has been knocked down by a car. In *They Were Sisters*, Vera is punished for her infidelity by having to surrender her daughter when she joins her lover in South Africa. Other kinds of desires in mothers are castigated. In D.H. Lawrence's short story, *The Rocking Horse Winner* (1949) adapted and directed by Anthony Pelissier, Paul (John Howard Davies) is desperate to make his profligate and selfish mother Hester (Valerie Hobson) happy, and literally rides his rocking horse to death when he discovers that it has the power to predict winning horses. This tragic end to her son's life makes Hester order that the winnings and the rocking horse are burnt.

Perhaps the most interesting example of child neglect is explored in *No Room at the Inn* (1948, Daniel Birt). Joan Temple's play, first performed in July 1945 in London, was seen by 700,000 people, serialised in the *Daily Express* in November 1946, and dramatised on BBC Saturday Night Theatre, to which 10 million listeners tuned in.[119] Most of the film consists of a flash-back to wartime, when Mary, a motherless evacuee is delivered to the house of Mrs Voray (Freda Jackson), an avaricious, sluttish drunk. When she hires out her spare room as a brothel, the four children, Norma, Lily, Irene and Ronnie have to share a bed. They play truant, are crawling with nits, and steal food. Middle-class Mary, initially uncomfortable amongst the unwashed, ragged cockney children, gradually becomes drawn into their recidivist activities in order to survive. Mary's teacher discovers the truth about the children's situation and complains to a council committee about 'the squalor, and the tyranny and the evil – the horrible degradation'. When summoned, however, Voray appears sober in demeanour and dress, adamant that the children are well cared for, and is stoutly defended by her influential male friends in the community. The chairman feels that there is insufficient evidence to warrant further investigation, and a jubilant Voray leaves. Later, after locking Ronnie in the coal-hole for a trifling offence, she lies in a drunken stupor, but Norma and Mary manage to extract the key from beneath her pillow and free him. Voray wakes up, but still inebriated she stumbles down the stairs to her death.

Though the unsuitable 'mother' receives just punishment, the children do not escape unscathed. One of the British Board of Film Censors' examiners suggested that the film be given a contemporary setting because 'child cruelty was much in the news'.[120] The other aspect of the film, juvenile delinquency, was also making headlines, and was blamed on the disruption of the war. In *The Blue Lamp* and *I Believe in You* the delinquency of Diana, Tom Riley's girlfriend, and Norma and Charlie respectively is attributed to the loss of parents during the war. In Temple's play, the adults are held responsible for the children's predicament, and one of the closing remarks is 'if there's a wave of juvenile crime after the war we shan't be free from blame'.[121] The play also has a more optimistic ending, in which Norma, who has stolen Mary's watch, returns it and delivers the last line: 'I must be turning over a new leaf, eh ducks?'[122] The film, however, is more emphatic about delinquency. Possibly as a concession to the BBFC, but certainly to stress its relevance to post-war society, the film has a prologue and epilogue, and the main narrative is seen as a flashback. In the epilogue, Mary, now working in a department store, witnesses Norma's arrest for shoplifting and she intervenes on her behalf, saying, 'I remember Norma. I'll help you.' Working-class Norma clearly has little hope of leading a normal life, and was, as *Today's Cinema* declared, 'clearly destined for a life of crime',[123] whereas Mary's temporary delinquency permits her to operate from a position of middle-class wisdom. *Today's Cinema* also recognised the narrative as an indictment of a 'wartime social scourge' and remarked on the 'type of landlady who took in evacuee children during the war'.[124] There is no doubt that despite its 'sordid'[125] theme the film was admired for its exposure of the 'ugly facts'.[126] Its revelations contrasted sharply with the notion promulgated during wartime of an army of benevolent foster mothers in every community willing to receive city evacuees. There were also women who were motivated by the financial benefits of accommodating evacuees, rather than doing so in a spirit of co-operation and goodwill.

Although nudging middle age, Mrs Voray is a 'good-time girl', a familiar wartime character. On screen, there appeared to be a smooth shift between the wartime 'good-time girl' to the post-war 'good-time mother'. 'Good-time mother' Babs (Jane Hylton) in *The Weak and the Wicked* (1953, J. Lee Thompson) goes out dancing, leaving her two children alone, one of whom suffocates in his cot. She spends her first days in prison agonising over the prospect of her other child being taken into care. Young wife and mother Bridget (Peggy Cummins) in *Street Corner* is a 'good-time mother' but is persuaded by a woman detective to return to her husband and 'look after him and the family'. In the same film, the sluttish Mrs Dawson goes out to work and leaves her small step-daughter alone and vulnerable to all manner of dangers. However, a WPC tracks down the child's real mother and they are reunited. Babs and Bridget are both married, but for unmarried mothers there was the added stigma of being a 'fallen woman'. In *The Boys in Brown* (1949, Montgomery Tully), a borstal governor, anxious to rehabilitate one of the inmates, discovers the whereabouts of the boy's real mother, who is now respectably married with legitimate children. He tries to persuade her to give her son a home by explaining that his adoptive mother is 'a drunk... and worse', but she refuses, saying that her husband is unaware of her illegitimate child. Both women are thereby presented as culpable for the boy's delinquency through their sexual 'deviancy'.

The unwed mothers in *Women of Twilight* (1952, Gordon Parry) live in a boarding house, and while they go out to work their babies are looked after by a blackmailing, scheming landlady, played by Freda Jackson in another 'wicked' role. The majority of the women are defined by their sexual experiences: Olga the 'good-time girl', Jess the promiscuous mother of four, and Vivianne the mistress of a condemned killer. The 'saintly' Christine is the only middle-class character, and the only woman seen with her baby, which thus juxtaposes class with ideal motherhood. Furthermore, in the tradition of melodrama, she demonstrates stoic self-sacrifice, in not telling her fiancé of her pregnancy for fear of compromising his career. While the film embraces the literary stereotype of the 'fallen woman', it also blames the landlady for preying on women made vulnerable because of the state's neglect of their situation, rather than the women themselves.[127]

According to 1950s cinema culture, few mothers have careers. An exception is *Lost* (1955, Guy Green), in which an American couple's child goes missing while in his nanny's care. The mother, a dress designer, is accused of neglect by an unscrupulous newspaper, which, after sympathetically interviewing her, publishes headlines asking, 'Can a career woman be a mother as well?' However, the negative portrait of the intrusive woman journalist counteracts the effect of the headline, and the mother is not blamed for her son's disappearance. In *Cage of Gold* (1950, Basil Dearden) Judith (Jean Simmonds) is both an unmarried mother and a career woman. Indeed Judith is confronted by the same choices mentioned at the beginning of this chapter as being emblematic of those faced by some British women. An artist, she is swept off her feet by charming former lover Bill, and breaks with her fiancé Alan. Bill abandons pregnant Judith when he discovers that she is penniless, and she eventually marries Alan, now an NHS doctor in his father's old practice in working-class Battersea, and a far more worthy father to young Nicky. Judith also surrenders her paintbrush to devote herself to her family, and all traces of her former career are eradicated. Yet at the beginning of the film, Judith displays considerable independence in refusing a 'safe' marriage with Alan in favour of an uncertain but exciting life with Bill. In some respects, as Robert Murphy has suggested, Judith's new life with Alan, her duty towards not only Nicky but her bedridden father-in-law are appropriate reminders of the sacrifice and social responsibility of the wartime period.[128]

From this limited but varied range of films made between 1945 and the late 1950s, it can be seen that the representation of women is not quite so rigidly defined as some writers have argued. The situation for women emerging from the war years was far from simple, and thus films about women and for women had to offer more than the 'romance and a good cry' recommended by the *Daily Mirror*'s film critic in 1946.[129] Films like *Perfect Strangers*, *The Years Between*, *The Loves of Joanna Godden*, *White Corridors*, *Blanche Fury* and *Woman in a Dressing Gown* which represent a cross-section of women's lives, be they careerists or housewives, powerfully resonate with the changes underway for women in British post-war society. These women were individuals whose relationships with their partners and husbands, and with the communities in which they served or lived, were diverse and complex.

There has not been the space here to discuss films which showed the real-life heroines of war whose sense of social responsibility outweighed regard for their own lives, such as the SOE agent Odette Sansom in *Odette* (1950, Herbert Wilcox) and *Carve Her Name with Pride* (1958, Lewis Gilbert), the story of Violette Szabo, who was shot by the Gestapo in 1943. In the following chapter, we will see that the irony of the story of *Odette* is that an English film-maker chose to dramatise her life rather than one of her own countrymen. The fictional heroines of *A Town Like Alice* (1956, Jack Lee) and *Ice Cold in Alex* (1958, J. Lee Thompson) are not covered here, and yet provided very strong roles for relatively unknown British actresses. The contributions of women – like directors and producers Muriel Box, Wendy Toye and Betty Box, production designer Carmen Dillon and screenwriters Anne Burnaby and Janet Green and countless actresses – to the film industry are testament to the fact that despite the difficulties described by Muriel Box, women were experiencing a period of empowerment in reality, which was in a sense being reflected on screen.

7

'Liberation' and *Les Femmes Françaises*

If women's status in Britain changed through greater participation in economic and political life, then it was doubly so for Frenchwomen. Approximately 57 per cent of the two million men captured in June 1940 were married, 39 per cent had children,[1] and nearly half of them spent five years or more in German prisoner-of-war camps.[2] The wives and families of about one in every seven Frenchmen waited for husbands and sons to return.[3] Meanwhile women not only worked and looked after home and family, and cooked with meagre rations, but worried about their captive husbands. Frenchwomen were enfranchised in October 1944, the culmination of over forty years of campaigning by feminist groups,[4] though the commonly held view, one particularly held by the Communist Party (PCF), was that votes for women were a reward for their Resistance activities. Women's political voices were now voluble, a considerable change from the occupation era, when being female meant being a component of Vichy's slogan 'travail, famille, patrie', and when cinema stressed motherhood and the family. How, then, were the great changes of the liberation era being reflected in contemporary cinema, now free from the practical and ideological restrictions of the occupation?

The representation of women in French cinema has been perceived in very narrow terms. Susan Hayward remarks that in the 1930s and 1940s women were reduced to a simplistic dualism, being 'either the agent of danger or salvation'.[5] Of the 1950s, she concludes that images of women were equally misogynistic, either 'fallen (or about to fall), adulterous, ensnaring or scheming'. Vichy's mother-figure was replaced by the 'proto-mother', an unthreatening, 'unsexualised' but 'caring, wise and all-knowing mature woman' who supported the male protagonist.[6] In their study of cinema's 'war between the sexes', Noël Burch and Geneviève Sellier explore the idea that following the 'destabilising' liberation era there was a 'replacement of the patriarchal order', when films manifested misogynistic themes.[7] The reason for these films is apparent. Surrounding the events of 1940 to 1944 there was a 'social gendering of the public domains', in which men, who alone wielded power in the political, economic and military spheres, were held responsible for the profoundly ignominious situation in which France found itself.[8] This humiliation was compounded by the fact that the first female votes were cast during the municipal elections of April 1945, when two-and-a-half million men were still absent.[9] Therefore, Burch and Sellier argue, the considerable shift in women's post-war social status was compensated by predominately male-led narratives in the liberation era.[10] However, in 1954 Jacques Doniol-Volcroze conducted a survey of 60 films made between 1945 and 1954 with substantive female roles, in an attempt to define the nature of female representation. In British, American and Swedish cinema, he argued, there were two or three 'types' in each who conveyed a true sense of their nation, whereas French films did not easily capture French womanhood.[11] This comment suggests that rather, than 'dualism', female roles were much more difficult to define.

During the occupation, the practical task of taking on responsibility for the household or for a small business or farm was accompanied by Vichy's veneration of 'l'éternal féminin'.[12] The 'cult' of femininity involved the dissemination of the notion that woman had a vital 'natural' essence which should be nurtured and contained,[13] a 'containment' which included draconian laws on abortion, which became a capital crime in February 1942 under the 300 Law.[14] Unsurprisingly, the most powerful images of France to appear in this era were feminine and virginal: Jeanne D'Arc, France's greatest heroine, was glorified by the Vichy regime as representing the wounded nation.[15] Marianne, symbol of the Republic, was particularly conspicuous around the liberation period, when one poster showed her hands marked with stigmata, suggesting the pain and suffering of France.[16] Marianne, however, actually masked the masculine nature of the republican tradition,[17] a paradox echoed by the fact that the 'feminine' was denigrated as well as revered.

After the war intellectual definitions of collaboration and resistance assumed sexual terms.[18] Sartre genderised collaborators, and in his essay 'Qu'est-ce qu'un collaborateur?', published in 1945, he defined the relationship between France and Germany as sexual, based on a feminine (or homosexual) desire to 'seduce' the strong invader.[19] Indeed the greatest fear of prisoners of war was that their wives were conducting adulterous affairs with Germans.[20] Claude Morgan's novel *La Marque de l'homme*, set in a prison camp, describes a French woman being attracted by the virile masculinity and cultural acumen of her captor, but she does not submit.[21] Vercors' clandestine novel *Le Silence de la mer*[22] (filmed in 1949 by Jean-Pierre Melville) adopted a similar approach in its description of the unspoken attraction between a young woman and a German officer billeted on her uncle. Werner von Ebrennac, a cultured francophile, believes fervently that music, literature and poetry can unite the two countries. His efforts at conversation are, however, met with stony silence, a silence constituting their resistance to his, and by implication the German, presence.

Perhaps the most sexualised phenomena of the liberation period were 'les femmes tondues'. These women had 'visibly and publicly enjoyed benefits denied the majority' by indulging in *collaboration horizontale*, sexual liaisons with the enemy.[23] Yet even the most innocuous services provided to the occupiers, regardless of the degree of coercion, were interpreted 'through a prism of sexuality',[24] and women in some communities were subjected to the same drastic punishment for having served a German in a shop or cleaned his accommodation. *Les femmes tondues* were humiliated by having their heads sheared in public, adorned with swastikas, jeered at and sometimes stripped before being paraded in the town square.[25] As the practice of head-shearing had since the Middle Ages been perpetrated on adulterous women, its deployment in the liberation era can be seen as retribution for woman's 'betrayal' of France.[26] The shearings halted as abruptly as they had begun, and although many photographs were taken it soon became unmentionable.[27] The silence which followed was echoed by lack of reference to it on screen until Henri-Georges Clouzot's updated *Manon* (1949) and, more memorably, Alan Resnais's sharply contemporary *Hiroshima mon amour* (1959). Resnais, a highly idiosyncratic film-maker, set the film in Hiroshima, where a French actress, 'Elle', is making a film about peace. Elle meets a Japanese architect, 'Lui', and they begin an affair. The repercussions of the atomic bomb, seen early on in a montage of newsreels, photographs and museum exhibits, combined with the intensity of the affair, revives Elle's repressed memories of her wartime love for a young German soldier. As she gradually reveals to Lui, her lover was shot, and died a slow, painful death cradled in her arms. As punishment, her head was shaved, she was incarcerated in a cellar until her hair grew back, and then left her home town, Nevers, for a new life in Paris. As Elle's love for the soldier was motivated by passion not by materialism, her treatment is presented as unjust, and her fate at the hands of the community ignominious. Like the phenomenon itself, this traumatic and long-buried event has been painfully repressed.

This reticence applied to other areas of life in which women had been involved during the occupation, particularly the Resistance. The significance of the Resistance is remarkably enduring. As late as 1983, a poll conducted by *L'Histoire* in anticipation of the fortieth anniversary of the liberation, asked readers which was the most significant force out of the Americans, the British, the Soviets and the French to the liberation. While the top answer was the US at 40 per cent, the next highest was for the French at 34 per cent, split between the Free French and the *Maquisards*. Henry Rousso considers this an 'incredible response', as it was nine times higher than the vote for the British.[28] Forty years earlier, when France was economically shattered, the 'cult of the Resistance' was vital to shoring up national self-esteem after years of division. Yet General de Gaulle rebuilt post-war France on the basis of a myth, 'that, essentially, the eternal France had never accepted defeat'[29] and consequently had resisted. Crucially, as Roderick Kedward argues, by August 1944 resistance activity was perceived as having been the 'normal' behaviour of all French people.[30] But while men were being embraced into a 'community' of *résistants*, films tended to ignore women's contributions, whether active or passive.

Resistance scholarship has tended to overlook the part women played because of its very nature.[31] Female presence in the Resistance is difficult to quantify, as women had to have actively served for a minimum of 90 consecutive days to be nominated for inclusion in the dossiers of the Combattants Volontaires de la Résistance. From these dossiers alone, it appears that up to 12 per cent of Resistance workers were female.[32] But resistance constituted far more than active consistent service; it was, as Paula Schwartz has shown, 'a system of action supported by many ... a series of small imperceptible elements which formed a larger construct'.[33] Within that construct, women's contributions were varied, either as full-time clandestine operators or, more often, capitalising on their roles as wives and mothers, with homes being used as meeting places, arms stores or hideaways.[34] Recent research has shown that in rural areas housewives were vital to support networks, not least for their 'protective decoy role of the woman at the doorway'.[35] Furthermore, women who worked in administration, nursing, teaching or as concierges had access to resources which supported the Resistance.[36]

Resistance films played a crucial part in de Gaulle's vision of France, and directors were eager to make them. Former *résistants* encouraged the making of films with qualities of 'truth, sober eloquence and restraint' which would inspire the audience with a Resistance spirit.[37] By the end of 1946, 15 films with Resistance themes had been made. While they comprise only 10 per cent of the total output for 1945 and 1946, the figure is significant given that between 1947 and 1958 only 11 were produced.[38] Resistance films showed collective endeavour which had not been possible during the occupation, although this endeavour was usually male-orientated, as in *Jéricho* (1945, Henri Calef) and *La Bataillon du ciel* (1945, Alexandre Esway), both of which are Anglo–French tales of bravery. An important Resistance text involving women was Christian-Jaque's *Boule de suif* (1945), a combination of two of Guy de Maupassant's short stories, *Boule de suif* and *Mademoiselle Fifi*.[39] Boule de suif, 'Dumpling', is a prostitute who, during the Prussian invasion of 1870, finds herself travelling across Normandy by coach with a group of *bourgeois* snobs and two nuns. The good-hearted Boule de suif shares her food with her fellow passengers, who briefly smother their contempt for her to satisfy their appetites. Having pressurised her to sleep with a Prussian officer to ensure their safe passage onwards, they then ignore her once more. As she watches them gorge themselves from bulging food hampers, she reflects bitterly that they have 'cast her aside as a thing unclean, for which they had no further use'.[40] 'Mademoiselle Fifi' is one of a group of brutal Prussian officers who are occupying a fine chateau. When they send out for prostitutes, one of the girls stabs Fifi and manages to escape.

Boule de suif was, according to critic André Bazin, the first feature film about the occupation.[41] While De Maupassant's heroine is described as 'short and rotund, as fat as a pig', though possessing 'magnificent dark eyes',[42] in the film she is played by the beautiful Micheline Presle, who endows her with glamour and sensuality. When Presle hides a fugitive Frenchman in her bedroom, she is quickly established as the heroine of the film. Both the literary and screen versions of Boule de suif possess far more nobility than any of her grand compatriots on the coach. As the coach's passengers represent a microcosm of French society,[43] in much the same way as various groups in British wartime film had symbolised the nation, so the presence of unpleasant characters is significant. Though she experiences the same humiliation as Maupassant's Boule de suif, Presle is allowed the satisfaction of revenge. After the coach is hijacked and the women are taken off to the occupied chateau, Boule de suif alone stands up to the ruthless Fifi, and kills him with complete impunity. Thus the film gives, in Carrie Tarr's words, 'an exemplary role as an active, articulate and effective figure of resistance',[44] a woman who is prepared to sacrifice her dignity in order to serve the wider community.

Possibly the most celebrated Resistance film of the era was *La Bataille du rail* (1945, René Clément), which powerfully conveys the notion of a 'Resistance community' in France. The film is a documentary-style account of the efforts by SNCF workers, *les cheminots*, to sabotage freight trains requisitioned by the Germans. Research has shown that of workers who actively resisted, *les cheminots* were the most powerful and showed great comradeship and solidarity.[45] Indeed the SNCF was collectively awarded the Légion d'honneur in 1949 for its commitment and sacrifice during the war.[46] The very nature of their work put them in a unique position in respect of Resistance activities. '[Y]ou railwaymen have in your hands,' advised the *Bulletin des chemins de fer*, 'the most powerful instrument against the enemy'.[47] The film is set on the demarcation line, the line between Vichy and Occupied France, at Châlon-sur-Saône, and shows acts of sabotage perpetrated by *les cheminots* and the brutal reprisal for their actions, then a group of workers sabotaging an armoured train. Finally, France is newly liberated and all the groups within the narrative are united in joyous celebration.

La Bataille du rail is mainly concerned with SNCF workers, the most intense point of which is a fine sequence which took 11 days to shoot,[48] in which six *cheminots* are executed for sabotage. Burch and Sellier argue that the film presents an exclusively masculine version of Resistance, but this is not strictly true,[49] particularly as Colette Audry, a novelist known for her redoubtable heroines, co-wrote the screenplay. Burch and Sellier refer to the only female character in the film being negative, the wife of a rather elderly stoker who protests that her husband is too old.[50] The film certainly presents the SNCF as an entirely male domain, despite the fact that women agents organised clandestine trains and warned other agents of enemy presence on the platform,[51] but several women are shown carrying out acts of resistance. Firstly, women are equally the victims of German oppression: a mother's hand snatches her daughter from a train window as a German officer passes, and passengers watch as a Jewish woman and her child are seen being 'escorted' down the platform. Active female resistance is demonstrated in that one of the *Maquisards* who helps with the sabotage of an armoured train is a girl, her belt hung with two hefty hammers. Passive resistance is also indicated: a woman collecting her dog from a special compartment sees a man hiding there but says nothing. Towards the end, a young woman opens a carriage door but slams it shut in disgust when she notices it is occupied by two German soldiers.

La Bataille du rail was praised almost unanimously by the critics, in particular for its authenticity and its value as factual evidence of the Resistance.

'Without doubt,' wrote Jean Néry in *Le Monde*, 'France owed it to itself to leave this document to the world'.[52] According to Alain Spenlé, *La Bataille du rail* was 'unquestionably the first valid document on the French Resistance'.[53] The Commission de contrôle, which provided exhibition visas for films, commented that it should be exported because it showed 'the true and magnificent face of the Resistance'.[54] It was one of the most popular films of 1946, and also won the Grand Prix at the 1946 Cannes Film Festival. Part of its authentic feel was surely that it acknowledged, albeit fleetingly, the contribution that women had made to the notion of France as a community of *résistants*.

Younger women in Resistance films were usually the daughters or sweethearts of Resistance fighters, as in *Le Père tranquille* (1946, René Clément), which was a big commercial success. Monique, like her mother and brother Pierre, is unaware that her father, M. Martin (Noël-Noël), a mild-mannered insurance agent who seems more concerned about his orchids than their German occupiers, is the head of the local Resistance. Nevertheless, Monique reveals her spiritual link with the Resistance, even though it is Pierre who joins the *Maquis,* more exasperated at his father's apparent 'cowardice' than committed to the cause. Monique realises that the secretive meetings her father holds with groups of men who come to the house are on weightier matters than insurance. When Martin returns home late one night, she confronts him, and he admits the truth. They watch together for several hours from a bedroom window until an explosion goes off successfully. Monique's role is dismissed by Burch and Sellier, who argue that her admiration for her father's heroic status merely reconstitutes the father–daughter configuration on the father's terms.[55] However, although she does not take an active part in the Resistance, she is ideologically connected, a link strengthened by her subsequent engagement to Martin's deputy. Also, a minor but important female role is that of a cleaner at the German HQ, who reads a document giving details of a big delivery to a nearby factory and passes this on to her female informant, who runs the *tabac*. This film is very much a Gaullist project in its suggestion that underneath every ordinary Frenchman is the potential for resistance, but it also endorses the part Frenchwomen played.

The courage and bravery of individuals, liaison agents and members of the Special Operations Executive (SOE) have been documented,[56] and yet their extraordinary experiences were practically ignored by film-makers. The life of resistance fighter Lucie Aubrac was not filmed until 1997 by Claude Berri as *Lucie Aubrac*, and was based on her memoir, *Ils Partiront dans l'ivresse*, published in 1984. It should also be noted that the story of Odette Sansom was filmed in 1950 by Herbert Wilcox, a British director better known for his historical melodramas and musical comedies. In August 1946, Anna Neagle, Wilcox's wife, read in the *London Gazette* of the award of the George Cross to Odette Marie-Céline Sansom, a Frenchwoman married to an Englishman, who had been recruited by the SOE. Odette worked undercover in France, was captured and tortured by the Gestapo at their infamous Avenue Foch headquarters in Paris and incarcerated at Ravensbruck, where she narrowly escaped death.[57] Wilcox bought the film rights to the book, but as Neagle professed she lacked the personal experience to 'get inside the heart and mind of Odette', he offered the role first to Ingrid Bergman and then Michèle Morgan.[58] Both actresses turned it down, and so Neagle took the part herself and gave a convincing and moving performance. Although Odette claims several times in the film to be 'an ordinary woman', a housewife and mother of three girls, her courage was truly extraordinary. *Cinématographie française* seemed content to interview Odette, who accompanied the film crew to Annecy in Haute Savoie, without expressing regret that it had not been done by one of her countrymen.[59] The fact that this uplifting account was not included in the canon of Resistance films deemed so important to rebuilding national prestige seems indicative of the reluctance to acknowledge all but the most generalised contributions made by women.

Charles de Gaulle's much vaunted support for women's rights was largely for tactical reasons; he was convinced that women were innately conservative and would vote for the Mouvement Républicaine Populaire (MRP), which was committed to the church and supporting the family.[60] As early as 1942, de Gaulle made it clear that once France was liberated men and women would elect a new government; the ordinance issued from his base in Algiers in April 1944 included an amendment enfranchising women.[61] However, public reaction was by no means universally supportive. In November 1944, when respondents to the national opinion poll were asked whether they approved of women's suffrage, 64 per cent replied yes, 29 per cent no and 3 per cent approved conditionally. A gender-based analysis reveals that 58 per cent of men were in favour while considerably more women, 69 per cent, approved.[62] That said, the numbers of men *and* women not in favour are still significant: of those who expressed an opinion, 34 per cent of men and 26 per cent of women disapproved,[63] though 54 per cent of those questioned felt that women would change the next election result.[64] This mixed picture gives some indication of the rather convoluted perception of women's status as a whole. Simone de Beauvoir's *Le Deuxième Sexe*, published in 1949, seems to arouse some difference of opinion even today. Robert Gildea claims that it was 'little read or understood at the time',[65] yet Gallimard issued the ninety-seventh reprint in 1955.[66]

Nonetheless, the long years of being politically powerless had left its legacy. It is also worth remembering that until 1965, when major reforms were introduced, the part of the 1804 Code Napoléon that considered women as minors was still valid.[67] Despite their new citizenship, even women who had been active in the underground movement were reluctant to be politically pro-active, arguing that modern politics, unlike the Resistance, lacked a common goal. In post-war France, many women simply found that their concerns were not being addressed by the major parties. Where female participation did occur, it tended to be at community level rather than national, where issues had a direct effect on their lives.[68] Nevertheless, some women may well have seen the vote more as a well-deserved reward for surviving the rigours of the occupation: the absent husbands, the rationing, the endless queuing, and for many an ever-present enemy. So how far did political liberation have an impact on women's sexual, social, cultural and economic status in the immediate post-war years, and how was it represented in post-war cinema?

In 1954, film-maker Jacques Becker remarked that 'the occupation marked the beginning of a certain "emancipation" of young better-off women',[69] an allusion to Micheline (Micheline Presle) in his film *Falbalas* (1944), who forgoes the chance of a safe, lucrative marriage with Daniel and also rejects a sexually passionate relationship with couturier and philanderer Philippe. Becker added that sexual liberation had gone too far, as even girls from poorer backgrounds, who traditionally tended to have stricter morals, were now more likely to be sexually active before marriage.[70] Becker's provocative comment raises the issue of whether other films represented female sexual 'emancipation', as he described it? There were certainly more films about prostitutes or 'morally loose' women in the liberation era, in contrast to Vichy's emphasis on woman as wife and mother. The *femme fatale* was not new but a stereotype well known to pre-war cinema. But was her reincarnation in post-war film an indication of a new-found sexual liberation, or did it represent some kind of vengeance on the female sex for the crisis of masculinity brought about by the occupation?

During the occupation, Vichy heroines were motivated by duty and sacrifice rather than pleasure and desire. Only occasionally was there a sense of female sexual emancipation, as in *Falbalas,* and in the example of Thérèse

(Jany Holt), who seeks refuge in a convent after committing a *crime passionnel* in Robert Bresson's *Les Anges du péché* (1943). Virtue, however, did not accurately reflect reality, as there was a huge increase in illicit sexual activity and, as in Britain, the number of prostitutes proliferated. The difference was that there had been licensed brothels in France since the early nineteenth century.[71] An American GI, enquiring about the location of the local brothel in a Wiltshire town, was told, 'We don't have brothels in England, you'll have to wait until you get to France'.[72] In 1935 there were between 300,000 and 400,000 prostitutes in the whole country, but by 1940 there were 100,000 in Paris alone, 2000 of them working in authorised brothels.[73] *Les maisons de tolérance* were strictly regulated, and their workers underwent regular and rigorous health checks in order to prevent venereal disease spreading to their German *clientèle*.[74] However, impecunious housewives, including prisoner-of-war wives living on allowances that were less than their husband's pay, took to streetwalking to supplement their incomes.[75] After the war, despite support for keeping brothels open on the grounds that controlling prostitution was beneficial to public safety, the Loi Marthe Richard (a municipal councillor in Paris concerned with 'moral purification') was passed in 1946, shutting down the 1500 venues still operational.[76] For prostitutes, the closures meant economic vulnerability, but rather than disappearing, prostitution merely became a clandestine profession.[77]

The popular perception in British films of Frenchwomen was that they were passionate and sexually assertive. Consider *Cage of Gold*, in which there is a sexual dichotomy in Bill Glennon's two lovers: Judith, whose pregnancy leads to marriage and for him the disagreeable prospect of a conventional life, and his long-term mistress Madeleine, a singer at the Parisian night-club Cage of Gold, to whom he constantly returns but who eventually kills him in a *crime passionnel*. Possibly the most famous actress in this respect was Simone Signoret, whose reputation for playing sensual women was such that in 1958, aged 37, she was recruited to play Alice Aisgill, the older, married 'loving friend' of ambitious Joe Lampton in Jack Clayton's *Room at the Top*, which she described as 'one of the best parts in the contemporary English cinema to be played by a Frenchwoman'.[78] 'Signoret,' wrote *Picturegoer*, 'puts more sizzling sex in a Mother Hubbard nightgown than a dozen undressed Bardots',[79] Brigitte Bardot then being the protégé of director Roger Vadim.

Long before Signoret's appearance on screen, however, Arletty was the most famous *poule,* in films like *Hôtel du Nord* (1938) and *Le Jour se Lève*

(1939) both directed by Marcel Carné, and *Fric-Frac* (1939, Claude Autant-Lara). Even Arletty's greatest role, which she played at the age of 46 in *Les Enfants du paradis*, the enigmatic, alluring and emotionally self-sufficient Garance, was still reliant on male patronage. Nevertheless, Arletty believed Garance to be 'the spirit of a woman...a complete woman'.[80] Garance belonged to the *demi-monde*, described by Simone de Beauvoir as a world in which the woman's protector endowed her with a social reputation, but added that the social and economic changes of the twentieth century had forever destroyed that 'flamboyant type'.[81] In post-war films, whores were still in demand, but the reasons for their inclusion were more complex. Signoret, Arletty's successor in the late 1940s, was an actress of great depth whose sexuality was, or invariably bordered on, the forbidden. For instance, her (frequent) lighting of a cigarette and placing it on her highly glossed full lips was an erotic overture in itself. The characters she played invariably lived outside respectable society, women who symbolised the darker side of life during the occupation: the betrayals, the suspicion and the collusion.

After a few minor roles from 1942, and playing a Belgian Resistance worker in Ealing's *Against the Wind* (1948, Charles Crichton), Signoret was given the role of a whore in *Macadam* (1946, Marcel Blistène), a film that successfully evoked a *quartier* of Montmartre. *Dédée d'Anvers* (1948), directed by Yves Allégret, her future husband, brought her to the serious attention of the French public. Dédée is the most expensive prostitute in René's (Bernard Blier) bar in the Belgian port of Anvers, but despite her status is bullied by her sadistic pimp Marco. Though confined to the bar's claustrophobic milieu, Dédée's world is turned upside down when she meets an Italian sailor, Francesco. Their attraction is mutual and immediate, and they plan to leave Anvers together. René, infuriated by Marco's treatment of Dédée, unthinkingly tells him, and Marco sets out to kill Francesco. Dédée and René pursue Marco, and at the dockside René knocks him unconscious and Dédée orders René to run over him in his car, her hand gripping the steering wheel as they drive over his inert body.

As heroic men are absent in the film, *Dédée d'Anvers* could be interpreted as symptomatic of the post-war crisis of masculinity.[82] Yet it is also about Dédée's resoluteness, in which from a position of being dominated and abused by Marco, her body bought nightly by strangers, she becomes a figure of authority and controller of her own destiny. Indeed, in the last sequence her previously feminine mode of dress changes to a workman-like trenchcoat. For Signoret, the success of *Dédée d'Anvers* meant several years of being 'catalogued as a whore', but she believed the character to be sympathetic, a 'victim of society'.[83] *Dédée d'Anvers* also demonstrated that she was 'always the subject not the object of her own desire', an actress whose physicality predominated, in her acting and her expressive face and gestures.[84]

Signoret's character in *Manèges* (1949, Yves Allégret) was quite different, the ruthless Dora, a 'real whore without a sidewalk and without a pimp',[85] although effectively her mother is the latter. This time, Blier plays Dora's husband Robert, blind to Dora's many infidelities and the fact that his riding school is in debt because of her profligacy. The depths to which Dora will stoop are revealed when she tells *Maman* offhandedly that one of her wealthy conquests has been imprisoned for 'dealings with the Krauts' during the war. Robert, who worships Dora, discovers the truth when she lies paralysed after an accident and she urges her mother to 'tell him everything... everything'. As Robert is a former *prisonnier* whose greatest friend died in the camp, her betrayal seems all the more wounding. Dora has no hesitation when trying to impress a potential lover in using Robert's experience to imply that he cannot satisfy her sexually: 'You know how it is, you have to be patient'. Her confession gives the false impression that she was one of the dutiful 'waiting wives' who were embraced by Vichy as being vital to the post-war 'renovation' of France.[86] A similar theme had been used in *Le Diable au corps*, in which the adulterous Marthe (Micheline Presle) tears up a letter from her husband, who is serving at the front during the First World War. As Presle observed, in 1946–47 this act was deeply shocking, coming so soon after the enforced separation of soldiers from their wives during the occupation.[87]

Dora is drastically punished for her duplicity through permanent paralysis and Robert's abandonment of her at the end of the film. Even though Burch and Sellier argue that the film privileges the masculine point of view,[88] she has been a commanding presence, and appears in the majority of the narrative. Nevertheless, it is a film of unremitting bleakness in which there are no victors. According to *L'Écran français*, it showed that film noir had 'reached its lowest point'.[89] Leahy and Hayward write that while various readings can be made of such a complex narrative, it is principally a representation of the deeply troubled relationships between men and women who were victims of 'economic and sexual insecurities and the confused need for retribution'.[90] The confusion is best illustrated by Signoret herself, who recalled the reaction from audiences: 'it upset them. And they detested me. I don't mean the critics. I mean the people in the street.'[91]

According to Burch and Sellier, *Manèges* belongs to the 25 per cent of films made between 1945 and 1955 which feature a 'sale garce', an 'evil bitch', who 'uses her powers of seduction to exploit, enslave and/or destroy men'.[92] These women display deeply anti-social tendencies, the most common being revenge. In *Les Dames du bois de boulogne* (Robert Bresson, 1945) based on Diderot's eighteenth-century story, the most satisfying form of revenge the wealthy Hélène (Maria Casarès) can inflict on a former lover who has spurned her is to engineer a love affair with Agnès, a young impoverished relative who has become a prostitute. Jean dutifully falls in love with Agnès and a marriage is arranged. Hélène then reveals the truth about his bride's unsavoury past, but to her dismay love triumphs. The forgiveness of past sexual misdemeanours is significant given the almost simultaneous phenomenon of *les femmes tondues,* for whom there was no such clemency. Interestingly, in 1951 André Bazin considered that a modern audience (unlike Diderot's readers) would find the 'abstract premise' of vengeance incomprehensible.[93] Perhaps this mass amnesia is proof of the 'conspiracy of silence'[94] that followed the wave of shearings in 1944. Other films about vengeful women, such as *Panique* (1947, Julien Duviver), were discussed earlier, and in Jean Cocteau's updated *Orphée* (1950), Death was a woman (Maria Casarès again). But in general, by the early 1950s the obsession with vengeance for its own sake had clearly waned. In Julien Duvivier's *Marie-Octobre* (1958), former *résistante* Danielle Darrieux's

12. *Manèges* (1949, Yves Allégret), with Simone Signoret and Bernard Blier. © 1949 Studiocanal Image/Celia Film.

planned retribution on a comrade who betrayed their chief many years before seems justified. Otherwise, most film-makers were preoccupied with contemporary matters.

As in Britain, reconstructing family life was extremely important to the greater task of rebuilding France. Divorce rates peaked in 1946, reaching 64,064, compared to 37,718 in 1945, due to the lifting of Vichy's restrictions and the inevitable marital breakdowns that followed the war.[94] As was the case in Britain, some women's experience of being independent, albeit enforced, had changed them in some respects, particularly wives of prisoners of war. Sarah Fishman's research indicates that most families successfully reunited because of a very persuasive propaganda campaign which encouraged waiting wives to be self-effacing.[96] Other marriages suffered because repatriated husbands found that their wives had altered, or worse. In *Retour à la vie, Le Retour de René* (1949, Jean Dréville), is a humorous account of a *prisonnier*, René, who returns from Germany to find his wife has disappeared and there are interlopers living in their apartment. By the end of the sketch, however, the 'intruders', who consist of a young pretty widow and her two children, have become very attached to René, and so his readjustment revolves around his new family.

Even established marriages were shown to be fragile, and a few films showed marital stability being threatened by a younger woman. Hayward argues that compared with the 1940s, the 1950s offer more sustained images of women as agents of their own desire.[97] However, films of both decades are critical of male infidelity in marriage. In *Les Amoureux sonts seuls au monde* (1948, Henri Decoin) famous composer Gérard Favier and his wife Sylvia (Louis Jouvet and Renée Devillers) are happily married. They meet a young pianist, Monelle (Dany Robin), who admires Gérard and becomes his protégé. Gossip quickly starts in the press, but though Monelle has fallen in love with Gérard, he does not share her feelings. When a scurrilous newspaper claims that Gérard is to be divorced, Sylvia offers him his freedom. Although he strenuously denies the affair, she commits suicide. The producers of *Les Amoureux sonts seuls au monde* were obliged by the censor to film an alternative ending in which the couple were reunited, on the basis that foreign cinemas would not show suicide.[98] The British version certainly had a 'happy ending'.[99] The original therefore has a much more pessimistic tone and acts as a warning to husbands that even contemplating adultery can have devastating consequences. The theme of *Des Gens sans importance* (1955, Henri Verneuil) is similar, but the victim is the 'other woman'. Jean, a truck driver (Jean Gabin), a faithful husband though unhappily married, meets a waitress from a roadside café, who seduces him. Far from enriching his life, however, Jean's affair is a depressing, claustrophobic relationship which echoes his marriage in that Clothilde (Françoise Arnoul) is as downtrodden as his wife is a drudge. Jean then loses his job, Clothilde becomes pregnant and dies following an illegal abortion. Clearly, in this example, female sexual independence does not come with impunity.

In an earlier film starring Arnoul, *La Rage au corps* (1953, Ralph Habib), a young wife (Clara) who has had previous lovers is (rather too easily) lured into prostitution while her husband is on a business trip. She attempts suicide when she faces the reality of her actions, but with psychiatric help and her husband's love, she recovers. As Burch and Sellier point out, Clara's sexuality is diagnosed as 'nymphomania', requiring medical treatment, while the promiscuousness of her lovers and her one 'client' are vindicated by means of the ubiquitous 'double standard'.[100] There are echoes of this notion in Roger Vadim's *Et Dieu créa la femme* (1956), in which it is suggested to orphaned Juliette (Brigitte Bardot) that if she passes a medical examination she might avoid being returned to the orphanage as punishment for her wanton behaviour.

Films about younger married couples were usually far more optimistic. Jacques Becker's *Antoine et Antoinette* (1947) and *Edouard et Caroline* (1951) deal with young newly married couples. Becker has been called a '*cinéaste social*', an epithet gleaned from his 1954 interview with *Cahiers du cinema*.[101] Admitting some truth in this, he stressed his concern for characters and relationships over dramatic plots, props and decor.[102] Even in *Casque D'Or* (1952), a *fin-de-siècle* romantic drama, the characters, Marie (Simone Signoret) and Manda (Serge Reggiani) take precedence over the costumes. As well as his interest in characterisation, Becker favoured female writers: Françoise Giroud for *Antoine et Antoinette* and Annette Wademant for *Edouard et Caroline*. Françoise Giroud, co-founder of *Elle* in 1945, was highly critical of what she saw as Simone de Beauvoir's 'detachment' from 'everyday women', and considered her 'the example incarnate of a woman living for and through a man', which was now an irrelevance in the modern world.[103] The combination of Becker's belief in women's sexual liberation and Giroud's espousal of genuine female autonomy mean that the characters of Antoinette and Caroline (both cited in Doniol-Valcroze's list)[104] are never subordinate to the men in the narrative.

Antoine and Antoinette Moulin are a young working couple. Becker's interest in Italian neo-realism[105] created an authentic chronicle of married life, 'its little pleasures, its routines and its irritations', which was particularly admired by left-wing critics.[106] Antoinette (Claire Mafféi) is a sales assistant at Prisunic, pursued (unsuccessfully) by various men, and is an independent modern young woman. Conversely, Antoine (Roger Pigaut), who works in a printing factory, reflects post-war male anxiety, in that he frequently succumbs to childish jealousy about his young wife. When he loses a winning lottery ticket, he is ashamed and tortures himself with images of Antoinette being enticed into a wealthy lifestyle by Monsieur Roland, the neighbourhood *épicier* who has designs on her. Though middle-aged and un-attractive, Roland is significant, as grocers wielded considerable power over the ration books. Even after the occupation, during which housewives had coped with food shortages by means of *le système débrouillard* (being resourceful) and queuing for several hours a day,[107] rationing on basic food-stuffs was still in force until 1949, and coffee until 1950,[108] and in some areas shops opened only three or four days a week due to lack of produce. Antoinette is thus potentially vulnerable to Roland's unwelcome attentions.

The ending of the original story, as told to Becker, was rather different from the film version.[109] The couple have a young daughter. The lost lottery ticket is never found and the humiliated husband does not return home. Several years have passed, and the wife has formed a new relationship, when the husband finds the ticket and the family is finally reunited. Becker considered that the husband's disappearance was far too 'Russian', and that no *Frenchman* would ever desert his home.[110] Finally, therefore, the ticket found, we see the couple speeding along on Antoine's long-held dream, a motorbike and sidecar, materially better off and fully prepared for the family ahead of them. Antoinette is an ideal wife, the 'spirit' of the film, who is clearly in love with her husband. She is also deeply forgiving, which enables Antoine's wounded pride to heal quickly after the disaster of the lost ticket.

Though the two films are both about tribulations between loving young married couples, *Edouard et Caroline* is quite distinct from *Antoine et Antoinette* in several ways. *Edouard et Caroline* is shot entirely indoors, adopting the style of 1930s American marital comedies. While Antoine and Antoinette are both from a *milieu populaire*, Edouard and Caroline have *bourgeois* pretensions, and despite their lack of money Caroline does not work. The *mode de vie* of the couple in the earlier film resonates still with the occupation, but Edouard and Caroline appear completely detached from that era. Caroline's (Anne Vernon) rich uncle has promised that he will introduce Edouard (Daniel Gélin), a gifted pianist, into Parisian bourgeois society, which will help his career to flourish. At the story's centre, however, is Caroline's dress, which she re-models in the style of designer Jacques Christian. But when Edouard sees it, he considers the *décolletage* far too low, they argue bitterly, and Edouard slaps Caroline. She demands a divorce and he goes to the *soirée* alone. At her uncle's, Caroline makes a grand entrance on her cousin Alain's arm, and her dress is a triumph. Edouard too has a highly successful evening, during which, although some of the guests are clearly bored, he is later offered the chance of a concert tour by a wealthy American. The couple go home sullen and uncommunicative, but they are quickly reunited when Caroline appears in a seductive negligée.

Compared to Becker's previous film, the story is slight, and the elite circle in which the couple wish to be initiated is a far cry from the hard-working community where the Moulins live. Admittedly, its aim is quite different to that of *Antoine et Antoinette*, in satirising the indolence of the bourgeoisie and suggesting that, rather than being cultured, they behave with shocking vulgarity.[111] However, the question of the dress, and indeed the negligée, is important in looking at how women were being represented. While the dress, which is for public consumption, angers Edouard, suggesting his insecurity, the other highly feminine creation, the negligée, to which only he is privy, is the agent of their reconciliation. To an extent, the film succumbs to stereotype as Caroline uses her feminine wiles to mollify her petulant husband, and as Burch and Sellier argue, the fact that she is idle and snobbish seems to indicate Becker's 'regression' since *Antoine et Antoinette*.[112] Indeed, Georges Sadoul, writing in *L'Humanité*, wished that the director would return to documenting the 'reality of our people'.[113] Nonetheless, *Edouard et Caroline* reflects women's renewed participation and interest in fashion, glamour and sheer femininity after long years of privation.

One of the ways in which France was revitalised was through *haute couture*. The first sign of a re-launch was in March 1945, when an exhibition was staged at the Louvre displaying wire dolls dressed and coiffured by the top couturiers and stylists of the day, demonstrating to the world that France had retained its reputation for fashion.[114] As the 'military' cut of wartime clothing was still the norm, the two gowns made by Christian Dior aroused particular interest, having 'waspish' nipped-in waists and voluminous skirts.[115] Dior's first proper collection was unveiled in February 1947, and changed the face of fashion forever with his extravagant use of fabric.[116] The Dior 'look' is shown in one of the episodes of Julien Duvivier's *Sous le ciel de Paris* (1950), in which models pose by the fountains of the Palais de Chaillot. However, in 1947 not everyone was enthused by such displays of luxury. In Britain, MP Mabel Ridealgh complained that it was 'too reminiscent of the "caged bird attitude"', and designers should be aware of 'the new *outlook* of women',[117] which required that they had freedom of movement. Judging by Dior's ill-fated decision to conduct a photographic session at a street market in Montmartre, where a group of women stall-holders attacked the model, pulling her hair and tearing the clothes from her back,[118] the frivolity and extravagance of Dior's designs were clearly too much for women for whom the occupation had meant years of drudgery and deprivation.

For most women, one of the discourses being most energetically directed at them was that of 'la femme au foyer', the art of being a housewife. The 'domestic ideal' was taught to girls in school on the basis that, as one 1953 textbook proposed, 'true happiness was to be found in the home'.[119] Indeed, there was a 400 per cent increase in spending on household appliances between 1949 and 1957.[120] The women's press also endorsed 'la femme au foyer'. Out of the four biggest-selling magazines, *Marie-Claire*, *L'Écho de la mode*, *Elle* and *Les Femmes d'aujourd'hui*, the two last (and most recent), had the largest proportion of their pages devoted to 'conseils pratiques', advice on 'everything that constituted women's traditional work',[121] so clearly were not interested in representing the newly enfranchised Frenchwoman. They also had the lowest number of pages on 'romance'.[122] Ménie Grégoire noted that in 1958 a new quarterly periodical, *Femme Pratique,* boasted that it was 'the technical journal for the housewife', a magazine with no serials and 'no romance'.[123] The lack of fiction was significant, as the 'roman feuilleton', the serialised novel, had always been an integral part of nearly all the popular women's magazines.[124] The appeal of housekeeping, as opposed to matters of the heart, was suggested by the fact that its first issue sold 250,000 copies, but the second almost double that number, 450,000![125]

Notwithstanding the importance of housekeeping and the 'domestic ideal', the 'new look' had huge repercussions on the design of women's fashion. It certainly influenced the increased 'sexualisation' of the female body in 1950s films. Simultaneously this was also the case in Britain with the appearance of Diana Dors. In an inversion of the assumed 'carnality' of *Les françaises*, *Passport to Shame* (1959, Alvin Rakoff), shows a naïve French girl (Odile Versois) being drawn into prostitution while the 'professional' Dors spends much of her time standing shimmering in doorways, showing off her curvaceous figure to its best advantage. In France, the *cinéma du qualité*,[126] which attempted to rival Hollywood's 'super-productions', used a preponderance of expensive costume dramas that permitted actresses to be tightly laced and corseted, accentuating their curves, or dressed in flimsy Empire-line gowns, exposing their *décolletage*. Yet the work of Jacqueline Audry, whose films include adaptations of her sister Colette's novels, indicates that the costume drama could effectively convey gender relationships without placing gratuitous emphasis on the period settings.[127]

Conversely, Martine Carol's role in the most successful film of that year, *Caroline Chérie* (1950, Richard Pottier), as a young aristocrat in revolutionary France, paid little heed to such subtleties, but rather marked Carol's debut as the first 'sex symbol *à la française*'.[128] As Alan Williams remarks, some of her films seem to have been made purely in order to 'display the Carolian figure'.[129] In 1954, André Bazin wrote with some irritation that she had initiated 'the feminine myth of the Fourth Republic', completely undermining Cécile Saint-Laurent's original heroine. 'From her feet to... her blonde hair, rounded buttocks and brown tipped breasts,' he complained, 'Caroline is Martine Carol Chérie for millions of French males'.[130] Appropriately, in Doniol-Volcroze's 1954 list, each of Carol's films are defined as 'érotique'.[131] Two films about courtesans unquestionably focus on the female body. In *Nana* (1955, Christian-Jaque), the rampant sexuality of Zola's heroine's is enough to destroy fortunes and families, and in Max Ophuls's *Lola Montès* (1955), Lola, a former courtesan whose lovers range from a king to a composer, is reduced to selling kisses from a golden cage in a circus ring, the ultimate voyeur's dream. *Caroline Chérie* signalled the replacement of the one-dimensional *garce* of the 1940s by the unthreatening sexy woman in thrall to a patriarchal figure of the 1950s.[132] Indeed, a perusal of the two beautifully illustrated catalogues compiled by Maurice Bessy and his colleagues reveal a remarkable number of stills from historical and contemporary films featuring young actresses posing in underwear or even half-naked.[133] The extreme example of Burch and Sellier's paradigm is of course Roger Vadim's *Et Dieu créa la femme*, in which Bardot's sinuous nymphette has a quasi-father–daughter relationship with the older, protective Kurt Jürgens.

These seemingly trivial films could not be further removed from the aesthetic of the liberation era, which concentrated on subjects that would help to restore a sense of national community. Another part of the 'restorative' agenda was to encourage women to produce children. In March 1945, de Gaulle made a speech in which he stressed the need for 12 million 'beautiful babies' in the next 10 years.[134] Thus wartime family policy continued in respect of child allowances, bonuses on the birth of first babies and strict laws on abortion and contraception. As one of the least controversial Vichy programmes, politicians were easily able to appropriate it as part of the peacetime settlement.[135] As in Britain, due to the emphasis placed on child-rearing, policies towards female employment verged on the contradictory, but a major difference in government policy towards childcare provision was that in France wartime nurseries were not withdrawn. Although there were still insufficient crèches, the ongoing debates about this issue suggest that there was a desire for married women to be able to work.[136] In France, female employment was more common: between 1906 and 1946 women represented more than 40 per cent of the working population.[137] According to the pre-war census, the proportion of women working was higher than in Britain, Germany, Holland and the US, mainly due to the importance of rural labour.[138]

There are paradoxes, nevertheless, in the practical and ideological constraints on women working. Firstly, the severe shortages of raw materials meant that in some traditionally female sectors there was considerable unemployment, particularly textiles,[139] for which, ironically, British women were being recruited across the Channel. Secondly, as with other areas of women's lives, female employment was rigidly prescribed by the archaic Code Napoléon. Until 1965, a woman had to obtain permission from her husband to work outside the home if he considered that such activity would constitute a threat to the family.[140] The results of a survey by the national opinion poll in 1947 indicate considerable support for women staying at home. To the question, 'Is it better that a woman works outside the home or devotes herself exclusively to running the house-hold?', 71 per cent thought the latter option was preferable.[141] Despite the considerable cultural and economic differences in attitudes between France and Britain towards women's work and childcare, there were, as in Britain, a number of important films that were concerned with neglected or vulnerable children.

The black-clad orphans who appear in 'crocodile' formation four times to symbolise the theme of maternal neglect in Jean Grémillon's *Le Ciel est à vous* (1943) were prescient images. Post-war films about orphans reflect the idea that for children whose parents were lost during *l'exode*, in prisoner-of-war camps, from deportation or from bombing raids, their childhood had been stolen.[142] Neglected or orphaned youngsters appear in *Le Visiteur* (1946, Jean Dréville), *La Fille du diable* (1946, Henri Decoin), *Impasse des deux anges* (1948, Maurice Tourneur), *Une si Jolie petite plage* (1948, Yves Allégret), *Au Royaume des cieux* (1949, Julien Duvivier) and *Jeux Interdits* (René Clément, 1952). The orphans in *Le Visiteur*, who hero-worship their benefactor Sauval, who is actually a criminal, convince him that their morally upright little community is superior to his corrupt *mode de vie*. While his criminality is attributed to his own orphan status, he ensures that the boys never know the truth about him. Lacking the support network of other parentless children, Isabelle, *La Fille du diable*, is not so fortunate, and when her illusions are shattered about Saget, the crook she has admired from afar, she kills herself. *Impasse des deux anges* features a curious young girl who lives apparently alone behind a ruined fence, surviving by selling black-market goods on 'no-man's land'. Marianne (Simone Signoret), who was also once an isolated, frightened girl, thus becomes a surrogate mother/sister figure when she appears.

These last two films in particular reflect the continuing anxiety about juvenile delinquency in France during the occupation, which in 1945 had prompted the penal authorities to create special courts and judges for under-eighteens.[143] They also invoke considerable compassion for the confused young victims of destabilisation. Nicole Védrès reported in 1947 that part of the return of French cinema to 'present-day situations' was demonstrated by the fact that Marcel Carné had dropped the idea of making *Candide* and instead was opting for a contemporary subject, about a 'revolt amongst a community of juvenile delinquents'.[144] *Fleur de l'âge* would have been his last collaboration with Jacques Prévèrt. Unfortunately the production in which the inmates rebel against authority ran into funding difficulties, and Carné was forced to abandon the project.

Films also reflected the anxiety that without a stable parental background orphans might become criminalised. At the beginning of *Au Royaume des cieux* (1949, Julien Duvivier) a young girl whose mother is killed in the Rouen bombing is placed with a peasant family by the state orphanage, L'Assistance Publique, and is ill-treated. She fares little better with an urban family, and ends up in a reform school. Yves Allégret's *Une si Jolie petite plage* (1948) alarmed the censor with its apparent suggestion that orphans were naturally irresponsible. Pierre (Gérard Philipe), a former orphan who revisits the Normandy hotel where he spent an unhappy summer being exploited by the proprietress, finds that another boy from L'Assistance Publique is being used in a similar way. In censorship files, there is a note about a scene in which the hotelier tells Pierre that 'You have to be careful ... we don't know where they come from ... where they were born ... they're rotten from birth ... The consequences of sin.'[145] Despite Allégret's insistence that because the character speaking the dialogue is 'odious', the public would not empathise with his sentiments, its mere presence in the scene was sufficient to make the censor insist that it be cut.[146] It nevertheless remains an extremely bitter film in which the young man, desperately isolated, commits suicide before the police reach him. It clearly censures the maltreatment of children from state orphanages by both men and women.

Jeux Interdits, a captivating film beautifully acted by its two young protagonists, is uncompromising about the fate of six-year-old Paulette (Brigitte Fossey). In a vivid opening sequence, she and her parents are amongst the mass of refugees fleeing south from Paris in June 1940. Near the Loire, their car breaks down, and when German aircraft fire at the ragged trail of people, Paulette's parents are both killed. Seizing her dead puppy, Paulette runs off and is eventually taken in by the Dolle family, and is befriended by their 11-year-old son Michel (Georges Poujoly), who is neglected by his parents. Paulette and Michel bury the puppy in a cemetery they build in a derelict mill, and to keep him company they collect other dead animals, whose graves they decorate with little crosses, shells and flowers. Finally, gendarmes arrive to take Paulette to the Red Cross, where, amidst a teeming throng of displaced people, she is duly labelled and told, 'you'll be with lots of other little girls like you who have been very sad, but together you'll be happy again'. Paradoxically, the children's obsession with death has up to this point shielded them from the terrifying reality that exists outside

13. *Jeux Interdits* (1952, René Clément), with Georges Poujoly and Brigitte Fossey. © 1952 Studiocanal Image.

172   Film and Community: Britain and France

their make-believe world. From the mutual security and warmth of Michel's friendship, Paulette suddenly finds herself alone and cries, 'Michel!' As her panic deepens, she is jolted into the present and screams, 'Maman!' and as she runs down the packed hall, the film ends. This negative representation of adults through children's eyes, in addition to the emphasis on the recent traumatic past, meant that while the film was critically acclaimed, it was not well received by the public.[147]

Finally, in what ways did films tackle the question of career women? Like their British counterparts, the number of women actually working in key positions in the film industry itself was small, and due to restrictions within it, notably its dominance by men, women directors like Jacqueline Audry and Andrée Feix tended to be given traditionally 'feminine' subjects.[148] Feix's first film was *Il Suffit d'une fois* (1946), which, in 'screwball comedy' mode, featured Edwige Feuillière as a talented sculptress who gives up her art for her lover. After her second film, however, *Le Capitaine Blomet* (1947), Feix went into editing.[149] Nicole Védrès earned praise for her documentaries *Paris 1900* (1948) – 'pure cinema,' enthused Andre Bazin[150] – and *La Vie commence demain* (1949), which featured an impressive array of cultural figures, including Le Corbusier, Sartre and Picasso. Agnès Varda wrote and directed *Le Pointe courte* in 1954, the story of a couple whose marriage is on the point of collapse and who find their differences resolved in the calm of a fishing village. Varda continued to make critically acclaimed shorts, and was much admired by François Truffaut, who described her film *Cléo de 5 à 7* (1962), about a woman wandering Paris while she awaits the result of a test for cancer, as 'poetic and intellectual'.[151] But women directors were rarely given the opportunity to create a consistent body of work like their male counterparts.

Unsurprisingly, films about career women were uncommon. Some films showed women forced to choose between love and work, a theme usually conveyed by means of a highly melodramatic narrative. In the British film *The Red Shoes* (1948, Michael Powell and Emeric Pressburger), ballerina Ludmilla Tcherina is compelled to leave the *corps* when she marries, which anticipates the tragic end of *prima ballerina* Vicky. In *Grand gala* (1952, François Campaux), Tcherina is again forced to make that choice, but as this time she is in the leading role, it is an anguished decision. In *La Maternelle* (1949, Henri Diamant-Berger), the *directrice* of a school for underprivileged children is so devoted to her work that she declines a marriage proposal from the man she loves. When he falls in love with another teacher, she realises too late that she has missed her chance. When in the last scene she murmurs, 'this school is my whole life,' she is clearly comforting herself.

Like the British production *White Corridors* (1951, Pat Jackson) Jean Grémillon's *L'Amour d'une femme* (1954), which he also wrote is about a doctor, unmarried and by implication childless. Grémillon was defined as one of the avant garde of French post-war cinema, a film-maker who had been France's 'principal social conscience'.[152] He had also made two films during the occupation in which the leading female character had a career: *Lumiére d'été* (1943), in which Madeleine Renaud runs a hotel, and *Le Ciel est à vous* (1944), discussed in chapter 2, where Renaud plays a *garagiste's* wife who becomes a record-breaking pilot. The link between *Le Ciel est à vous* and *L'Amour d'une femme* is the importance of career against home and family. Indeed, in the film's resumé, Grémillon wrote that 'women today ought to work'.[153] Though Marie (Micheline Presle) is in love with an Italian engineer, she prioritises her career as a doctor over marriage. She believes even more strongly than Sophie Dean that she can make a contribution to the world through her work. Grémillon was interested in the isolation felt by career women and the contradiction between the supposed 'emancipation' of professional women and men's inability to deal with the repercussions.[154] Unlike Neil, Sophie's fiancé who is completely supportive of her career, André demands that Marie leave her job so they can marry. Significantly, the film was never given a general distribution, which Burch and Sellier argue could be attributed to its documentary style and minimal dramatic narrative. However, as Laurent Marie notes, there were only a handful of unreservedly enthusiastic critics, and good reviews came from the left-wing press like *Les Femmes françaises*. Mainstream women's magazines, however were unconvinced by Marie's decision.[155] Considering the conspicuous lack of films about female careerists, and Grémillon's own curiosity about the rather complicated assumptions held about women and work, the latter response seems the most likely reason for its limited distribution.

This survey of a variety of films in the post-war years has intended to highlight the ways in which women's status in society was interpreted in film. Film-makers wanted to present a France which had acted nobly, but in the Resistance films that proliferated, women seemed to play only minor parts. Although Burch and Sellier's criticism of the few women in Resistance films is too extreme, apart from *La Bataille du rail*, contemporary films failed to acknowledge the crucial elements of support that women had been able to give from their private, domestic sphere. However, *Boule de suif* must not be underestimated. As the first film about the occupation, albeit in allegorical form, it is a stirring tribute to a woman who sacrifices herself for France, metaphorically represented by the passengers of the coach.

Boule de suif's status as a prostitute has been seen as conforming to stereotype, but, as in other post-war films, whores often signify assertiveness and independence, as in *Dédée D'Anvers*. In *Manèges*, the awful revenge Dora inflicts on her cuckolded husband is inextricably bound up with the intricacies of the strained relationships between men and women in the aftermath of the occupation. Happy marriages were shown under stress, young women were threats, infidelity was at best pointless, at worst devastating.

As the 1950s approached, female sexuality became less dangerous as films showed women's bodies idealised and feminised. Concern about familial stability and deprived children also waned as the genuinely troubled youngsters in *La Fille du diable, Une si Jolie petite plage* and *Jeux interdits* metamorphosed into Juliette in *Et Dieu créa la femme,* in which her sexual proclivities are attributed to her parentless state. The image of Bardot, pouting, nubile and sexually liberated, has tended unfairly to overshadow other themes in French cinema of the time, which was, after all, on the brink of the *nouvelle vague*. There were clearly some difficulties with female representation. Women had traditionally formed a significant proportion of the workforce, and a national survey in 1947 revealed that 84 per cent of people questioned felt that women should receive the same salary as men doing the same job.[156] However, there was still a reluctance to concede their capabilities as careerists, as demonstrated by the interesting case of *L'Amour d'une femme*. Grémillon is very much a lone voice in this respect, and the fate of his film seems to validate de Beauvoir's argument that 'today it is very difficult for women to accept at the same time their status as autonomous individuals and their womanly destiny,' adding that 'this is the source of the blundering and restlessness which sometimes cause them to be considered a "lost sex"'.[157] At this final juncture, women in post-war French film appear to represent that 'lost sex', the casualties of outdated laws, attitudes and assumptions which ensured that identifying their place within society was a task of great complexity, and one which, with a few exceptions, film-makers approached with trepidation.

8

Conclusion

The aim of this book has been to examine how film-makers interpreted community during the war, when it was used to encourage a sense of unity, and during its aftermath, when Britain and France were experiencing the repercussions of large-scale disruption. Films have a special intensity of meaning, and those which were made during this period are particularly revealing both in terms of the response they elicited from their audiences and in their reflections on the society which produced them. Furthermore, films naturally evoke the era in which they were made, regardless of their genre, and do not need to be either popular or artistic to warrant the attention of the historian. While the inclusion of a particular star in a feature film unquestionably attracted audiences, there are lesser-known British and French productions whose analysis was prevented here by lack of space, which would certainly help to extend our current understanding of culture, society and community during the 1940s and 1950s.

Community was a familiar image in Britain's wartime cinema culture, in its embrace of the populace, civilians and service personnel alike, and in its emphasis on 'pulling together'. An investigation of film of the post-war period, however, has enabled the identification of shifts in its interpretation. Although community was a device that was consciously and explicitly used by wartime film-makers to convey a sense of popular synthesis, its deeper significance only became clear in post-war film. While historians of French film have been concerned to identify the 'Vichy' dimension of films, it has been illuminating to move beyond the political stereotypes in order to explore film in terms of the kinds of images of community they were presenting. Analysis has established how film-makers were able to convey a strong sense of the divisions in society during the occupation, as well as a desire for national reunification. The post-war era liberated not only the population but also film-makers, who contributed to national regeneration and renewal by visualising a 'Resistance community'. However, the diversity of images of community evoked the complex repercussions of the occupation.

During the war and occupation, although their modes of operation were similar in the two countries, film-makers were subject to different agendas. British producers energetically engaged with the notion of projecting consensus, 'more than those of any other nation',[1] in films like *In Which We Serve* and *The Gentle Sex*. Conversely, the notion of projecting national solidarity in France seemed a questionable project. Film-makers were faced with the fact that, in being occupied, France had lost its identity, which created a 'schizophrenic mentality'.[2] However, film-makers in both the occupied and unoccupied zones were able to express and articulate 'France' in terms of a community. Unlike the harmonious groupings of British films, however, the impressions of community in *L'Assassin habite au 21*, *Le Ciel est à vous* and *Le Corbeau* were contradictory, ambiguous and positively dark. Some historians have stressed the evasive nature of the cinema of the occupation, yet even an allegorical film like *Les Visiteurs du soir* incorporated a sub-text exuding loyalty and hope within a narrative which focused on a community riven by cruelty and mistrust.

Rural and urban imagery were used to articulate particular visions of community. Although the promulgation of the rural myth was common to both countries, the countryside and its people were perceived very differently in the context of war and occupation. The main distinction was that British films like *A Canterbury Tale*, *Tawny Pipit*, *Millions Like Us* and *They Came to a City* showed the landscape as an evocative but ultimately symbolic space, and used it to instil patriotism and to enable the expression of ideas about the future. French films, however, prioritised and idealised *les paysans*. Whereas most historians have claimed that French rural films merely bowed to Vichy peasant politics, in *Jeannou*, *La Fille du puisatier*, *Monsieur de Lourdines* and *Goupi Mains Rouges* rural ideology operated in tandem with another separate discourse that connected rural and regional France to the capital and thus bestowed a semblance of 'unity' on a deeply fractured nation.

The representation of urban Britain and France centred almost entirely on their capital cities. Yet they were deeply contrasting images consonant with the fact that London was the proud heart of the nation while Paris was occupied. London was delineated in terms of small identifiable communities, like those in *The Bells Go Down* and *Waterloo Road*, films whose 'realism' delighted the critics. Whereas Britain's capital was recognisable, contemporary Paris was largely invisible. The deserted boulevards where the cyclists ride in *Falbalas* were a very rare glimpse indeed of occupied Paris. Whereas British historical films which were based in London referred to a glorious past, as in *Young Mr Pitt*, French costume dramas which centred on the country's capital city tended to be evasive. Yet *Les Enfants du paradis* firmly reasserted the status of Paris in ostentatious and voluptuous style. Above all, it rejected the countryside appropriated by Vichy in favour of the faults and flaws, the low life and the *grandeur* of Paris. By celebrating Paris, France appeared to be restored.

There was a considerable difference between the depiction of rural and urban in the wartime period and that projected after the war. In contrast to the largely symbolic function of British wartime cinema, post-war films focused strongly on communities and contemporary rural politics. Films explored the neglected Celtic fringes and their traditional communities, echoing the contemporary interest in regionalism. More importantly, historical films like *Captain Boycott, Jassy* and *Blanche Fury* examined the antagonistic relationship between the autocratic owner and the democratic community. Landowners were portrayed as brutish and irresponsible, while their tenants, by implication, were the natural beneficiaries of the surrounding landscapes. In France, where the rural population outweighed the urban, the increase in films about regional and rural communities indicated a desire to reconstruct regional and national identities that had been ruptured by the occupation. Yet the rural world was changing. In the post-war 'cinéma du paysan', *Farrebique* was key in its juxtaposition of continuity with the need for modernisation. *Le Café du cadran* and *Faits divers à Paris* made such sharp cultural distinctions between rural and urban that they suggested an attempt to realign a population dispersed by the war. Films presented city and countryside as indelibly linked, but also as culturally separate spheres.

The urban imagery of British post-war film continued to focus on the communities and neighbourhoods of London, despite bombing on a nationwide scale. Films used London's bomb-sites and landmarks, its working-class neighbourhoods, its underworld and its chic West End. Ealing continued its wartime ethos of earthy realism in *It Always Rains on Sunday,* and also conveyed whimsical images of London's communities in *Hue and Cry, Passport to Pimlico* and *The Lavender Hill Mob*. The film noir emerged as a powerful new genre in which the city was pre-eminent, from *They Made Me A Fugitive* to *Night and the City* (1950, Jules Dassin), whose

American style, it was said, had created a 'never-never city' which was decidedly not London.[3] Yet these depictions of 'urban sleaze' were tempered by the very popular 'Mayfair Cycle', films which treated war-weary audiences to the sheer escapism of an elite corner of the city.

Urban France had suffered much destruction, and a significant percentage of the population had been rendered homeless as a result. Yet unmarked Paris provided rich material. Marcel Carné's *Les Portes de la nuit* was unusual in its revelations of collaboration and betrayal. The French critical reaction was largely hostile, as the film exuded a mood of fatalism and pessimism that they believed to be inappropriate. Contemporary Paris was more happily evoked by Jacques Becker in *Antoine et Antoinette*, which provided a great contrast to the evasive urban imagery of occupation cinema. It also echoed British wartime films in its focus on a co-operative, mutually interdependent community. As C.A. Lejeune wrote, it was 'one of those films that are so true in their evocation of a neighbourhood one can almost feel the moving sun warming the pavestones and smell coffee and bicycle tyres and the steam of ironing in the air'.[4] The film noirs that appeared from 1947 related to darker aspects of the community. In *Quai des Orfèvres* and others like *Copie Conforme* and *Entre onze heures et minuit*, detectives and victims alike are solitary figures in city locales. The fondly remembered *Impasse des deux anges* hides a 'no-man's land' and is juxtaposed with a *bourgeois faubourg* to emphasise its derelict status within the city's topography. These and other films tacitly confronted the recent past by suggesting the dispersal and dislocation caused by the occupation.

The key event of 1945 was the return of millions of people to their countries and communities. In Britain, the rehabilitation of those who had served in the army, navy and airforce was anticipated as a difficult re-adjustment only by enlightened members of the medical profession and veterans associations. Film-makers, however, were unhesitant about positing the ex-serviceman as disillusioned at best and dangerous at worst. The damaged heroes of *Great Day*, *They Made Me A Fugitive*, *Cage of Gold* and *The League of Gentlemen* all longed for a sense of purpose. They missed the camaraderie of service life and sought compensation by entering into the criminal fraternity, for which they were marginalised by mainstream society. The notion of social exclusion also applied to civilians in films exploring the wartime ideal of the benevolent community. *Frieda* tested not only Denfield's altruism, but the tolerance levels of British audiences towards Germans, whilst *The Franchise Affair* depicted a small community which ostracised with alacrity two blameless female outsiders. As the decade progressed, there appeared a nostalgia for wartime communality. Indeed, Thorold Dickinson remarked in 1950 that British cinema only began to hold its own 'when we were having great emotional stress'.[5] It is surely no coincidence that the director of *Passport to Pimlico*, the most memorable evocation of wartime solidarity, spoke of the lack of 'purposeful emotion' in contemporary life shortly after the film's release. The resistance in *The Happy Family* to the Festival of Britain, the last great demonstration of Attlee's Britain, appeared to yearn for Churchill. The presence on the Festival's Film Panel of Ealing's Michael Balcon indicated that the community ethos was still thought to be desirable. As the organisers announced, '1951 should mark a revival in the spirit of the individual and collective enterprise'.[6] For film-makers like Balcon, it had never died.

Le retour was considered to be crucial to the reconstruction of France. Whereas there was little doubt about the role of British servicemen to the prosecution of the war, French soldiers had been quickly defeated and captured in 1940. *Les prisonniers* symbolised an unhappy period in the country's recent history, and as they returned their presence undermined the simplistic notion of a national community which was being promoted by the liberation government. French film-makers were reticent on the subject of *le retour*, preferring either to provide distractions or images of resistance. The underlying tensions with regard to the French military were nevertheless evident in *Le Diable au corps*, whose narrative of betrayal and guilt suggested remorse at the blame being placed on the army for the occupation. It was almost five years before the appearance of *Retour à la vie*, which dealt directly with the return of *prisonniers* and *déportés*, a film condemned by critics and censors as too pessimistic. Civilian readjustment was embraced in themes about guilt, betrayal and revenge. Unwelcome outsiders became familiar figures in *La Fille du diable* and *Nuit sans fin*, which reiterated the complex relationship between city and countryside as incompatible but linked. These films presented a disturbing picture of French society, its communities divided by suspicion, fear and doubt. Yet like rural films of this period, they suggested that to dispel such anxieties and reunite the nation, the population must remain in their proper cultural spheres.

The representation of women in the post-war era demonstrates a time of enormous shifts and changes. Women in British wartime films had functioned not merely as sacrificial lambs, suffering from loving, losing and grieving in *Millions Like Us*, *The Gentle Sex* and *The Way To The Stars*. Indeed, just as many men made sacrifices, as shown in *In Which We Serve*, *The Bells Go Down* and *The Way Ahead*. While there has been much debate about the extent to which films avoided articulating the 'liberating' effects of war in favour of a 'domesticising' agenda, what most writers do agree on is that those made during the immediate post-war period are informed by the rather uncertain atmosphere in which they appeared. Post-war women thus emerged on screen in a diversity of roles which speak for themselves: not only the careerists – the sheep farmer, the doctor, the probation officer, the policewoman, the politician – but also the 'domestics' – the restless wives, the loyal wives, the good mothers, the bad mothers, the corrupt 'surrogate' mothers, not to mention the array of heroines in films made in the 1950s. In every case, without exception, the woman's role with the community, with society, was brought under scrutiny.

Cinema of the liberation was suffused with a network of cultural and ideological complexities. Liberation meant not only deliverance, but also confrontation with an unpleasant recent past which meant a frenetic search for scapegoats at liberation. Sexual collusion by women was seen not only as a blatant betrayal of absent men but more shamefully of the country as a whole. Women's enfranchisement served to increase the sense of inadequacy and failure felt by men on their return to France. Though the more enlightened film-makers strove to include them in the *résistant* community and to acknowledge their newly acquired independence, even women who were portrayed as deceitful, vengeful and duplicitous were assertive and self-assured. By the mid-1950s, women appeared to be restored to the screen as innocuous objects of desire, alluring and unthreatening, yet somehow still indefinable. Jacques Doniol-Valcroze's study of women and film on the cusp of that era,[7] prompted by his inability to find the true cinematic Frenchwoman, seems therefore highly suggestive of de Beauvoir's enigmatic 'lost sex'.[8]

In summary, then, community has provided an excellent way to explore the ways in which film captured two societies undergoing searing and contrasting experiences. While community was a ubiquitous and highly successful conduit for the transmission of ideas about harmony and consensus in wartime Britain, it was a deeply problematic notion in a France which was enduring the bitter consequences of enemy occupation: conflict, division and rupture. British films made after the war demonstrate that community was an awkward concept to translate into the post-war years, yet its attraction for film-makers lay in its rich ambiguity. Film-makers used it to confront issues which were germane to British post-war rural politics, to depict the ex-serviceman's alienation as due to the deprivation of a communal lifestyle, to point out that communities were both intolerant and insular, and to exhibit intense nostalgia for the wartime community spirit. In France, community was expressed less explicitly but no less boldly. Contrary to the perception of Vichy cinema as evasive and detached, films suggested the need for a sense of community in their delineation of rural and urban, whilst also being unafraid to confront the divisiveness, suspicion and hatred rife in contemporary society. The realignment of a physically and psychologically dislocated population is most evident in post-war films, where rural and urban are replaced in their proper environments. The return of *prisonniers* and *déportés* was more painful, and was an issue which encapsulated, possibly more than any other, the underlying trauma of the occupation and the long, difficult years which followed. In Britain, community had been evoked and celebrated for six years, and film-makers were now free to examine it more closely. French film-makers, on the other hand, were only just embarking on the difficult task of rediscovering and reasserting their national community on screen.

Notes on the Text

Chapter 1

1   Neil Rattigan, *This is England: British Film and the People's War, 1939–1945* (Associated University Presses/Farleigh Dickinson, 2001); Robert Murphy, *British Cinema and the Second World War* (Continuum, 2000); Christine Geraghty, *British Cinema in the Fifties: Gender, Genre and the 'New Look'* (Routledge, 2000); James Chapman, *The British at War: Cinema, State and Propaganda* (I. B. Tauris, 1998).

2   Ulrike Sieglohr (ed.), *Heroines without Heroes: Reconstructing Female and National Identities in European Cinema, 1945–51* (Cassell, 2000).

3   Two exceptions are: Tim Bergfelder, 'The Production Designer and the Gesamtkuntswerk: German Film Technicians in the British Film Industry of the 1930s', in Andrew Higson (ed.), *Dissolving Views: Key Articles on British Cinema* (Cassell, 1996); Kevin Gough-Yates, 'Exiles and British Cinema', in Robert Murphy (ed.), *The British Cinema Book* (British Film Institute Publishing [hereafter BFI], 1997).

4   Gough-Yates, ibid., p.104.

5   Richard Cobb, *French and Germans, Germans and French: A Personal Interpretation of France under Two Occupations, 1914–1918 and 1940–1944* (University Press of New England, 1983).

6   Philippe Burrin, *La France à l'heure allemande 1940–1944* (Éditions du Seuil, 1995).

7   Ian Ousby, *Occupation: The Ordeal of France 1940–1944* (John Murray, 1997); Julian Jackson, *France: The Dark Years: 1940–1944* (Oxford University Press, 2001).

8   P.M.H. Bell, *France and Britain, 1940–1944: The Long Separation* (Longman, 1997), p.3.

9   *Picture Post*, 21 October 1944.

10 *Kinematograph Weekly*, [hereafter *KW*] 11 January 1945.

11   *Film français*, 15 December 1944.
12   *Film français*, 26 January 1945.
13   *Cinémonde*, 17 December 1946.
14   Quoted in John W. Young, 'Henry V, the Quai d'Orsay and the Well-Being of the Franco–British Alliance, 1947', *Historical Journal of Film, Radio and Television*, vol. 7, no 3, 1987, p.320.
15   *L'Écran français*, 8 July 1945.
16   *Cinémonde*, 30 September 1947.
17   *Sequence*, December 1946.
18   *Observer*, 4 June 1995.
19   Arthur Marwick, *Class, Image and Reality in Britain, France and the USA since 1930* (Collins, 1980), Chapter 11.
20   Rattigan, *This is England*.
21   Ibid., pp.83–84.
22   Jeffrey Richards, 'In Which We Serve', in Anthony Aldgate and Jeffrey Richards, *Britain Can Take It: British Cinema in the Second World War* (Edinburgh University Press, 1994), p.203.
23   Rattigan, op. cit., p.316.
24   Jeffrey Richards, *Films and British National Identity; From Dickens to Dad's Army* (Manchester University Press, 1997), p.192.
25   Joanna Bourke, *Working-Class Cultures in Britain, 1890–1960* (Routledge, 1994), p.137.
26   Quoted in Dennis E. Poplin, *Communities: A Survey of Theories and Methods of Research* (Macmillan, 1972), p.9.
27   David W. Minar and Scott Greer, *The Concept of Community: Readings with Interpretations* (Aldine Publishing Co., 1969), p.140.
28   Raymond Williams, *Keywords: A Vocabulary of Culture and Society* (Croom Helm, 1976), p.66.
29   Andrew Higson, *Waving the Flag: Constructing a National Cinema in Britain* (Clarendon Press, 1997), p.243.
30   Benedict Anderson, *Imagined Communities: Reflections on the Origin and Spread of Nationalism* (Verso, 1983).
31   Ibid., p.16.
32   Ibid., p.131.
33   Raymond Williams, *The Country and the City* (Chatto and Windus, 1972), p.165.
34   James Hanley, *No Directions* (Faber & Faber, 1943); Robert Greenwood, *The Squad Goes Out* (J.M. Dent and Sons, 1943).
35   Adrian Alington, *These Our Strangers* (Chatto and Windus, 1940); Susan Ertz, *Anger in the Sky* (Hodder and Stoughton, 1943).
36   Evelyn Waugh, *Put Out More Flags* (Chapman and Hall, 1942).
37   J.B. Priestley, *All England Listened* (Chilmark Press, 1967), p.55.
38   'Do Listeners like Priestley?', *Picture Post*, 22 March 1941.
39   *Daily Mail*, 2 July 1940.

40   J.B. Priestley, 'Britain's Silent Revolution', *Picture Post*, 27 June 1942 (emphasis in the original).

41   Kingsley Martin, 'Reflections on Air Raids', *Political Quarterly*, 12, 1941, pp.66–80.

42   Angus Calder and Dorothy Sheridan (eds), *Speak for Yourself: A Mass Observation Anthology* (Jonathan Cape, 1984), p.120.

43   Kenneth Clark, *Henry Moore Drawings* (Thames & Hudson, 1974), p.149.

44   'The Home Front', episode 6 of 'The World At War', Thames Television, 1974, produced by Jeremy Isaacs.

45   Quoted in Stephen Brooke, *Reform and Reconstruction: Britain after the War 1945–1951* (Manchester University Press, 1995), p.36.

46   See Philippe Pétain, *La France Nouvelle: Principes de la Communauté* (Fasquelle Éditeurs, 1941).

47   Quoted in Philippe Burrin, 'Vichy', in Pierre Nora (ed.), *The Realms of Memory: Rethinking the French Past*, vol. 1: *Conflicts and Divisions* (Columbia University Press, 1992), p.194.

48   Georges Duby, *Histoire de la France rurale*, vol. 3: *De 1914 à nos jours* (Seuil, 1976), pp.440–42.

49   Maurice Larkin, *France Since the Popular Front: Government and People 1936–1986*, (Oxford University Press, 1988), p.46.

50   Paul Simon, *One Enemy Only – the Invader* (Hodder & Stoughton, 1942). Simon wrote his account from exile in London during 1941–42.

51   Evelyn Ehrlich, *Cinema of Paradox: French Filmmaking under the German Occupation* (Columbia University Press, 1985), p.11.

52   Quoted in Charles Rearick, *The French in Love and War: Popular Culture in France 1914–1945* (Yale University Press, 1997), p.252.

53   Burrin (1996) op. cit., p.196.

54   Amitai Etzioni, *The Spirit of Community: Rights, Responsibilities and the Communitarian Agenda* (Fontana Press, 1995), p.ix.

55   Ibid.

56   Angus Calder, *The Myth of the Blitz* (Pimlico, 1992), p.xiv.

57   See Henry Rousso, *The Vichy Syndrome: History and Memory in France Since 1944,* translated by Arthur Goldhammer (Harvard University Press, 1994).

58   Eric Williams, *The Wooden Horse* (Collins, 1949); P.R. Reid, *The Colditz Story* (Hodder and Stoughton, 1952).

59   Ken Worpole, *Dockers and Detectives: Popular Reading: Popular Writing* (Verso, 1983), p.54.

60   Neil Rattigan, 'The Last Gasp of the Middle Classes: British War Films of the 1950s', in Andrew Higson (ed.), *Dissolving Views: Key Articles on British Cinema* (Cassell, 1996); John Ramsden, 'Refocusing "The People's War": British War Films of the 1950s', *Journal of Contemporary History*, vol. 33, no 1, 1998; Geraghty, *British Cinema in the Fifties*, chapter 10.

61   Stanley Hoffman (ed.), *In Search of France* (Harvard University Press, 1963), p.36.

62   Ibid., p.37.

63   Jean-Pierre Rioux, *The Fourth Republic*, translated by Geoffrey Rogers (Cambridge University Press, 1987), p.41.

64   J.M. Guillon and P. Laborie (eds), *Mémoire et Histoire: La Résistance* (Éditions Privat, 1995), p.43.

65   Claude Morgan, 'Le Démocratie et ceux qui en parlent', *Les Lettres françaises*, 16 December 1944.

66   Quoted in Tony Judt, *Past Imperfect: French Intellectuals 1944–1956*, (University of California Press, 1992), p.35.

67   Laurence Wylie, *A Village in the Vaucluse* (Harvard University Press, 1957), p.30.

68   Gavin Lambert, 'French Cinema: The New Pessimism', *Sequence*, Summer 1948, pp. 8–12.

69   Rousso, *The Vichy Syndrome*, p.4.

70   Andrew Clay, 'Men, Women and Money: Masculinity in Crisis in the British Professional Crime Film 1946–1965', in Steve Chibnall and Robert Murphy (eds), *British Crime Cinema* (Routledge, 1999).

71   Megan Koreman, 'A Hero's Homecoming: The Return of the Deportees to France, 1945', *Journal of Contemporary History*, vol. 32, no 1, January 1997, p.51.

72   Esther Delisle, book review of Michael Kelly, *The Reconstruction of Masculinity at Liberation*, in H.R. Kedward and Nancy Wood (eds), *The Liberation of France: Image and Event* (Berg, 1995), H-Net French History Discussion Group, December 1998.

73   The subject was not addressed again fully until Alain Resnais's film *Nuit et brouillard* (1956).

Chapter 2

1   Coined by Tom Wintringham, the founder of the Local Defence Volunteers, which became The Home Guard, in *Picture Post*, 15 June 1940.

2   Milton Dank, *The French Against the French: Collaboration and Resistance* (Cassell, 1978).

3   Robert Murphy, *Realism and Tinsel: Cinema and Society 1939–49* (Routledge, 1989), p.4.

4   Evelyn Ehrlich, *Cinema of Paradox: French Filmmaking under the German Occupation* (Columbia University Press, 1985), p.1.

5   Jill Forbes, *Les Enfants du paradis* (BFI, 1997), p.15.

6   *KW*, 7 September 1939.

7   The 1938 Act established a quota of 15 per cent for distributors (renters) and 12.5 per cent for exhibitors, Julian Petley, 'Cinema and State', in Charles Barr (ed.), *All Our Yesterdays: 90 Years of British Cinema* (BFI, 1986), pp.33–34.

8   Margaret Dickinson and Sarah Street, *Cinema and State: The Film Industry and the Government 1927–84* (BFI, 1985), pp.103–9.

9   Mass Observation, Topic Collections, Box 4, File A, 'Interviews': Interview with Mr Sydney [Sidney] Cole, Assistant Editor of *Cine Technician*, by Len England, 22 November 1939.

10   Memorandum dated 4 June 1940, quoted in Ian McLaine, *Ministry of Morale: Home Front Morale and the MOI in World War II* (Allen and Unwin, 1979), p.63.

11   James Chapman, *The British at War: Cinema, State and Propaganda* (I.B.Tauris, 1998), p.250.

12   Anthony Aldgate and Jeffrey Richards, *Britain Can Take It: The British Cinema in the Second World War* (Edinburgh University Press, 1994), p.3.

13   Mass Observation File Report, Box 5 File A, letter (undated).

14   Mass Observation File Report, Box 5 File A, letter dated 8 November 1940.

15   Kathleen Box and Louis Moss, *Wartime Social Survey: The Cinema Audience* (MOI, 1943).

16   PRO, INF 1/178: Memorandum, 'Security Censorship of Films', 6 September 1939.

17   *KW*, 11 January 1940.

18   PRO, INF 1/867: Co-ordinating Committee Paper no 1, 'Programme for Film Propaganda' (undated).

19   Chapman, op. cit., p.62.

20   Mass Observation, File Report 394, 'Mass Observation Film Work', 10 September 1940.

21   Charles Barr, Ealing Studios (Studio Vista, 1993), p.13.

22   *L'Écran français*, 14 November 1945.

23   T.E.B. Clarke, *This is Where I Came In* (Michael Joseph, 1974), p.149.

24   Michael Balcon, *Michael Balcon Presents…A Lifetime in Film* (Hutchinson, 1969), p.150.

25   Ibid.

26   *L'Écran français*, 14 November 1945.

27   *Johnny Frenchman* press book, BFI.

28   Roger Manvell, 'The British War Film', in Michael Balcon, Ernest Lindgren, Forsyth Hardy and Roger Manvell, *Twenty Years of British Film 1925–1945* (Falcon Press, 1947), p.85.

29   Andrew Higson, '"Britain's Outstanding Contribution to the Film": The Documentary-Realist Tradition', in Barr (ed.), *All Our Yesterdays*, p.84.

30   Geoffrey McNab, *J. Arthur Rank and the British Film Industry* (Routledge, 1993), p.93.

31   Geoffrey McNab, 'Looking for Lustre: Stars at Gainsborough', in Pam Cook (ed.), *Gainsborough Pictures* (Cassell, 1997), p.111.

32   Michael Sadleir, *Fanny By Gaslight* (Constable and Co., 1940).

33   Geoff Brown, 'Paradise Lost and Found: The Course of British Realism', in Robert Murphy (ed.), *The British Cinema Book* (BFI, 1997), p.192.

34   Arthur Marwick, *Class, Image and Reality in Britain, France and the USA since 1930* (Collins, 1980), chapter 11.

35   Jeffrey Richards, 'In Which We Serve', in Aldgate and Richards, *Britain Can Take It*, p.202.

36   Sheridan Morley, *A Talent to Amuse: A Biography of Noel Coward* (Penguin edition, 1974), p.272.

37   John Ellis, 'The Quality Film Adventure', in Andrew Higson (ed.), *Dissolving Views: Key Articles on British Cinema* (Cassell, 1996).

38   Dilys Powell, *Films Since 1939* (Longmans–British Council, 1947), p.26.

39   Quoted in Dorothy Sheridan and Jeffrey Richards, *Mass Observation at the Movies* (Routledge & Kegan Paul, 1987), pp.276, 280.

40   1944, written by Noel Coward, directed by David Lean, a family saga covering 1918–39.

41   Quoted in J.P. Mayer, *British Cinemas and their Audiences* (Dennis Dobson, 1948), p.211.

42   *Documentary News Letter*, no 5, January–February 1944, p.2.

43   Quoted in Morley, op. cit., p.279.

44   Christine Gledhill and Gillian Swanson, 'Gender and Sexuality in Second World War Films – A Feminist Approach', in Geoff Hurd (ed.), *National Fictions: World War Two in British Films and Television* (BFI, 1984); Janet Thumim, 'The Female Audience: Mobile Women and Married Ladies', in Christine Gledhill and Gillian Swanson (eds), *Nationalising Femininity: Culture, Sexuality and British Cinema in the Second World War* (Manchester University Press, 1996); Andrew Higson, *Waving the Flag: Constructing a National Cinema in Britain* (Clarendon Press, 1997).

45   Angus Calder, *The People's War: Britain 1939–45* (Panther Books Ltd, 1971), p.62.

46   *The Gentle Sex* press book, BFI.

47   PRO, INF 1/867, Memorandum: Co-ordinating Committee Paper no 1, 'Programme for Film Propaganda', 29 January 1940.

48   Quoted in David Matless, 'Taking Pleasure in England: Landscape and Citizenship in the 1940s', in Richard Weight and Abigail Beach (eds), *The Right to Belong: Citizenship and National Identity in Britain, 1930–1960* (I. B. Tauris, 1998), p.199.

49   PRO, INF 1/224, Letter from Noel Coward to Brendan Bracken, 12 October 1942.

50   Eric Ambler, *Here Lies Eric Ambler* (Weidenfeld & Nicolson, 1988), p.184.

51   PRO, INF 1/224, Letter from David Niven to Brigadier E. O'Donnell, Office of the Adjutant General, War Office, 27 November 1942.

52   PRO INF 1/224, Niven to O'Donnell.

53   John Ellis, *The Sharp End: The Fighting Man in World War Two* (Pimlico, 1993), p.340.

54   C.A. Lejeune, *Chestnuts in her Lap, 1936–1946* (Phoenix House, 1947), p.124.

55   Henry Rousso, *The Vichy Syndrome: History and Memory in France Since 1944*, translated by Arthur Goldhammer (Harvard University Press, 1994), p.4.

56   *Cinématographie française*, 2 September 1939.

57   Roy Armes, *French Cinema* (Secker & Warburg, 1985), p.129.

58   *Cinématographie française*, double issue, 14–21 October 1939.

59   Paul Leglise, *Histoire de la politique du cinéma français*, tome II: *Le Cinéma entre deux républiques 1940–1946* (L'Herminier, 1969), p.41.

60   In 1936, American films totalled 231 out of a total of 448 shown. See Ginette Vincendeau and Keith Reader (eds), *La Vie est à nous: French Cinema of the Popular Front 1935–1938* (BFI, 1986), p.79.

61   Jean-Pierre Jeancolas, *15 ans d'années trente* (Stock, 1983), pp.308–9.

62   Diary entry for 15 May 1942, Lochner, Louis (ed.), *The Goebbels Diaries (1942–1943)*, translated by Louis Lochner (Doubleday & Co., 1948), p.215.

63   Quoted in Jeancolas, op. cit., p.309.

64   Ehrlich, *Cinema of Paradox,* op. cit., p.xiii.

65   Colin Crisp, *The Classic French Cinema 1930–1960* (Indiana University Press, 1997), p.44.

66   Charles Ford, *Pierre Fresnay: gentilhomme de l'écran* (Paris, Éditions France-Empire, 1981), p.76.

67   Representing 14 per cent of the total made during 1940–44, and comprising: thrillers, 10; comedies, 7; dramas, 6; musicals, 2; historical drama, 5.

68   Crisp, op. cit., p.49.

69   Quoted in Ehrlich, op. cit., p.107.

70   J.H. Weiss, 'An Innocent Eye? The Career and Documentary Vision of Georges Rouquier', *Cinema Journal*, Spring 1981, p.48.

71   Ibid., p.50.

72   Jeancolas, op. cit., p.319.

73   Jacques Siclier, *La France de Pétain et son cinéma* (Henri Veyrier, 1981), p.21.

74   André Bazin, *French Cinema of the Occupation and Resistance*, translated by Stanley Hochman, (Frederick Ungar, 1981), pp.95–96.

75   Miranda Pollard, 'Femme, Famille, France: Vichy and the Politics of Gender', PhD thesis, University of Dublin, 1989.

76   Lindsay Anderson, 'Some French Films – and a Forecast', *Sequence*, December 1946.

77   Ibid.

78   François Guérif, *Le Cinéma Policier Français* (Veyrier, 1981), p.19.

79   Ibid., p.79.

80   *L'Écran français*, 10 March 1944, quoted in Olivier Barrot, *L'Écran français 1943–1953: histoire d'un journal et d'une époque* (Les Éditeurs Français Réunis, 1979), p.14.

81   Action Catholique française: Centrale Catholique du Cinéma et radio (CCR), *Films français parus pendant l'occupation avec leur analyse morale* (CCR, 1945), p.25.

82   Louis Daquin interviewed by Evelyn Ehrlich in Ehrlich, *Cinema of Paradox*, op. cit., p.177.

83   Letter from Lt Colin-Reval of DGSS Sécurité Militaire to M. le Président de la Commission d'Épuration du Cinéma, 10 October 1944, Archives Scénaristiques, Le Corbeau, Chavance 03 II, BIFI.

84   As noted by *Film français*, 19 September 1947, when it was finally re-released.

85   Ian Ousby, *Occupation: The Ordeal of France 1940–1944* (John Murray, 1997), p.146.

86   J.F. McMillan, *Dreyfus to De Gaulle: Politics and Society in France, 1889–1969* (Edward Arnold, 1985), p.133.

87   Jean Dutourd, *Au Bon Beurre* (Gallimard, 1952), p.32.

88   Ibid., p.33.

89   'Affaire de Tulle: un cas typique d'anonymographie', *L'Avenir Medical*, July/August 1923, (sent by Edmond Locard to Chavance), Archives scenaristiques, *Le Corbeau*, Chavance 03 I (B1), BIFI.

90   'Archives scénaristiques: documentation pour le scénario', *Le Corbeau*, Chavance 03 I (B1), BIFI.

91   *L'Illustration*, 1 November 1943.

92   Note on the script, 'Archives scénaristiques: continuité dialogue', Chavance 03 I (B1), BIFI.

93   Pollard, 'Femme, Famille, France', pp.278–302; Cheryl A. Koos, '"On les aura!": the gendered politics of abortion and the Alliance nationale contre la depopulation, 1938–1944', *Modern and Contemporary France*, 7 (1) (1999), pp.21–22.

94   See p.8.

95   See Alain Brossat, 'Images des femmes tondues', *L'Histoire*, no 179, July–August 1994; Corran Laurens, '"La Femme au Turban": les Femmes tondues', in H.R. Kedward and Nancy Wood (eds), *The Liberation of France: Image and Event* (Berg, 1995), pp.155–79.

96   *L'Écran français*, 10 March 1944, quoted in Barrot, *L'Écran français 1943–1953*, p.15.

97   Ibid.

98   Jeanie Semple, 'Ambiguities in the film *Le Ciel est à vous*', in H.R. Kedward (ed.), *Vichy France and the Resistance: Culture and Ideology* (Croom Helm, 1985); Margaret Atak, 'Le Corbeau and Le Ciel est à vous: Entre le spectacle esthétique et la connaissance'. *Contemporary French Civilisation* 23 (1999): 337–54.

99   Quoted in Barrot, *L'Écran français*, op. cit., p.15.

100   *Les Nouveaux Temps*, 5 February 1944.

101   Archives scénaristiques: *Le Ciel est à vous*, CJ 0304 B237, BIFI, p.1.

102   Archives scénaristiques, scénario: *Le Ciel est à vous*, 0587 B171, BIFI, p.132, states that the song is the last verse of 'Pont de Nantes'.

103   Cited in Semple, op. cit., p.125.

104   Jeancolas, *15 ans d'années trente*, p.321.

105   Alan Williams, *Republic of Images: A History of French Film* (Massachusetts: Harvard University Press, 1992), p.259.

106   Bazin, Poésie, in *French Cinema of the Occupation and Resistance*, p.95.

Chapter 3

1   Nicola Lambourne, *War Damage in Western Europe: The Destruction of Historical Monuments During the Second World War* (Edinburgh University Press, 2001), pp.44–46.

2   Sheila Ferguson and Hilde Fitzgerald, *The History of the Second World War: Studies in the Social Services: United Kingdom Civil Series* (HMSO, 1955), p.4.

3   Quoted in Georges Duby, *Histoire de la France rurale*, tome 4: *De 1914 à nos jours* (Paris: Seuil, 1976), p.101.

4   Henry C. Warren, *England is a Village* (London: Eyre & Spottiswoode, 1940), p.5, "England's might is still as her fields and villages, and though the whole weight of her mechanised armies rolls over them to crush them in the end they will triumph".

5   Robert Colls and Philip Dodd (eds), *Englishness: Politics and Culture, 1880–1920* (Croom Helm, 1986).

6   Rachel Knappet, *Pullet on the Midden* (Chivers, 1946), p.9.

7   Annie Moulin, *Peasantry and Society in France since 1789* (Cambridge University Press, 1991), p.151.

8   Jean-Pierre Azéma, *From Munich to the Liberation, 1938–1944* (Cambridge University Press, 1984), p.38.

9   Nicole Ollier, *L'Exode sur les routes de l'an 40* (R. Laffont, 1970), p.162.

10   H.R. Kedward, *In Search of the Maquis* (Oxford University Press, 1993), p.25.

11   Gordon Wright, *Rural Revolution in France: The Peasantry in the Twentieth Century* (Stanford University Press, 1964), p.93.

12   *Daily Mail*, 2 September 1939.

13   Richard Titmuss, *The History of the Second World War: Problems of Social Policy: United Kingdom Civil Series* (HMSO, 1950), p.102.

14   Raymond Williams, *The Country and the City* (Chatto & Windus, 1972), 1990 edition, p.1.

15   James Lehning, *Peasant and French: Cultural Contact in Rural France During the Nineteenth Century* (Cambridge University Press, 1995), p.3.

16   Today, Parisians are observed referring to *La France profonde* with a mixture of 'mockery, embarrassment and longing': Richard Bernstein, *Fragile Glory: A Portrait of France and the French* (Bodley Head, 1991), p.23.

17   Sadie Ward, *War in the Countryside* (Cameron Books, 1988), p.8.

18   Moulin, *Peasantry and Society*, chapter 4.

19   Ward, op. cit., p.154.

20   Keith A.H. Murray, *History of the Second World War: Agriculture: United Kingdom Civil Series* (HMSO, 1955) pp.235–36.

21   Alison Woodeson, '"Going Back to the Land": Rhetoric and Reality in Women's Land Army Memories', *Oral History,* vol. 21, no 2, Autumn 1993, p.54.

22   Angus Calder, *The People's War: Britain 1939–1945* (Panther, 1971), p.496.

23   Arthur Marwick, *The Home Front* (Thames and Hudson, 1976); John Macnicol, 'The Evacuation of Schoolchildren', in Harold L Smith (ed.), *British Society in the Second World War* (Manchester University Press, 1986).

24   'Evacuation: The True Story', BBC Radio 4 1999, produced by David Prest.

25   See B.S. Johnson, *The Evacuees* (Gollancz, 1968).

26   Macnicol, op. cit.; *Daily Mirror,* 16 September 1940.

27   *News Chronicle,* 20 October 1939.

28   Titmuss, *The History of the Second World War,* op. cit., pp.506–8.

29   Travis L. Crosby, *The Impact of Civilian Evacuation in the Second World War* (Croom Helm, 1986).

30   *Picture Post,* 30 November 1940: 'Is this just? What evacuation often means: Two families crowd a cottage, while big country houses stand empty'.

31   See Chapter 6.

32   Alun Howkins, 'The Discovery of Rural England', in Colls and Dodd, *Englishness,* p.81.

33   Robert Hewison, *Under Siege: Literary Life in London 1939–1945* (Weidenfeld & Nicolson, 1977), pp.124–25.

34   For example, James Agate, *Speak for England: An Anthology of Prose and Poetry for the Forces* (Hutchinson, 1939).

35   J.B. Priestley, broadcast, 9 June 1940, in *Postcripts* (Wm Heinemann Ltd, 1940), pp.6–7.

36   *Daily Mirror,* 12 September 1940.

37   Mass Observation Report 13 January 1941, File A, Box 5.

38   *Picturegoer,* 18 January 1941.

39   PRO INF 1/867, Co-ordinating Committee Paper, 'Programme for Film Propaganda', 29 January 1940.

40   *New Statesman,* 4 November 1939.

41   Ibid.

42   *Spectator,* 3 November 1939.

43   Ian McLaine, *Ministry of Morale: Home Front Morale and the MOI in World War II* (Allen and Unwin, 1979), p.5.

44   Williams, *The Country and the City,* p.120.

45   Interestingly, this scene was re-enacted by Crawford and Portman in March 1946 at the first National Film Awards, as one of the 'outstanding British films' of the war; Peter Noble (ed.), *The British Film Yearbook 1947–1948* (Skelton Robinson, n.d.), p.132.

46   Andrew Higson, *Waving the Flag: Constructing a National Cinema in Britain* (Clarendon Press, 1997), p.239.

47   In August 1946, Eric Portman told *Picturegoer* that his ideal film would be 'a picture that dealt seriously with … showing how social conditions have changed and demonstrating how all classes are now merging would provide

not only excellent entertainment...but also...a valuable record of contemporary life in Britain'.

48   In 1944, there were 376 American films compared to 62 British. *KW*, 26 December 1946.

49   Quoted in Anthony Aldgate and Jeffrey Richards, *The Best of British: Cinema and Society, 1930–1970* (Blackwell, 1983) op. cit., p.340.

50   *New Statesman,* 31 October 1942.

51   Aldgate and Richards, op. cit., pp.125–26.

52   *KW*, 11 January 1945.

53   Publicity leaflet, BFI, microfiche.

54   Office letter from Michael Balcon to Hugh Findlay (Ealing's Press Representative), 14 July 1942: '..."They Came in Khaki" was changed because we did not desire to suggest that our story dealt primarily with our enemy. Indeed it deals mainly with our English villagers.' Michael Balcon Collection, F7, BFI.

55   Graham Greene, 'The Lieutenant Died Last', *Colliers*, 29 June 1940, pp.9–10, 24.

56   Ibid., p.9.

57   The ringing of church bells was prohibited during the war.

58   Quoted in Elizabeth Sussex, 'Cavalcanti in England', *Sight and Sound*, vol. 44, no 4, Autumn 1975, p.210.

59   Penelope Houston, *Went the Day Well?* (BFI, 1992), p.42.

60   Sue Harper, 'The years of total war: propaganda and entertainment', in Christine Gledhill and Gillian Swanson (eds), *Nationalising Feminity: Culture, Sexuality and the Cinema in the Second World War* (Manchester University Press, 1996), pp.201–2.

61   Charles Barr, *Ealing Studios* (Studio Vista, 1993), p.31.

62   Dilys Powell, *Sunday Times*, 14 May 1944, found 'the exterior work of the film is enchanting', but otherwise 'a witty piece of muddle'; William Whitebait, *New Statesman*, 13 May 1944, thought it 'a slow-moving and often beautiful film', but concluded, 'I carried away from *A Canterbury Tale* an enjoyment I was loath to examine too closely'.

63   Michael Powell in *Arena*, BBC2, 17 November 1981, quoted in Aldgate and Richards, *The Best of British*, p.3.

64   James Chapman, *The British at War: Cinema, State and Propaganda* (I.B. Tauris, 1998).

65   See Steve Jones, 'Caravans and Slide Shows: Rural Modernism in A Canterbury Tale', *Rural History*, 12, 2, 2001, pp.211–27.

66   Press book, *A Canterbury Tale*, BFI.

67   Nannette Aldred, '*A Canterbury Tale*: Powell and Pressburger's Film Fantasies', in David Mellor (ed.), *A Paradise Lost: The Neo-Romantic Imagination in Britain, 1935–1955* (Lund Humphries, 1987), p.118.

68   *MFB*, 30 June 1944.

69   Quoted in Georges Duby, *Histoire de la France rurale*, p.443.

70   Philippe Pétain, *La France nouvelle: principes de la communauté* (Fasquelle, 1941), p.142, 'Message aux Paysans: 20 Avril 1941'.

71   Miranda Pollard, 'Femme Famille, France: Vichy and the Politics of Gender', PhD thesis, University of Dublin, 1989, pp.40–44.

72   Marcel Arland, *Le Paysan français à travers la littérature* (Stock, 1941); Henri Pourrat, *Le Paysan français* (Clermont, 1941); Albert Dauzat, *Le Village et le paysan de France* (Gallimard, 1941); Louis Barjon, *Le Paysan* (Le Puy: Xavier Mappus, 1942).

73   Marc Bloch, *L'Étrange défaite: témoignage écrit en 1940* (Gallimard, 1990), pp.80–81, first published in 1946.

74   Duby, op. cit., p.44.

75   H.R. Kedward, *Occupied France: Collaboration and Resistance, 1940–1944* (Blackwell, 1985), p.14.

76   Wright, *Rural Revolution in France*, p.75.

77   Azéma, *From Munich to the Liberation*, p.234.

78   Maurice Toesca, 'L'Occupation', in Jacques Meyer (ed.), *Vie et morts des français* (Tallendier, 1980), pp.127–32.

79   Ian Ousby, *Occupation: The Ordeal of France, 1940–1944* (John Murray, 1997), p.118.

80   Jean-Pierre Rioux, 'La France a faim!', *L'Histoire*, no 179, July–August 1994, p.38.

81   Duby, op. cit., pp.444–45.

82   Jean-Pierre Jeancolas, *15 ans d'années trente: Le cinéma français, 1929–1944* (Stock, 1983) p.323.

83   Archives scénaristiques: continuité dialogue, *Chavance* 03 I (B1), BIFI.

84   Christian Bosseno, '84 ans de cinéma paysan', *Cinémaction*, no 16, 1981.

85   In 1928, Poirier made *Verdun, visions d'histoire*. In order to achieve authenticity, veterans (French and German) of the day battle volunteered to act in the film. Philippe Pétain, the French commander at the time, played himself.

86   Jeancolas, op. cit., p.298, François Garçon, *De Blum et Pétain: Cinema et société française, 1936–1944*, (Les éditions du cerf, 1984), p.96.

87   This sequence was deleted after the liberation.

88   Noël Burch and Geneviève Sellier, *La Drôle de guerre des sexes du cinéma français (1930–1956)* (Éditions Nathan, 1996), p.184.

89   Evelyn Ehrlich, *Cinema of Paradox: French Filmmaking of the German Occupation* (Columbia University Press, 1985), p.34.

90   Pierre Véry, *Goupi Mains-Rouges* (Éditions J'ai lu, 1959), p.14, first published in 1937.

91   *Je suis partout*, 23 April 1943.

92   Véry, op. cit., p.14.

93   Florianne Wild, 'The Case of the Undead Emperor: Familial and National Identity in Jacques Becker's *Goupi Mains Rouges*', in Elizabeth Ezra and Sue Harris (eds), *France in Focus: Film and National Identity* (Berg, 2000), p.158.

94   *Grand écho du Midi*, 29 November 1943, quoted in Garçon, op. cit., p.73.

95   Raphael Samuel, *Theatres of Memory*: vol. 1: *Past and Present in Contemporary Culture* (Verso, 1996), p.210.

96   Herman Lebovics, *True France: The Wars Over Cultural Identity, 1900–1945* (Cornell University Press, 1992), p.26.

97   Véry, op. cit., p.149.

98   Ibid., p.132.

99   Alan Williams, *Republic of Images: A History of French Film* (Harvard University Press, 1992), p.259.

100   *Film français*, 24 August 1945.

101   J.B. Priestley, *English Journey* (Penguin, 1977), pp.66–67, 80, first published in 1934.

102   Ferguson and Fitzgerald, *Studies in the Social Services*, p.4.

103   An image immortalised by Herbert Mason's photograph published in the *Daily Mail* on 31 December with the caption 'War's greatest picture'.

104   Williams, *The Country and the City*, p.165.

105   Seven hundred and ninety-three firemen and twenty-five firewomen were killed and seven thousand seriously injured during the war. Calder, *The People's War*, p.241.

106   Jeffrey Richards, 'Dearden at Ealing', in Alan Burton, Tim O'Sullivan and Paul Wells (eds), *Liberal Directions: Basil Dearden and Postwar British Film Culture* (Flicks Books, 1997), p.17.

107   PRO INF 6/895 Memorandum from Ian Dalrymple, Crown Film Unit to the MOI: 'Could you possibly arrange the West End show with GFD [General Film Distributors] as I am afraid we may be forestalled by Ealing', dated 22 October 1942; Letter from Balcon to S. Cole, film editor requesting 'an emergency job on Bells' dated 6 October 1942, F37, Michael Balcon Collection, BFI.

108   Quoted in Richards (1997), op. cit., p.17.

109   *Picture Post*, 28 September 1940.

110   *Picture Post*, 19 October 1940.

111   Gareth Stedman Jones, 'The "Cockney" and the Nation', in David Feldman and Gareth Stedman Jones (eds), *Metropolis, London: Histories and Representations since 1800* (Routledge, 1989), p.278.

112   Letter to S.C. Balcon, 5 November 1942, F37, Michael Balcon Collection, BFI.

113   Press book, *The Bells Go Down*, BFI.

114   *News Chronicle*, 17 April 1943.

115   Robert Murphy, *Realism and Tinsel: Cinema and Society 1939–49* (Routledge, 1989), p.40.

116   *Sunday Times*, 18 April 1943.

117   Quoted in Nicholas Pronay and Jeremy Croft, 'British Film Censorship During the Second World War', in James Curran and Vincent Porter (eds), *British Cinema History* (Weidenfeld & Nicolson, 1983), pp.148–49.

118   Thirty-eight drawings were published in *Bombed London* (Cassell, 1947).

119   Quoted in Richards, 'Dearden at Ealing', op. cit., pp.17–18.

120   Letter from Michael Balcon to S.C. Balcon, 5 November 1942: 'They [shots of the control rooms] should also establish that the Blitz is going on all over London but that the Whitechapel area where our story takes place is a particularly bad spot'. F37, Michael Balcon Collection, BFI.

121   *KW*, 21 December 1945 records that it was the sixth most popular British film out of a total of 42.

122   More than half the men in the services were married and some of those marriages collapsed under the strain of separation. See Paul Addison, *Now the War is Over: A Social History of Britain, 1945–51* (Pimlico, 1995), pp.16–17; 'Forbidden Britain: Affairs', BBC, 1994, produced by Steve Humphries.

123   Geoff Brown, *Launder and Gilliat* (BFI, 1977), p.110.

124   *The Times*, 15 January 1945.

125   *News Chronicle*, 31 January 1945.

126   Gilliat in Brown, op. cit., p.111.

127   Murphy, 'The Spiv Cycle', in *Realism and Tinsel* .

128   David Hughes, 'The Spivs', in Philip French and Michael Sissons (eds), *The Age of Austerity* (Hodder & Stoughton, 1964), p.89.

129   *KW*, 11 January 1945.

130   Philippe Burrin, 'Vichy', in Pierre Nora (ed.), *The Realms of Memory: Rethinking the French Past*: vol. 1: *Conflicts and Divisions* (Columbia University, 1992), p.181.

131   Robert Paxton, *Vichy France: Old Guard and New Order 1940–1944* (Barrie and Jenkins, 1972), pp.54, 98–99.

132   Jean-Paul Sartre, 'Paris sous l'occupation', *Situations III* (Gallimard, 1949), p.18.

133   Ibid., p.21.

134   Pierre Sorlin, 'The Struggle for Control of French Minds', in K.M. Short (ed.), *Film and Radio Propaganda in World War II* (Croom Helm, 1983), p.260.

135   Ginette Vincendeau, 'Community, Nostalgia and the Spectacle of Masculinity', in *Screen*, November–December, 1985, p.21.

136   Susan Hayward, *French National Cinema* (Routledge, 1993), p.146.

137   François Guérif, *Le Cinéma policier français* (Veyrier, 1981), p.79.

138   Patrick Marnham, *The Man Who Wasn't Maigret: A Portrait of Georges Simenon* (Penguin, 1993), p.207.

139   Dominique Veillon, *La Mode sous l'occupation: débrouillarde et coquetterie dans la France en guerre (1939–1945)* (Éditions Payot, 1990), p.28.

140   Claude Naumann, *Jacques Becker* (Bibliothèque du film/Durante, 2001), p.13.

141   Anthony Beevor and Artemis Cooper, *Paris after the Liberation* (Hamish Hamilton), 1994, p.305.

142   Veillon, op. cit., p.130.

143   Burch and Sellier, *La Drôle de guerre des sexes*, p.203.

144   *Film français*, 10 August 1945.

145   Press book, *Falbalas*, BFI.

146   Beevor and Cooper, op. cit., p.305.

147   Veillon, op. cit., p.248.

148   Micheline Presle, *L'Arrière memoire: conversation avec Serge Toubiana* (Flammarion, 1994), pp.86–87.

149   Georges Sadoul, *French Film* (Falcon Press, 1953), pp.103–4.

150   *Le Film* 1 April 1944 reported that '*Les Enfants du paradis* is finished … the director the technicians and the actors immediately returned to Paris where the editing is being carried out.'

151   Jean-Pierre Jeancolas, 'Beneath the Despair, the Show Goes On: Marcel Carné's *Les Enfants du Paradis* (1943–1945)', in Susan Hayward and Ginette Vincendeau (eds), *French Film: Texts and Contexts* (Routledge, 1990), p.124.

152   Jill Forbes, *Les Enfants du Paradis* (BFI, 1997), p.18.

153   *The Radio Times,* 3 and 4 August 1948 lists the screening of *Les Enfants du paradis* in two parts and was the first full-length feature film ever to appear on BBC TV.

154   Pierre Sorlin, *European Cinemas, European Societies* (Routledge, 1991), p.70.

Chapter 4

1   Keith A. Murray, *History of the Second World War: Agriculture: United Kingdom Civil Series* (HMSO, 1955), pp.235–36.

2   Nuffield College, *Britain's Town and Country Pattern: A Summary of the Barlow, Scott and Uthwatt Reports* (Faber & Faber, 1944), p.101.

3   Christian Bosseno, 'Le Cinéma du paysan', *Cinémaction*, no 16, 1981, p.35.

4   Jean-Pierre Azéma, *From Munich to the Liberation, 1938–1944* (Cambridge University Press, 1984), p.100.

5   Arthur Vesselo, 'Films of the Quarter', *Sight and Sound*, Autumn 1947, p.120.

6   *KW*, 11 January 1945.

7   Howard Newby, *Country Life: A Social History of Rural England* (Weidenfeld and Nicholson, 1987), chapter 10.

8   Flora Thompson, *Larkrise to Candleford* (Oxford University Press, 1945).

9   Mollie Panter-Downes, *One Fine Day* (Virago, 1989), p.8. first published in 1947.

10   Angela Thirkell, *Peace Breaks Out*, 1946; *Love Among the Ruins*, 1948; *The Old Bank House*, 1949 (Hamish Hamilton).

11   Ronald Millar, *Frieda* (English Theatre Guild, 1947).

12   Alan Burton, 'Love in a Cold Climate: Critics, Film-makers and the British Cinema of Quality – the Case of the Captive Heart', in Alan Burton, Tim O'Sullivan and Paul Wells (eds), *Liberal Directions: Basil Dearden and Post-war British Film Culture* (Flicks Books, 1997).

13   *Observer*, 31 March 1946.

14   *KW*, 19 December 1946.

15   Sheila Kaye-Smith, *Joanna Godden* (Cassell and Company Ltd, 1921).

16   Of the 7,750,000 women working in 1943, 43 per cent were married: see Penny Summerfield, *Women Workers in the Second World War: Production and Patriarchy in Conflict* (Croom Helm, 1984), pp.29–30.

17   Hilton Tims, *Once a Wicked Lady: A Biography of Margaret Lockwood* (Virgin, 1989), p.133.

18   Sadie Ward, *War in the Countryside* (Cameron Books, 1988), pp.24–25.

19   Martin's father quotes from Shakespeare's sonnet: 'Though rough winds do shake the darling buds of May and summer's lease hath all too short a day'. Bates's novel *The Darling Buds of May* was published in 1958.

20   See Jeffrey Richards on Vaughan Williams and 'Englishness', in *Films and British National Identity: From Dickens to Dad's Army* (Manchester University Press, 1997), pp.283–325.

21   Kaye-Smith, op. cit., p.125.

22   *MFB*, June 1947.

23   George Orwell, 'The Lion and the Unicorn', in Sonia Orwell and Ian Angus (eds), *The Collected Essays, Journalism and Letters of George Orwell*, vol. 2: *My Country Right or Left* (Penguin, 1970), p.83.

24   Andrew Sinclair, *War Like a Wasp: The Lost Decade of the Forties* (Hamish Hamilton, 1989), p.265.

25   George Orwell, *The English People* (Collins, 1947), p.44.

26   *KW*, 11 January 1945.

27   *KW*, 22 August 1945.

28   *Sunday Times*, 6 July 1947.

29   David Bruce, 'Hollywood Comes to the Highlands', in Eddie Dick (ed.), *From Limelight to Satellite: A Scottish Film Book* (BFI, 1990), pp.71–82.

30   Richards, *Films and British National Identity*, p.191.

31   Neil Gunn, *The Silver Darlings* (Faber & Faber, 1941).

32   Richards, op. cit., p.198.

33   Kevin Gough-Yates, *Michael Powell, in Collaboration with Emeric Pressburger* (BFI, 1971), p.7.

34   Richards, op. cit., p.200.

35   Michael Powell, *A Life in Movies: An Autobiography*, (Methuen, 1987), p.465.

36   Emeric Pressburger Collection, Box 7, item 12, BFI.

37   Kevin Macdonald (Pressburger's grandson), *Emeric Pressburger: The Life and Death of a Screenwriter* (Faber & Faber, 1994), p.244; Ian Christie, *Arrows of Desire: The Films of Michael Powell and Emeric Pressburger* (Faber & Faber, 1994), p.54.

38   Peter Hennessy, *Never Again: Britain 1945–1951* (Vintage, 1993), p.89.

39   *Evening Standard*, 16 November 1944.

40   *The Scotsman*, 19 March 1946.

41   Nuffield College, *Britain's Town and Country Pattern*, p.101.

42   John R. Short, *The Post-war Experience: Housing in Britain* (Methuen, 1982), pp. 74–75.

43   Quoted in Robert Hewison, *Culture and Consensus: England, Art and Politics since 1940* (Methuen, 1995), p.22.

44   Alun Howkins, 'Mass Observation and Rural England, Rural History (1998) 9, 1, p.85.

45   Sadie Ward, *War in the Countryside*, p.179.

46   Catherine de la Roche, 'The Mask of Realism', *Penguin Film Review*, no 7, September 1948, p.35.

47   Sue Harper, *Picturing the Past: The Rise and Fall of the British Costume Film* (BFI, 1994), p.151.

48   Nuffield College, op. cit., p.101.

49   Press book, *Blanche Fury*, BFI.

50   Raymond Durgnat, 'Some Lines of Inquiry into Post-war British Crimes', in Robert Murphy (ed.), *The British Cinema Book* (BFI, 1997), p.91.

51   *Picturegoer*, 13 March 1948.

52   Alfred Cobban, 'France – A Peasant's Republic', *The Listener*, XLI, 1949, p.429.

53   Henri Mendras, *La Fin des paysans: innovation et changement dans l'agriculture* (S.E.D.E.I.S, 1984), p.28.

54   L. Bernot and R. Blanchard, *Nouville: Un village français* (University of Paris/Institut d'ethnologie, Musée de l'homme, 1953); Henri Mendras, *Études de sociologie rurale: Novis et Virgin* (Colin, 1953); Laurence Wylie, *Village in the Vaucluse* (Harvard University Press, 1957).

55   Jean-Pierre Rioux, 'La France a Faim!', *L'Histoire*, no 179, July–August 1994, pp.38–42.

56   Bernot and Blanchard, op. cit., p.240.

57   *Bulletin d'information de l'institut français d'opinion publique*, 1 February 1945.

58   Cited in Gordon Wright, *Rural Revolution in France: The Peasantry in the Twentieth Century* (Stanford University Press, 1964), p.231.

59   Annie Moulin, *Peasantry and Society in France since 1789* (Cambridge University Press, 1991), pp.162–63.

60   Isabel Boussard, 'L'État de l'agriculture française aux lendemains de l'occupation, (1944–1968)', *Revue d'histoire de la deuxième guerre mondiale*, no 116, October 1979, p.79.

61   *Revue du cinéma*, no 3, January 1947.

62   J.H. Weiss, 'An Innocent Eye?: The Career and Documentary Vision of Georges Rouquier', interview with Georges Rouquier, 1978, in *Cinema Journal*, Spring 1981, p.50.

63   Georges Duby, *Histoire de la France rurale*, tome 4: *De 1914 à nos jours* (Seuil, 1976), p.12 (emphasis in the original).

64   Laurence Wylie, 'Social Change at the Grass Roots', in Stanley Hoffmann (ed.), *In Search of France* (Harvard University Press 1963), p.167.

65   Cadre de l'Action, scenario, CJO551/B70, BIFI.

66   Albert Dauzat, *La Vie rurale, des origines à nos jours* (Presses Universitaires, 1946), p.119.

67   One of about 680,000 agriculturalists who were prisoners, according to an estimate by the Ministry of Agriculture in late 1941, in Sarah Fishman, *We Will Wait: Wives of French Prisoners of War* (Yale University Press, 1991), p.61.

68   Weiss, op. cit., p.56.

69   Mendras, *La Fin du paysans*, p.113.

70   *Cinémonde*, 4 February 1947.

71   Quoted in Jacques Chevallier, 'La caméra au champs', *Image et Son*, April 1959, p.6.

72   Philip Lowe and Henry Buller, 'The Historical and Cultural Contexts', in Philip Lowe and Maryvonnne Bodiguel (eds), *Rural Studies in Britain and France* (Bellhaven Press, 1990), p.16.

73   Marc Bloch, *French Rural History: An Essay on its Basic Characteristics* (Routledge & Kegan Paul, 1966), p.xxv, first published in 1931.

74   Wright, *Rural Revolution in France,* op. cit., p.89.

75   Jean-Pierre Rioux, *The Fourth Republic* (Cambridge University Press, 1980), p.438.

76   *L'Écran français*, 22 August 1945.

77   *Cinémonde*, 11 February 1947.

78   Laurence Wylie, 'Social Change at Grass Roots', p.174.

79   Boussard, 'L'État de l'agriculture française', p.79.

80   F. Raison-Jourde, *La Colonie auvergnate de Paris au XIX siècle* (Commission de travail historiques, 1976).

81   *Film français*, 11 July 1947.

82   The overhead panning shots of Paris were taken from a helicopter, a very expensive resource. As mentioned in the script: scénario 2521/B769, *Sous le ciel de Paris*, BIFI, p.1.

83   'Julien Duvivier ou l'artisan consciencieux', Philippe de Comes and Michel Marmin (eds), *Le Cinéma français 1930–1960* (Atlas, 1984), p.29.

84   Press book, *Sous le Ciel de Paris coule la Seine*, BFI.

85   Note in Archives scénaristiques: scénario 2521/B769, BIFI, p.35.

86   Richard Kuisel, *Seducing the French: The Dilemma of Americanization*, (University of California Press, 1993).

87   Rioux, *The Fourth Republic*, op. cit., p.19.

88   Danièle Voldman, 'La France en ruines', *L'Histoire*, no 179, July–August 1994, p.98.

89   W. Diville and A. Guilcher, *Bretagne et Normandie* (P.U.F., 1951); J. Gouthier, *Naissance d'un grand cité: Le Mans au milieu du XXe siècle* (Colin, 1953); Michel Quoist, *La Ville et l'homme: Rouen: étude sociologique d'un secteur prolétarien* (Les éditions ouvrières, 1952).

90   Georges Duby, *Histoire de la France urbaine*: tome 5 (Seuil, 1985).

91   Charles Rearick, *The French in Love and War: Popular Culture in France, 1914–1945* (Yale University Press, 1997), pp.273–75.

92   Ginette Vincendeau, 'Community, Nostalgia and the Spectacle of Masculinity', *Screen*, vol. 26, no 6, November–December 1985, p.20.

93   They were replaced by singer, Yves Montand and unknown actress Nathalie Nattier. Marcel Pierre, *Aux Portes de la nuit: La roman d'un film de Marcel Carné* (Nouvelle édition), 1946.

94   Marcel Carné, *La Vie à belle dents* (Jean-Pierre Olivier, 1975), p.89.

95   Susan Hayward, *French National Cinema* (Routledge, 1993), p.165.

96   Letter from Marlene Dietrich to the producers, quoted in *Paris Cinéma*, 20 February 1946.

97   *L'Écran français*, 10 December 1946.

98   Ibid.

99   Georges Sadoul, *French Film* (London: Falcon Press, 1953), p.113.

100   *Sunday Times*, 28 September 1947.

101   *Observer*, 28 September 1947.

102   Alan Williams, *Republic of Images: A History of French Film* (Cambridge, Masschusetts: Harvard University Press, 1992), p.285.

103   *Film français*, 13 February 1948.

104   Quoted in Miranda Pollard, 'Femme, Famille, France: Vichy and the Politics of Gender', unpublished PhD thesis, Trinity College, Dublin, 1989, p.355.

105   Fifty three per cent of respondents considered food provision the first necessity, *Bulletin d'information de l'institut français d'opinion publique*, 16 February 1946.

106   Jean Dutourd, *Au Bon Beurre* (Gallimard, 1952).

107   See Jane Root, 'Film Noir', in Pam Cook (ed.), *The British Cinema Book* (BFI, 1993), pp.95–96.

108   Jill Forbes, 'The Série Noire', in Brian Rigby and Nicholas Hewitt (eds), *France and the Mass Media* (Macmillan, 1995), p.89.

109   Archives scénaristiques: scénario, *Le Chanois* 046 B22, BIFI, p.82.

110   D.V. Donnison, *Housing Policy Since the War* (Penguin, 1960), p.141.

111   Robert Thorne, 'The Setting of St Paul's in the Twentieth Century', *London Journal*, 16 (2), 1991, p.118.

112   Roy Porter, *London: A Social History* (Hamish Hamilton, 1994), pp.341–42.

113   Paul Addison, *Now the War is Over: A Social History of Britain: 1945–1951* (Pimlico, 1995), p.74.

114   *Picturegoer*, 28 August 1945.

115   Edgar Anstey (ed.), *Shots in the Dark: A Collection of Reviewers' Opinions of some of the leading films released between January 1949–December 1951* (Allan Wingate, 1951), p.33.

116   *KW*, 22 July 1948.

117   *Observer*, 1 July 1951.

118   From the text of a BBC broadcast dated 15 October 1952, Michael Balcon Special Collection, BFI.

119   *KW*, 26 April 1945.

120   Norman Collins, *London Belongs to Me* (Collins, 1945).

121   Patrick Hamilton, *The Slaves of Solitude* (Cardinal, 1991), first published 1947.

122   *Observer*, 6 May 1945.

123   T.E.B Clarke, 'Just an Idea', in Roger Manvell (ed.), *The Cinema: 1951* (Penguin, 1951), p.150.

124   *Observer*, 23 February 1947.

125   Gareth Stedman Jones, 'The "Cockney" and the Nation, 1780–1988', in David Feldman and Gareth Stedman Jones (eds), *Metropolis, London: Histories and Representations Since 1800* (Routledge, 1989), p.315.

126   Pierre Sorlin, *European Cinemas: European Societies, 1939–1990* (Routledge, 1991), p.114.

127   Michael Young and Peter Willmott, *Family and Kinship in East London* (Routledge & Kegan Paul, 1957).

128   Charles Barr, *Ealing Studios* (Studio Vista, 1993), p.70.

129   David Hughes, 'The Spivs', in Philip French and Michael Sissons (eds), *The Age of Austerity* (Hodder & Stoughton, 1963).

130   *MFB*, December 1947.

131   *Observer*, 20 November 1947.

132   Arthur Vesselo, 'Films of the Quarter', *Sight and Sound*, Winter 1947–48, p.137.

133   Julian Petley, 'The Lost Continent', in Charles Barr (ed.), *All Our Yesterdays: 90 Years of British Cinema* (British Film Institute, 1986), p.111.

134   Terence Morris, *Crime and Criminal Justice Since 1945* (Blackwell, 1989), p.34.

135   The Bernstein Film Questionnaire 1946–47, April 1947, p.5.

136   British Board of Film Censors, Scenario Report, no 55, 4 March 1947, BFI.

137   Parliamentary Debates, House of Commons, 5th series (Hansard) 16 June 1948, vol. 452, p.775.

138   *KW*, 18 December 1947.

139   Sarah Street, *British National Cinema* (Routledge, 1997), p.133.

140   *KW*, 17 April 1947.

141   *KW*, 18 December 1947.

142   *Observer*, 6 July 1947.

143   *KW*, 25 March 1948.

144   Quoted in Robert Murphy, *Realism and Tinsel: Cinema and Society 1939–49* (Routledge, 1989), p.155.

145   *KW*, December 1947.

146   Geoff Brown, 'Which Way to The Way Ahead?: Britain's Years of Reconstruction', *Sight and Sound*, Autumn 1978, p.244.

Chapter 5

1   Peter Hennessy, *Never Again: Britain 1945–1951* (Vintage, 1993), p.62.

2   Angus Calder, *The People's War: Britain 1939–45* (Panther Books, 1971), p.631.

3   Mass Observation, *The Journey Home* (John Murray, 1944) p.106.

4   *Daily Mirror*, 4 July 1945.

5   'Forgotten Men?', *Picturegoer*, 21 July 1945.

6   *Picturegoer*, 30 March 1946.

7   Calder, op. cit., p.657.

8   *British Legion Journal*, March 1946.

9   Quoted in Barry Turner and Tony Rennell, *When Daddy Came Home: How Family Life Changed Forever in 1945* (Hutchinson, 1995), p.69.

10   Mass Observation, op. cit., p.52.

11   François Cochet, 'Français retour d'Allemagne', *L'Histoire*, no 179, July–August 1994, p.70.

12   Pieter Lagrou, 'Victims of Genocide and National Memory: Belgium, France and the Netherlands, 1945–1954', *Past and Present*, no 154, 1997, p.192.

13   Sarah Fishman, 'Grand Delusions: The Unexpected Consequences of Vichy France's Prisoner of War Propaganda', *Journal of Contemporary History*, vol. 26, 1991, p.229.

14   Philippe Burrin, *La France à l'heure allemande 1940–1944* (Éditions du Seuil, 1995), p.145.

15   Quoted in Fishman, op. cit., p.237.

16   François Ambrière, *Les Grandes vacances* (Éditions du seuil, 1956).

17   Henry Rousso, *The Vichy Syndrome: History and Memory in France Since 1944*, translated by Arthur Goldhammer (Harvard University Press, 1994), p.5.

18   Quoted in Edouard Lynch, 'Les conditions du retour dan la débâcle allemande', in Marie-Anne Matard-Bonucci and Edouard Lynch (eds), *La Libération des camps et le Retour des déportés* (Éditions Complexe, 1995), p.115.

19   John Ellis, *The Sharp End: The Fighting Man in World War Two* (Pimlico, 1993); Paul Fussell, *Understanding and Behaviour in the Second World War* (Oxford University Press, 1989); Angus Calder and Paul Addison (eds), *Time To Kill: A Soldier's Experience of War in the West, 1939–1945* (Pimlico, 1997).

20   Alan Bullock, *Hitler and Stalin: Parallel Lives* (Harper Collins, 1991), p.1086.

21   Ellis, op. cit., p.323.

22   Fussell, op. cit., p.36.

23   A. Crang, 'The British Soldier on the Home Front: Army Morale Reports, 1940–45', in Calder and Addison (eds), op. cit., pp.70–71.

24   'Forbidden Britain: Affairs', BBC2 1994, produced by Steve Humphries.

25   John Ellis, 'Reflections on the "Sharp End" of War', in Calder and Addison (eds), op. cit., p.16.

26   Quoted in Turner and Rennell, *When Daddy Came Home*, p.41.

27   Advertisement in the *People*, 9 March 1947.

28   J.B. Priestley, *Three Men in New Suits* (William Heinemann Ltd, 1945).

29   Labour Party, *Let Us Face the Future* (1945), quoted in Stephen Brooke, *Reform and Reconstruction: Britain after the War 1945–1951* (Manchester University Press, (1995), p.36.

30   Priestley, op. cit., p. 167.

31   *New Statesman*, 2 July 1949.

32   *Observer*, 7 May 1950.

33   *KW*, 11 January 1945.

34   *Picturegoer*, 3 February 1945.

35   J.P. Mayer, *British Cinemas and their Audiences* (Dennis Dobson, 1948), p.194.

36   Mass Observation, op. cit., p.47.

37   Peter Hutchings, 'The British Horror Movie: An Investigation of British Horror Production', PhD thesis, University of East Anglia, 1989, p.11.

38   Charles Barr, 'Projecting Britain and the British Character: Ealing Studios, Part One', *Screen*, vol. 15, no 1, Spring 1974, p.109.

39   *KW*, 16 December 1948.

40   Andrew Spicer, 'Male Stars, Masculinity and British Cinema, 1945–1960', in Robert Murphy (ed.), *The British Cinema Book* (BFI, 1997), p.146.

41   Lesley Storm, *Great Day* (English Theatre Guild), p.37.

42   Neil Rattigan, *This is England: British Film and the People's War 1939–1945* (Associated University Presses, 2001), pp.207–8.

43   Storm, op. cit., p.38.

44   Erwin Hiller was the cinematographer on both films.

45   Richard Hillary, *The Last Enemy* (Macmillan, 1942).

46   Calder, *The People's War*, p.601.

47   *Daily Mail*, 24 April 1946.

48   Ray Rochford, ex-Royal Navy, interviewed in 'Hooked', Channel 4 1998, produced by Steve Humphries.

49   British Board of Film Censors Scenario Report, 16 December 1946, BFI.

50   *News Chronicle*, 27 June 1947; *Picturegoer*, 16 August 1947.

51   Arthur Vesselo, 'The Quarter in Britain', *Sight and Sound*, Autumn 1947, p.120.

52   Jane Lewis, *Women in Britain Since 1945* (Blackwell, 1991), p.16.

53   Sheila Ferguson and Hilde Fitzgerald, *Studies in the Social Services: The History of the Second World War: United Kingdom Civil Series* (HMSO, 1955), p.3.

54   Paul Addison, *Now the War is Over: A Social History of Britain, 1945–51* (London: Pimlico, 1992), p.17.

55   Lewis, op. cit., p.17.

56   John Braine, *Room at the Top* (Signet, 1958).

57   Ibid., p.53.

58   Tim O'Sullivan, 'Not Quite Fit for Heroes: Cautionary Tales of Men at Work: *The Ship That Died of Shame* and *The League of Gentlemen*', in Alan Burton, Tim O'Sullivan and Paul Wells (eds), *Liberal Directions: Basil Dearden and Postwar British Film Culture* (Flicks Books, 1997), p.184.

59   Ferguson and Fitzgerald, op. cit., p.4.

60   Roy Porter, *London: A Social History* (Hamish Hamilton, 1994), p.342.

61   Patrick Hamilton, *The Slaves of Solitude* (Constable, 1972), p.26, first published in 1947.

62   Marcia Landy, *British Genres: Cinema and Society, 1930–1960* (Princeton University Press, 1991), p.270.

63   Who also played the only mean-spirited resident of 'The Red Lion' in *The Way to the Stars* and the unpleasant Mrs Vinten in *The October Man*.

64   Norman Longmate, *The G.I.'s: The Americans in Britain, 1939–1945* (Hutchinson, 1975).

65   Ronald Millar, *Frieda* (English Theatre Guild, 1947).

66   Tamsin Day Lewis (ed.), *Last Letters Home* (Macmillan, 1995), pp.212–17.

67   Press book, *Frieda*, BFI.

68   Press book; *KW*, 5 and 12 June 1947.

69   Press book.

70   Charles Barr, *Ealing Studios* (Studio Vista, 1977), p.75.

71   Ibid., pp.75–76.

72   Charlotte Brunsdon and Rachel Moseley, '"She's a Foreigner Who's Become a British Subject": *Frieda*', in Burton, O'Sullivan and Wells, *Liberal Directions*, pp.129–36.

73   Barr, *Ealing Studios*, op. cit., p.74.

74   Mass Observation Archive, Mass Observation File Reports, Box 15, File 1, report dated 26 July 1947.

75   Terry Lovell, 'Frieda', in Geoff Hurd (ed.), *National Fictions: World War Two In British Films and Television* (BFI, 1984), p.33.

76   Josephine Tey, *The Franchise Affair* (Penguin, 1951), first published in 1948.

77   Ibid., p.248.

78   *KW*, 15 December 1949.

79   Barr, *Ealing Studios*, op. cit., p.106.

80   Hennessy, op. cit., p.427.

81   Michael Frayn, 'Festival of Britain', in Philip French and Michael Sissons (eds), *The Age of Austerity* (Hodder & Stoughton, 1963), p.20.

82   Stephane Marchetti, *Affiches 1939–1945: Images d'une certaine France* (Edita, 1982), p.171.

83   Rousso, *The Vichy Syndrome*, p.24.

84   Lagrou, 'Victims of Genocide and National Memory', p.183.

85   Megan Koreman, 'A Hero's Homecoming: The Return of the Deportees to France, 1945', *Journal of Contemporary History*, vol. 32, no 1, January 1997, pp.11–12.

86   Lynch, 'Les conditions du retour dans la débâcle allemande', in Matard-Bonucci and Lynch (eds), *La Libération des camps*, pp.120–21.

87   Christophe Lewin, *Le Retour des Prisonniers de Guerre: Naissance et Developpement de la Fédération Nationale de Prisonniers de Guerre* (Publications de la Sorbonne, 1986), p.94.

88   François Cochet, 'Des Retours Décalés', in Christiane Franck (ed.), *La France de 1945: Resistances, Retours, Renaissances* (Presses Universitaires de Caen, 1996), p.144.

89   *Les Lettres françaises*, 16 December 1944.

90   Koreman, op. cit., pp.13–14.

91   Claire Duchen, *Women's Rights and Women's Lives in France 1944–1968* (Routledge, 1994), p.35.

92   Suzanne Collette-Kahn, *Femme, tu vas voter: comment?* (Éditions de la Liberté, 1945), p.2.

93   Lagrou, op. cit., p.201.

94   Stéphane Triqueraux, 'La Libération dans les temoignages écrits de 1945 à 1947', in Matard-Bonucci and Lynch (eds), op. cit., p.57.

95   J.M. Guillon, 'La Résistance, cinquante ans et deux mille titres après', in J.M. Guillon and P. Laborie (eds), *Mémoire et Histoire: la Résistance* (Éditions Privat, 1995), p.30.

96   Susan Hayward, *French National Cinema* (Routledge, 1993), p.189.

97   *Film français*, 13 July 1945.

98   *Cinémonde*, 19 August 1947.

99   Charles Rearick, *The French in Love and War: Popular Culture in France 1914–1945* (Yale University Press, 1997), p.258.

100 Raymond Radiguet, *Le Diable au corps* (Gallimard, 1982), first published in 1923.

101 Ibid., p.46.

102 Jean Aurenche, *La Suite à l'écran* (Institut Lumière, 1993), p.139.

103 Ibid., p.142.

104 Quoted in *Time*, 21 March 1949.

105 *Cinémonde*, 15 July 1947; *Figaro*, 24 July 1947.

106 Freddy Buache, *Claude Autant-Lara* (L'Age d'homme, 1982), p.45.

107 Carrie Tarr, 'From Stardom to Eclipse: Micheline Presle and Post-war French Cinema', in Ulrike Sieglohr (ed.), *Heroines without Heroes: Reconstructing Female and National Identities in European Cinema, 1945–51* (Cassell, 2000), p.72.

108 *Film français*, 5 December 1947.

109 Hayward, *French National Cinema*; Alan Williams, *Republic of Images: A History of French Film* (Harvard University Press, 1992).

110 Rousso, *The Vichy Syndrome*, p.186.

111 Jacques Prévert, *Le Crime de Monsieur Lange, Les Portes de la Nuit: Scénarios* (Gallimard, 1990), p.194.

112 Suzanne Langlois, 'La Résistance dans le cinéma français de fiction (1944–1994)', PhD thesis, McGill University, Quebec, 1996, p.207.

113 Annette Wieviorka, 'Rendez-vous a l'hôtel Lutétia', *L'Histoire*, July–August 1994, p.75.

114 Lynch, 'Les filtres successifs de l'information', in Matard-Bonucci and Lynch (eds), *La Libération des camps*, p.171.

115 Rousso, op. cit., p.25.

116 Herbert Lottman, *The People's Anger: Justice and Revenge in Post-Liberation France* (Hutchinson, 1986), p.14.

117 Langlois, op. cit., p.178.

118 Sarah Fishman, *We Will Wait: Wives of French Prisoners of War* (Yale University Press, 1991).

119   Langlois, letter to the author, 2 April 1999.

120   Rousso, op. cit., p.24.

121   Joseph Daniel, *Guerre et cinéma: grandes illusions et petits soldats 1895–1971* (Armand Colin, 1972), p.255.

122   Burrin, *La France a l'heure allemande*.

123   Quoted in Langlois, op. cit., p. 208.

124   *La Cinématographie française*, 15 October 1949.

125   *Sunday Times*, 23 April 1950.

126   *Observer*, 23 April 1950.

127   *Nuit et brouillard* (1956, Alain Resnais), about the Holocaust; *Passage du Rhin* (1959, André Cayatte), about *prisonniers*.

128   *Film français*, 19 September 1947.

129   Pierre Boileau and Thomas Narcejac, *D'Entre les morts*, published in Britain as *The Living and the Dead* in 1956.

130   Boileau and Narcejac, *Vertigo*, translated by Geoffrey Sainsbury (Bloomsbury Film Classics edition, 1997), p.61.

131   Ibid., p.96.

132   Danièle Voldman, 'La France en ruines', *L'Histoire*, no 179, July–August 1994, p.98.

133   Jean-Pierre Rioux, *The Fourth Republic*, translated by Geoffrey Rogers (Cambridge University Press, 1987), p.13.

134   Robin Buss, *French Film Noir* (Marion Boyars, 1994), p.13.

135   Gavin Lambert, 'The New Pessimism', *Sequence*, Summer 1948, pp.8–12.

136   Clouzot was permanently suspended by the Comité Regional Interprofessionel d'Épuration dans les Entreprises. This was later reduced to two years.

137   Martha Wolfenstein and Nathan Leites, *Movies: A Psychological Study* (The Free Press, 1950), pp.322–23.

138   Marcel Oms, 'Le charme discret du cinéma du Vichy', *Cahiers de la cinémathèque*, no 8, Winter 1973, p.68.

139   Noël Burch and Geneviève Sellier, *La Drôle de guerre des sexes du cinéma français 1930–1956* (Nathan, 1996), p.231.

140   Olivier Wieviorka, 'Les Mécanismes d'épuration', *L'Histoire*, July–August 1994, p.50.

141   Gordon Wright, *Between the Guillotine and Liberty: Two Centuries of the Crime Problem in France* (Oxford University Press, 1982), p.192.

142   *Cinémonde*, 30 April 1946.

143   Charles Ford, *Pierre Fresnay: gentilhomme de l'écran* (Éditions France-Empire, 1981), p.78.

144   Georges Simenon, *Les Fiançailles de M. Hire* (Fayard, 1933).

145   *Nouvelles Litteraires*, 16 January 1947; *Les Lettres françaises*, 24 January 1947.

146   *Film français*, 6 December 1946.

147   *L'Écran français*, 21 January 1947.

148   *Opéra*, 22 January 1947.

149   Ibid.
150   H.R. Kedward, 'Introduction', in H.R. Kedward and Nancy Wood (eds), *The Liberation of France: Image and Event* (Berg, 1995) p.6.
151   Lagrou, op. cit., p.190.
152   Rousso, *The Vichy Syndrome*, p.133.
153   Lagrou, 'Victims of Genocide and National Memory', p.193.
154   L. Bernot and R. Blanchard, *Nouville: un village français* (Université de Paris, 1953), p.376.
155   Quoted in Turner and Rennell, *When Daddy Came Home*, p.188.
156   J.B. Priestley, *Three Men in New Suits*, p.71.
157   *New Statesman*, 2 July 1949.
158   Barr, *Ealing Studios*, op. cit., p.106.
159   *Les Lettres français*, 16 December 1944.
160   Albert Camus, *The Outsider* (Penguin, 1982), afterword. First published in 1942.
161   Quoted in Rousso, op. cit., p.27.

Chapter 6

1   Sue Aspinall, 'Women, Realism and Reality in British Films, 1943–1953', in James Curran and Vincent Porter (eds), *British Cinema History* (Barnes & Noble, 1983), p.273.
2   Sue Harper, *Mad, Bad and Dangerous to Know: Women in British Cinema* (Continuum, 2000), chapter 4.
3   Christine Geraghty, *British Cinema in the Fifties: Gender, Genre and the 'New Look'* (Routledge, 2000), p.82.
4   Pam Cook, *Fashioning the Nation: Costume and Identity in British Cinema* (British Film Institute, 1996).
5   Sue Harper, 'From Holiday Camp to High Camp', in Andrew Higson (ed.), *Dissolving Views: Key Articles on British Cinema* (Cassell, 1996), p.103.
6   Geraghty, op. cit., p.86.
7   Cited in Harold Smith, 'The effect of the war on the status of women', in Harold Smith (ed.), *War and Social Change: British Society in the Second World War* (Manchester University Press, 1986), p.209.
8   Cited in Di Parkin, 'Women in the armed services, 1940–45', in Raphael Samuel (ed.), *Patriotism: The Making and Un-Making of British National Identity*, vol. 11: *Minorities and Outsiders* (Routledge, 1989), p.164.
9   Sheila Ferguson and Hilde Fitzgerald, *The History of the Second World War: Studies in the Social Services: United Kingdom Civil Series* (HMSO, 1955), p.4.
10   Penny Summerfield, '"It did me good in lots of ways": British Women in Transition from War to Peace', in Claire Duchen and Irene Bandhauer-Schffman (eds), *When the War Was Over: Women, War and Peace in Europe, 1940–1956* (Leicester University Press, 2000), p.13.
11   Monica Dickens, *One Pair of Feet* (Penguin, 1973), p.7. First published in 1942.

12   Penny Summerfield, *Women Workers in the Second World War: Production and Patriarchy in Conflict* (Croom Helm, 1984), p.29.

13   Joanna Bourke, *Working-Class Cultures in Britain 1890–1960* (Routledge, 1994), p.106.

14   Ibid., p.108.

15   Angus Calder, *The People's War: Britain 1939–45* (Panther Books Ltd, 1971), p.385.

16   Peter Lewis, *A People's War* (Methuen, 1986), p.133.

17   Janice Winship, 'Women's Magazines: Management of the Self in *Woman's Own*', in Christine Gledhill and Gillian Swanson (eds), *Nationalising Femininity: Culture, Sexuality and British Cinema in the Second World War* (Manchester University Press, 1996), p.130.

18   Lucy Noakes, *War and the British: Gender, Memory and National Identity* (I. B. Tauris, 1998), p.60.

19   Ibid., p.63.

20   Ben Wicks, *Welcome Home: True Stories of Soldiers Returning from World War Two* (Bloomsbury, 1991), p.32.

21   Summerfield, *Women Workers in the Second World War*, p.34.

22   Ibid.

23   Antonia Lant, 'Prologue: Mobile Femininity', in Gledhill and Swanson, op. cit., pp.15–16.

24   Calder, op. cit., p.384.

25   Summerfield, (1984), p.45.

26   Quoted in Penny Summerfield, 'The girl that makes the spring that drills the hole that holds the spring…': discourses of women and work in the Second World War', in Gledhill and Swanson, op. cit., p.36.

27   Vincent Porter and Chaim Litewski, '*The Way Ahead*': Case History of a Propaganda Film', *Sight and Sound*, Spring 1981, p.111.

28   Elisabeth Sadler, *Sleep and Cease Crying* (Big Ben Books, 1943).

29   Harper, *Mad, Bad and Dangerous to Know*, p.34.

30   Ferguson and Fitzgerald, op. cit., p.330.

31   Christine Gledhill, '"An Abundance of Understatement": Documentary, Melodrama and Romance', in Gledhill and Swanson, op. cit., p.212.

32   Calder, op. cit., p.62.

33   Cited in Parkin, op. cit., p.164.

34   Cited in ibid., p.165.

35   Ibid.

36   Lewis, *A People's War*, op. cit., p.135.

37   Cited in Parkin, 'Women in the armed services', p.168.

38   Delia Jarrett-MacCauley, 'Putting the Black Woman in the Frame: Una Marson and the West Indian Challenge to British National Identity', in Gledhill and Swanson, op. cit., p.121.

39   Brian McFarlane (ed.), *Sixty Voices: Celebrities Recall the Golden Age of British Cinema* (BFI, 1992), p.142.

40   *Sunday Times*, 11 April 1943.

41   Wicks, *Welcome Home*, p.139.

42   Summerfield, 'It did me good in lots of ways', op. cit., p.20.

43   Wicks, op. cit., pp.179–80.

44   Richard Titmuss, *Essays on the Welfare State* (Unwin, 1958); Arthur Marwick, *Britain in the Century of Total War: War, Peace and Social Change 1900–1967* (Bodley Head, 1968); Alva Myrdal and Viola Klein, *Women's Two Roles: Home and Work* (Routledge & Kegan Paul, 1956).

45   Press Book, *Perfect Strangers*, BFI.

46   Harper, *Mad, Bad and Dangerous to Know*, op. cit., p.40.

47   *MFB*, September 1945.

48   Ferguson and Fitzgerland, *The History of the Second World War*, p.4.

49   'Forbidden Britain: Our Secret Past 1900–1960; Affairs', BBC2, 1994, produced by Steve Humphries.

50   Ferguson and Fitzgerald, op. cit., p.18.

51   'Hidden Love: What Granny Did in the War', Channel 4, 1999, produced by Steve Humphries.

52   'Forbidden Britain', op. cit.

53   *KW*, 11 January 1945; *News Chronicle*, 13 January 1945.

54   Quoted in Wicks, *Welcome Home*, p.45.

55   *Picture Post*, 21 April 1945.

56   Cynthia P. White, *Women's Magazines, 1693–1968* (Michael Joseph, 1970), pp.133–34.

57   *Woman's Own*, 11 January 1951.

58   Penny Summerfield and Gail Braybon, *Out of the Cage: Women's Experiences in the Two World Wars* (Pandora Press, 1987), p.270.

59   Quoted in Barry Turner and Tony Rennell, *When Daddy Came Home: How Family Life Changed Forever* (Hutchinson, 1995), p.70.

60   Margaret Forster, *Daphne du Maurier* (Chatto and Windus, 1993), pp.178–79.

61   Jane Lewis, *Women in Britain since 1945: Women, Family, Work and the State in the Post-War Years* (Blackwell, 1992), pp.79–80.

62   Denise Riley, *War in the Nursery: Theories of the Child and the Mother* (Virago, 1983), p.166.

63   Daphne Du Maurier, 'The Years Between', in Fidelis Morgan, *The Years Between: Plays by Women on the London Stage, 1900–1950* (Virago, 1994), p.348.

64   Ibid., p.394.

65   *MFB*, April 1946.

66   Smith, 'The Effect of War on the Status of Women', p.211.

67   Summerfield and Braybon, op. cit., pp.263–64.

68   Alva Myrdal and Viola Klein, *Women's Two Roles: Home and Work* (Routledge & Kegan Paul, 1956), p.53.

69   Summerfield, *Women Workers in the Second World War*, p.187. (There was no census in 1941.)

70   Ibid., p.30.

71   Summerfield, 'It did me good in lots of ways', op. cit., p.14.

72   Elizabeth Wilson, *Women and the Welfare State*, (Tavistock, 1977), p.154.

73   Riley, *War in the Nursery*, p.122.

74   Wendy Webster, *Imagining Home: Gender, 'Race' and National Identity, 1945–64* (UCL, 1998), p.19.

75   Riley, op. cit., p.137.

76   Summerfield and Braybon, op. cit., pp.259–60.

77   Harper, *Mad, Bad and Dangerous to Know*, op. cit., p.91.

78   McFarlane, *Brian, An Autobiography of British Cinema*, (Methuen, 1997), p.140.

79   Ibid., p.140.

80   Ibid., p.42.

81   Ibid.

82   T.A. Critchley, *A History of the Police in England and Wales, 1900–1966* (Constable, 1967), p.215.

83   Clive Emsley, *The English Police: A Political and Social History* (Longman, 1991), p.158.

84   Malcolm Young, *An Inside Job: Policing and Police Culture in Britain* (Clarendon Press, 1991), p.202.

85   Muriel Box, *Odd Woman Out* (Leslie Frewin, 1974), pp.214–15.

86   Young, op. cit., p.207.

87   Ibid., p.203.

88   Catherine de la Roche, 'The Mask of Realism', *Penguin Film Review*, no 7, September 1948, p.38.

89   Janet Finch and Penny Summerfield, 'Social Reconstruction and the Emergence of the Companionate Marriage, 1945–59', in David Clark (ed.), *Marriage, Domestic Life and Social Change: Writings for Jacqueline Burgoyne (1944–88)*, (Routledge, 1991) pp.7–8.

90   Joseph Shearing, *Blanche Fury or Fury's Ape* (William Heinemann, 1939).

91   *Picturegoer*, 5 July 1947.

92   Ibid.

93   Harper, *Mad, Bad and Dangerous to Know*, op. cit., p.103.

94   Sheila Kaye-Smith, *Joanna Godden* (Cassell & Company Ltd, 1921); Arthur La Bern, *It Always Rains on Sunday* (Nicholson & Watson, 1945).

95   McFarlane, *An Autobiography of British Cinema*, p.235.

96   *Picturegoer*, 17 January 1948.

97   Kaye-Smith, op. cit., p.236.

98   Aspinall, 'Women, Realism and Reality', p.285.

99   McFarlane, *An Autobiography of British Cinema*, p.236.

100   *Observer*, 15 June 1947.

101   *Sunday Times*, 15 June 1947.

102   Aspinall, op. cit., p.273.

103   Geraghty, *British Cinema in the Fifties*, p.163.

104   Ibid., p.160.

105   Ibid., p.164.
106   Ted Willis, *Woman in a Dressing Gown and other TV Plays* (Barrie and Rockliff, 1959), p.12.
107   John Hill, *Sex, Class and Realism: British Cinema, 1956–1963* (BFI, 1986), pp.98–99.
108   *Woman's Own*, 8 February 1951.
109   *KW*, 26 September 1957.
110   *Sight and Sound*, September 1957.
111   Calder, *The People's War*, p.360.
112   Lewis, *Women in Britain Since 1945*, p.17.
113   Ibid.
114   Ibid, p.18.
115   White, op. cit., p.138.
116   Ibid., p.141.
117   *Woman's Own*, 4 January 1951.
118   Geraghty, *British Cinema in the Fifties*, p.133.
119   Publicity advertisement in *KW*, 23 September 1948.
120   James C. Robertson, *The BBFC: Film Censorship in Britain 1895–1950* (Croom Helm, 1985), p.172.
121   Joan Temple, *No Room at the Inn* (World Film Publications, 1948), p.232.
122   Ibid., p.234.
123   *Today's Cinema*, 21 September, 1948.
124   Ibid.
125   *MFB*, October 1948.
126   *KW*, 23 September, 1948.
127   Janet Fink and Catherine Holden, 'Representations of Spinsters and Single Mothers in the Mid-Victorian Novel, Inter-war Hollywood Melodrama and British Film of the 1950s and 1960s', *Gender and History*, vol. 11, no 2, July 1999, p.246.
128   Robert Murphy, 'Cage of Gold', in Alan Burton, Tim O'Sullivan and Paul Wells eds., *Liberal Directions: Basil Dearden and Postwar British Film Culture*, p.160.
129   *Daily Mirror*, 11 January 1946.

Chapter 7

1   Sarah Fishman, *We Will Wait: Wives of French Prisoners of War* (Yale: Yale University Press, 1991), p.xii.
2   Christophe Lewin, *Le Retour des prisonniers de guerre: naissance et developpement de la FNPG* (Publications de la Sorbonne, 1986), p.17.
3   Sarah Fishman, 'Grand Delusions: The Unintended Consequences of Vichy France's Prisoner of War Propaganda', in *Journal of Contemporary History*, vol. 26, 1991, p.229.

4   Hanna Diamond, *Women and the Second World War in France, 1939–1948* (Longman, 1999), p.178.

5   Susan Hayward, *French National Cinema* (Routledge, 1993), p.173.

6   Ibid., p.174.

7   Noël Burch and Geneviève Sellier, *La Drôle du guerre des sexes du cinema français, 1930–1956* (Nathan, 1996).

8   Michael Kelly, 'The Reconstruction of Masculinity at the Liberation', in H.R. Kedward and Nancy Wood (eds), *The Liberation of France: Image and Event* (Berg), p.119.

9   Diamond, op. cit., p.188.

10 Burch and Sellier, op. cit., p.224.

11 Jacques Doniol-Volcroze, 'Déshabillage d'une petite bourgeoisie sentimentale', *Cahiers du cinema*, no 31, January 1954.

12 Francine Muel-Dreyfus, *Vichy et l'éternel feminin* (Éditions de seuil, 1996).

13 Ibid., p.10.

14 Cheryl A. Koos, '"On Les Aura!": The Gendered Politics of Abortion and the Alliance Nationale Contre la Dépopulation, 1938–1944', *Modern and Contemporary France* (1999), 9 (1), p.22.

15 Margaret Collins Weitz, 'The Poster War: Propaganda on Paris Walls during the Occupation', *Contemporary French Civilisation*, 23, 1999, pp.321–23.

16 Kelly, op. cit., p.118.

17 Siân Reynolds, 'Marianne's Citizens?: Women, the Republic and Universal Suffrage in France', in Siân Reynolds (ed.), *State and Revolution: Essays on Power and Gender in Europe since 1789* (Wheatsheaf, 1986), p.102.

18 Tony Judt, *Past Imperfect: French Intellectuals 1944–1956* (University of California Press, 1992), p.49.

19 Jean-Paul Sartre, 'Qu'est-ce qu'un collaborateur?', *Situations* III (Gallimard, 1949), p.58.

20 Fishman, *We Will Wait*, op. cit., p.141.

21 Claude Morgan, *La Marque de l'homme* (Éditions de minuit, 1945).

22 Vercors, *La Silence de La Mer* (Éditions de Minuit, 1944)

23 Claire Duchen, 'Crime and Punishment in Liberated France', in Duchen and Irene Bandhauer-Schffman (eds), *When the War Was Over: Women, War and Peace in Europe, 1940–1956* (Leicester: Leicester University Press, 2000), p.234.

24 Karen H. Adler, 'Reading National Identity: Gender and "Prostitution" During the Occupation', *Modern and Contemporary France* (1999), 7 (1), p.47.

25 Duchen, op. cit., p.234.

26 Diamond, *Women and the Second World War*, p.136.

27 Corran Laurens, '"La Femme au Turban": les Femmes tondues', in Kedward and Woods, op. cit., p.155.

28 Henry Rousso, *The Vichy Syndrome: History and Memory in France Since 1944*, translated by Arthur Goldhammer (Harvard, Harvard University Press, 1994), p.280.

29   Eric Hobsbawm, *The Age of Extremes: The Short Twentieth Century, 1914–1991* (Michael Joseph, 1994), p.164.

30   H.R. Kedward, *Occupied France: Collaboration and Resistance, 1940–1944* (Oxford: Blackwell, 1985), p.77.

31   Paula Schwartz, 'Redefining Resistance: Women's Activism in Wartime France', in M.R. Higonnet, J. Jenson, S. Michel and M.C. Weitz (eds), *Behind the Lines: Gender and the Two World Wars* (Yale: Yale University Press, 1987), p.142.

32   Diamond, op. cit., p.98.

33   Schwartz, op. cit., p.142.

34   Diamond, op. cit., p.100.

35   H.R. Kedward, 'Rural France and Resistance', in Sarah Fishman, Laura Lee Downs, Ioannis Sinanoglou et al. (eds), *France at War: Vichy and the Historians* (Oxford, Berg, 2000), p.127.

36   Schwartz, op. cit., p.144.

37   Suzanne Langlois, 'Images that matter: The French Resistance in Film (1944–1946)', *French History*, December 1997, p.470.

38   Rousso, op. cit., p.228.

39   Guy de Maupassant, *Boule de Suif and Other Stories*, translated by H.N.P. Sloman, (Penguin 1949).

40   Ibid., p.56.

41   André Bazin, *French Cinema of the Occupation and Resistance*, translated by Stanley Hochman (Frederick Ungar, 1981), p.119.

42   De Maupassant, op. cit., p.22.

43   Carrie Tarr, 'From Stardom to Eclipse: Micheline Presle and Post-war French Cinema', in Ulrike Sieglohr (ed.), *Heroines without Heroes: Reconstructing Female and National Identities in European Cinema, 1945–51* (Cassell, 2000), p.69.

44   Ibid., p.70.

45   Christian Chevandier, 'La Résistance des cheminots: le primat de la fonctionnaire plus qu'une réelle spécificité', *Le Mouvement Social*, no 180, July–September 1997, p.147.

46   Ibid.

47   Quoted in ibid., p.152.

48   Archives du tournage, *La Bataille du rail*, CJ0150 B21, BIFI, note on sketch no 12.

49   Burch and Sellier, *La Drôle du guerre des sexes*, p.221.

50   Ibid.

51   Diamond, *Women and the Second World War*, p.104.

52   *Le Monde*, 5 March 1946.

53   *Revue du cinema*, October 1946.

54   Quoted in Suzanne Langlois, 'La Résistance dans le cinéma français de fiction (1944–1994)', PhD thesis, McGill University, Quebec, 1996, p.101.

55   Burch and Sellier, op. cit., p.223.
56   Rita Kramer, *Flames in the Field* (Michael Joseph, 1995); Schwartz, 'Redefining Resistance', in Higonnet, Jenson, Michel and Weitz, op. cit.
57   Anna Neagle, *There's Always Tomorrow* (Everest Pictures, 1974), p.161.
58   Ibid., p.162.
59   *Cinématographie française*, 25 March 1950.
60   Claire Duchen, *Women's Rights and Women's Lives in France 1944–1968* (Routledge, 1994), p.33.
61   Reynolds, 'Marianne's Citizens?', op. cit., pp.106–7.
62   *Bulletin d'information de l'institut français d'opinion publique*, 1 November 1944.
63   Ibid.
64   Ibid.
65   Robert Gildea, *France Since 1945* (Oxford University Press, 1993), p.122.
66   Burch and Sellier, *La Drôle du guerre des sexes*, p.258.
67   Fishman, op. cit., p.5.
68   Diamond, *Women and the Second World War*, pp.195–97.
69   Jacques Rivette and François Truffaut, 'Entretien avec Jacques Becker', *Cahiers du cinéma*, no 32, February 1954.
70   Ibid.
71   Theodore Zeldin, *France: 1948–1945*, vol. 1: *Ambition, Love and Politics* (Clarendon Press, 1973), p.307.
72   Norman Longmate, *The GIs: The Americans in Britain, 1942–1945* (Hutchinson, 1975), p.278.
73   Diamond, op. cit., p.39.
74   Philippe Burrin, *Living with Defeat: France under the German Occupation, 1940–1944*, translated by Janet Lloyd (Arnold, 1996), p.204.
75   Fishman, *We Will Wait*, 57.
76   Diamond, op. cit., p.166.
77   Ibid., p.167.
78   Simone Signoret, *Nostalgia Isn't What it Used to Be* (Harper & Row, 1978), p.221.
79   *Picturegoer*, 24 January 1959.
80   John Kobal, *People Will Talk: Personal Conversations with the Legends of Hollywood* (Aurum Press, 1986), p.116.
81   Simone de Beauvoir, *The Second Sex*, translated by H.M. Parshley (Penguin, 1972), p.578 (first published as *Le Deuxième Sexe* in 1949).
82   Sarah Leahy and Susan Hayward, 'The Tainted Woman: Simone Signoret, Site of Pathology or Agent of Retribution?', in Sieglohr (ed.), *Heroines Without Heroes*, p.80.
83   Signoret, op. cit., p. 79.
84   Leahy and Hayward, op. cit., p.77.
85   Signoret, op. cit., p. 79.
86   See Fishman, *We Will Wait*, chapter 7.

87   Micheline Presle, *L'Arrière Mémoire: conversation avec Serge Toubiana* (Flammarion, 1994), p.98.

88   Burch and Sellier, *La Drôle du guerre des sexes*, pp.280–82.

89   *L'Écran français*, 30 January 1950.

90   Leahy and Hayward, op. cit., p.86.

91   Signoret, op. cit., p.79.

92   Noël Burch and Geneviève Sellier, 'Evil Women in the Post-war French Cinema', in Sieglohr (ed.), *Heroines Without Heroes*, p.47.

93   *Cahiers du cinéma*, no 3, June 1951.

94   Ibid.

95   Duchen, *Women's Rights and Women's Lives*, p.28.

96   Fishman, op. cit., p.165.

97   Susan Hayward, *French National Cinema* (Routledge, 1993), p.176.

98   *Image et Son*, 57–58, November/December 1952.

99   *Observer*, 25 February 1951; *MFB*, May 1951.

100   Burch and Sellier, *La Drôle des guerre des sexes*, pp. 256–57.

101   Rivette and Truffaut, 'Entretien avec Jacques Becker'.

102   Ibid, p.8.

103   Quoted in Kristin Ross, *Fast Cars, Clean Bodies: Decolonisation and the Re-ordering of French Culture* (MIT Press, 1995), pp.68–69.

104   Jacques Doniol-Valcroze, 'Déshabillage d'une petite bourgeoisie senti-mentale', *Cahiers du cinema*, no 31, January 1954.

105   Claude Naumann, *Jacques Becker* (Bibliothèque du film/Durante, 2001), p.39.

106   Ibid., pp.42, 44.

107   Dominique Veillon, 'La Vie Quotidienne des femmes', in Françoise Bedarida and Jean-Pierre Azéma (eds), *Le Régime de Vichy et les Français* (Fayard, 1992), pp.631–32.

108   Duchen, *Women's Rights and Women's Lives*, p.17.

109   Rivette and Truffaut, op. cit., p.9.

110   Ibid., p.10.

111   Jean-Louis Vey, *Jacques Becker ou la fausse évidence* (Aléas, 1995), p.37.

112   Burch and Sellier, *La Drôle des guerre des sexes*, p.262.

113   Quoted in Naumann, op. cit., p.41.

114   Dominique Veillon, *La Mode sous l'occupation: débrouillardise et coquetterie dans la France en guerre (1939–1945)* (Éditions Payot, 1990), p.250.

115   Anthony Beevor and Artemis Cooper, *Paris after the Liberation, 1944–1949* (Penguin edition, 1995), pp.306–7.

116   Ibid., p.313.

117   Quoted in Harry Hopkins, *The New Look: A Social History of the Forties and Fifties in Britain* (Secker & Warburg, 1963), p.95 (emphasis in the original).

118   Beevor and Cooper, op. cit., p.315.

119   Quoted in Claire Duchen, 'Occupation Housewife: The Domestic Ideal in 1950s France', *French Cultural Studies*, II (1991), p.4.

120   Richard Kuisel, *Seducing the French: The Dilemma of Americanisation* (University of California, 1993), p.105.

121   Ménie Grégoire, 'La Presse feminine', *Esprit*, July–August 1959, p.22.

122   Ibid.

123   Ibid., p.24.

124   Evelyne Sullerot, *La Presse féminine* (Armand Colin, 1963), pp.127–44.

125   Grégoire, op. cit., p.24.

126   See Roy Armes, *French Cinema*, (Secker & Warburg, 1985), Chapter 9; Alan Williams, *A Republic of Images: A History of French Film* (Harvard: Harvard University Press, 1992), chapter 12.

127   Burch and Sellier, *La Drôle du guerre des sexes*, pp.248–51.

128   Susan Hayward, *French National Cinema* (Routledge, 1993), p.161.

129   Williams, ibid., p.280.

130   André Bazin, 'De la Carolisation de la France', *Esprit*, February 1954.

131   Doniol-Valcroze, 'Déshabillage d'une petite bourgoisie', pp.8–9.

132   Burch and Sellier, *La Drôle du guerre des sexes*, op. cit. p.61.

133   Maurice Bessy, Raymond Chirat and André Bernard, *Histoire du cinéma français: encyclopédie des films 1951–1955* and *1956–1960* (Éditions Pygmalion-Gérard Watelet, 1989, 1990).

134   Duchen, *Women's Rights and Women's Lives*, op. cit., p.29.

135   Fishman, *We Will Wait*, op. cit. p.171.

136   Diamond, *Women and the Second World War*, p.172.

137   Dreyfus, *Vichy et l'eternel féminin*, p.119.

138   De Beauvoir, *The Second Sex*, p.148.

139   Diamond, op. cit., p.169.

140   Jane Jenson, 'The Liberation and New Rights for French Women', in Higonnet, Jenson, Michel and Weitz, *Behind the Lines*, p.275.

141   *Bulletin d'information de l'institut français d'opinion publique*, 16 January 1947.

142   François Guérif, *Le Cinéma policier français* (Veyrier, 1981), p.94.

143   Gordon Wright, *Between the Guillotine and Liberty: Two Centuries of the Crime Problem in France* (Oxford: Oxford University Press, 1983), p.192.

144   Nicole Védrès, 'French Cinema Takes Stock', *Penguin Film Review*, 3, 1947, p.82.

145   Archives Nationales, Ministère de l'information, 'La Censure', F41 2385, letter from Ministre de la Santé Publique et de la Population to M. le President du Conseil des Ministres, 15 December 1948.

146   Ibid.

147   Charles Ford, *Histoire du cinéma français contemporaine* (Éditions France-Empire, 1977), p.61.

148   Carrie Tarr, 'Women, the Cinema and (the) Liberation', in Kedward and Woods, *The Liberation of France,* op. cit., p.105.

149   Ford, op. cit., p.145.

150   Olivier Barrot, *L'Écran français, 1943–1953: histoire d'un journal et d'une époque* (Les Éditeurs français réunis, 1979), p.229.

151   François Truffaut, *Letters*, translated by Gilbert Adair (Faber & Faber, 1990), p.176.

152   Doniol-Valcroze, 'De L'Avant garde', in H. Agel, J.L. Barrot, A. Bazin et al., *Sept ans du cinéma français* (Éditions du cerf, 1953), p.21.

153   Quoted in Laurent Marie, 'La Réception critique de *L'Amour d'une femme*', *1895*, October 1997, p.84.

154   Burch and Sellier, *La Drôle du guerre des sexes*, p.261.

155   Marie, op. cit., pp. 86–87.

156   *Bulletin d'information de l'institut français d'opinion publique*, 16 November 1947.

157   De Beauvoir, *The Second Sex*, p.292.

Chapter 8

1   Quoted in Roy Armes, *A Critical History of British Cinema* (Secker & Warburg, 1978), p.147.

2   Susan Hayward, *French National Cinema* (Routledge, 1993), p.157.

3   Arthur Vesselo, 'Films of the Quarter', *Sight and Sound*, Autumn 1947, p.120.

4   *Observer*, 5 September 1948.

5   'Round Table on British Films', *Sight and Sound*, May 1950.

6   Quoted in File H33, 'Festival of Britain': Michael Balcon Special Collection, BFI (no page number).

7   Jacques Doniol-Valcroze, 'Déshabillage d'une petite bourgeoisie sentimentale', *Cahiers du cinema*, no 31, January 1954, pp.4–5.

8   Simone de Beauvoir, *The Second Sex*, translated by H.M. Parshley (Penguin, 1972), p.292.

Sources and Bibliography

Archival and unpublished sources

Public Record Office (Kew, London)
INF 1/178 – Ministry of Information. Memorandum, 'Security Censorship of Films', 6 September 1939.
INF 1/867 – Co-ordinating Committee Paper No. 1, 'Programme for Film Propaganda', 29 January 1940.
INF 1/224 – Letter from David Niven to the War Office, 27 November 1943.
INF 1/224 – '*The Way Ahead*', Memorandum, 29 June 1943.
INF 6/895 – Memorandum from the Crown Film Unit to the Ministry of Information, 22 October 1942.
BT 64/2178 – Board of Trade. Manpower requirements for the film industry, September 1945–January 1946.
BT 64/2229 – Supplementary Statement to the Committee for Reciprocity Information, January 1947.
BT 64/2370 – Negotiations with the American Film Industry for removal of ad-valorem duty, March 1948.
BT64/2398 – Appointment of Committee of Enquiry on Distribution and Exhibition of Films, July–November 1948.

Archives Nationales (Paris)
F41 /2376–2385 – Ministère d'état à l'information, La Censure, 1944–1949.
F41/ 2702 – Ministère d'état à l'information: Centre National du Cinématographie, November–December 1947.
F41/2707–8 – Exploitation, relations avec l'étranger.
F41/2712 – Industrie – généralités.
F42/136 – Fichiers de films, 1941–1946.

Bibiothèque de l'image – Filmothèque (BIFI)
0183/B53, Archives scénaristiques, *L'Assassin habite au 21*.
Chavance 03 I, Documentation pour le scénario, *Le Corbeau*.
Chavance 03 II, Letter from Sécurité Militaire to the Commission d'Épuration du Cinéma, 10 October 1944, *Le Corbeau*.
CJ 0304 B237, Archives scénaristiques, *Le Ciel est à vous*.
Le Chanois, 046 B22, Archives scénaristiques, *Impasse des deux anges*.
1944/B5778, Archives scénaristiques, *Nuit sans fin*.
CJ0551/ B70, Archives scénaristiques, *Farrebique*.

British Film Institute (BFI)
The Bernstein Film Questionnaire (1946–47).
Michael Balcon Collection.
Emeric Pressburger Collection.
Filippo Del Guidice Collection.
British Board of Film Censors Scenario Reports, 1944–49.

Museum of Modern Art, New York – Film Study Centre
Farrebique – reviews collection.

The Tom-Harrisson-Mass Observation Archive, University of Sussex
Harper, Sue and Vincent Porter, 'Weeping in the Cinema in 1950: A Re-assessment of Mass-Observation Material', Mass Observation Archive Occasional Paper no 3, 1995.
Topic Collection: Box 4, File A, 'Interviews'.
Topic Collection: Box 5, File A, 'Letters to *Picturegoer* Weekly', 1940–1941.
File Report 394, 'Mass Observation Film Work', 10 September 1940.
Box, Kathleen and Louis Moss, 'The Wartime Social Survey: The Cinema Audience, An Enquiry for MOI', 1943.
Box, Kathleen, 'The Social Survey: The Cinema and the Public: An Enquiry into Cinemagoing Habits and Expenditure made in 1946', Mass Observation, 1946.

Published Sources

Parliamentary Debates: House of Commons, 5th Series, Hansard, 1939–1950.
Action Catholique française: Centrale Catholique du Cinéma et radio (CCR), *Films français parus pendant l'occupation avec leur analyse morale*, CCR: Paris, 1945.
L'Institut français d'opinion publique, 1944–50.

Books

Unless otherwise indicated, the places of publication for books in English is London and for books in French, Paris.

Addison, Paul, *Now the War is Over: A Social History of Britain, 1945–51*, Pimlico, 1992.
— *The Road to 1945: British Politics and the Second World War*, Pimlico, 1994.
Agate, James, *Speak for England: An Anthology of Poetry and Prose for the Forces*, Hutchinson & Co., 1939.
Agel, Henri (ed.), *Sept ans du cinéma français*, Éditions du Cerf, 1953.
Ahrenfeldt, R.H., *Psychiatry in the Second World War*, Routledge, 1958.
Aldgate, Anthony and Jeffrey Richards, *The Best of British: Cinema and Society, 1930–1970*, Oxford: Blackwell, 1983.
— *Britain Can Take It: The British Cinema in the Second World War*, Edinburgh: Edinburgh University Press, 1994.
Ambler, Eric, *Here Lies Eric Ambler*, Weidenfeld & Nicolson, 1988.
Amouroux, Henri, *La Vie des français sous l'occupation*, Le Livre de Poche, 1961.
— *La Grande histoire des français sous l'occupation*, 5 Volumes, Laffont, 1976–93.
Anderson, Benedict, *Imagined Communities: Reflections on the Origin and Spread of Nationalism*, Verso, 1983.
Andrew, Dudley J., *Mists of Regret: Culture and Sensibility in Classic French Film*, Princeton: Princeton University Press, 1995.
L'Année Politique 1946, Éditions le Grand Siècle, 1946.
Anstey, Edgar, Forsyth Hardy, Ernest Lindgren and Roger Manvell (eds), *Shots in the Dark*, Allan Wingate, 1951.
Arland, Marcel, *Le Paysan français à travers la littérature*, Stock, 1941.
Arletty, *La Défense*, La Table Ronde, 1971.
Armes, Roy, *A Critical History of British Cinema*, Secker & Warburg, 1978.
— *French Cinema*, Secker & Warburg, 1985.
Aron, Robert with Georgette Elgey, *Histoire de Vichy, 1940–1944*, Fayard, 1954.
Ascoli, David, *The Queen's Peace: The Origins and Development of the Metropolitan Police*, Hamish Hamilton, 1979.
Aurenche, Jean, *La Suite à l'écran*, Lyon: Institut Lumière, 1993.
Autant-Lara, Claude, *Le Diable au corps*, Collection Cinéma Classique, 1984.
Azéma, Jean-Pierre, *From Munich to the Liberation, 1938–1944*, Cambridge: Cambridge University Press, 1984.
Balcon, Michael, Ernest Lindgren, Forsyth Hardy and Roger Manvell, *Twenty Years of British Film 1925–1945*, Falcon Press, 1947.
Balfour, Michael, *Propaganda in War 1939–1945: Organisations, Policies and Publics in Britain and Germany*, Routledge & Kegan Paul, 1979.
Bandy, Mary Lea, *Rediscovering French Film*, New York: Museum of Modern Art, 1983.
Barjon, Louis, *Le Paysan*, Le Puy: Xavier Mappus, 1942.

Barr, Charles, *Ealing Studios*, Studio Vista, 1993, first published in 1977.

— (ed.), *All Our Yesterdays: 90 Years of British Cinema*, BFI, 1986.

Barrot, Olivier, *L'Écran français 1943–1953: histoire d'un journal et d'une époque*, Les Éditeurs Français Réunis, 1979.

Bazin, André, *French Cinema of the Occupation and Resistance*, translated by Stanley Hochman. New York: Frederick Ungar, 1981.

Beckett, Francis, *Clem Attlee: A Biography*, Richard Cohen Books, 1997.

Bédarida, F. and J.P. Azéma (eds), *Le Régime de Vichy et les français*, Fayard, 1992.

Beevor, A. and A. Cooper, *Paris after the Liberation*, Hamish Hamilton, 1994.

Bell, P.M.H., *A Certain Eventuality: Britain and the Fall of France*, Saxon House, 1994.

— *France and Britain, 1940–1944: The Long Separation*, Longman, 1997.

Bellanger, C. H. Michel and C. Lévy, *Histoire générale de la presse française de 1940–1944*, P.U.F., 1975.

Bergonzi, Bernard, *English Literature and its Background, 1945–1960*, Oxford: Oxford University Press, 1993.

Bernot, L. and R. Blanchard, *Nouville: un village français*, Université de Paris, 1953.

Bernstein, Richard, *Fragile Glory: A Portrait of France and the French*, Bodley Head, 1991.

Bertin-Maghit, Jean-Pierre, *Le Cinéma français sous Vichy: Les Films français de 1940–1944*, Ça Cinéma, 1980.

— *Le Cinéma sous l'occupation*, Olivier Orban, 1989.

Bessy, Maurice, Raymond Chirat and André Bernard, *Histoire du cinéma français: encyclopédie des films 1951–1955 & 1956–1960*, Éditions Pygmalion-Gérard Watelet, 1989 and 1990.

— *Histoire du cinéma français: encyclopédie des films 1940–1950*, Éditions Pygmalion-Gérard Watelet, 1994.

Bettelheim, Charles and Suzanne Frère, *Une Ville française moyenne: Auxerre en 1950*, Armand Colin, 1950.

Blackwell, Trevor and Jeremy Seabrook, *A World Still to Win: Reconstruction of the Post-War Working Class*, Faber & Faber, 1985.

Bliss, Edward (ed.), *In Search of Light: The Broadcasts of Ed Murrow, 1938–1961*, Macmillan, 1968.

Bloch, Marc, *French Rural History: An Essay on its Basic Characteristics*, translated by Janet Sondheimer, Routledge & Kegan Paul, 1966, first published in 1931.

— *L'Étrange défaite: témoignage écrit en 1940*, Gallimard, 1990, first published in 1946.

Bogarde, Dirk, *Snakes and Ladders*, Triad-Panther, 1979.

Bonnell, Réné, *Le Cinéma Exploité*, Éditions du Seuil, 1978.

— *Le Vingt-cinquième image: une économie de l'audiovisuel*, Gallimard, 1989.

Bourke, Joanna, *Working-Class Cultures in Britain, 1890–1960*, Routledge, 1994.

Box, Kathleen and Louis Moss, *Wartime Social Survey: The Cinema Audience*, MOI, 1943.

Box, Muriel, *Odd Woman Out*, Leslie Frewin, 1974.

Briggs, Asa, *The History of Broadcasting in the UK*, vol. III: *The War of Words*, Oxford: Oxford University Press, 1970.

—*The BBC: The First Fifty Years*, Oxford: Oxford University Press, 1985.

Briggs, Susan, *The Home Front: The War Years in Britain, 1939–1945*, Weidenfeld & Nicolson, 1975.

Brooke, Stephen, *Reform and Reconstruction: Britain After the War 1945–1951*, Manchester: Manchester University Press, 1995.

Brown, Geoff, *Launder and Gilliat*, BFI, 1977.

Buache, Freddy, *Claude Autant-Lara*, Lausanne: L'Age d'Homme, 1982.

Bullock, Alan, *Hitler and Stalin: Parallel Lives*, HarperCollins, 1991.

Burch, Noël and Geneviève Sellier, *La Drôle du guerre des sexes du cinema français, 1930–1956*, Nathan, 1996.

Burrin, Philippe, *La France à l'heure allemande 1940–1944*, Éditions du Seuil, 1995.

Burton, Alan, Tim O'Sullivan and Paul Wells (eds), *Liberal Directions: Basil Dearden and Postwar British Film Culture*, Trowbridge: Flicks Books, 1997.

Buss, Robin, *French Film Noir*, Marion Boyars, 1994.

Calder, Angus, *The People's War: Britain 1939–45*, Panther Books Ltd., 1971.

— *The Myth of the Blitz*, Pimlico, 1992.

Calder, Angus and Dorothy Sheridan (eds), *Speak for Yourself: A Mass Observation Anthology*, Cape, 1984.

Calder, Angus and Paul Addison (eds), *Time To Kill: A Soldier's Experience of War in the West, 1939–1945*, Pimlico, 1997.

Cantril, Hadley (ed.), *Public Opinion 1939–1946*, Princeton: Princeton University Press, 1951.

Carné, Marcel, *Les Visiteurs du soir*, Balland, 1974.

— *La Vie à belle dents*, Jean-Pierre Olivier, 1975.

Carter, Erica, James Donald and Judith Squires (eds), *Space and Place: Theories of Identity and Location*, Lawrence & Wishart, 1993.

Chapman, James, *The British at War: Cinema, State and Propaganda*, I. B. Tauris, 1998.

Charensol, Georges, *La Renaissance du cinéma français*, Éditions du Sagittaire, 1946.

Chevalier, Louis, *Les Paysans*, Denoël, 1947.

Chibnall, Steve and Robert Murphy (eds), *British Crime Cinema*, Routledge, 1999.

Chirat, Raymond and P.H. Chombart de Lauwe, *La Vie quotidienne des familles ouvrières*, CNRS, 1977.

Christie, Ian, *Arrows of Desire: The Films of Michael Powell and Emeric Pressburger*, Faber & Faber, 1994.

Churchill, Winston, *The War Speeches of the Rt. Hon. Winston S. Churchill*, compiled by Charles Eade, 3 vols, Cassell, 1951.

Clark, David (ed.), *Marriage, Domestic Life and Social Change: Writings for Jacqueline Burgoyne (1944–88)*, Routledge, 1991.

Clark, Kenneth, *Henry Moore Drawings*, Thames & Hudson, 1974.

Cobb, Richard, *French and Germans, Germans and French: A Personal Interpretation of France under Two Occupations, 1914–1918 and 1940–1944*, New Hampshire: University Press of New England, 1983.

— *A Second Identity: Essays on France and French History*, Oxford: Oxford University Press, 1969.

Cohen, Anthony P., *Belonging: Identity and Social Organisation in British Rural Cultures*, Manchester: Manchester University Press, 1982.

Cohen-Séat, Gilbert, *Essai sur les principes d'une philosophie du cinéma*, Presses Universitaires de France, 1946.

Collette-Kahn, Suzanne, *Femme, tu vas voter: comment?*, Éditions de la Liberté, 1945.

Colls, Robert and Philip Dodd (eds), *Englishness: Politics and Culture, 1880–1920*, Croom Helm, 1986.

Cook, Chris, and Alan Sked, *Post-War Britain: A Political History*, Brighton: Harvester Press, 1992.

Cook, Pam (ed.), *The Cinema Book*, BFI, 1985.

— *Fashioning the Nation: Costume and Identity in British Cinema*, BFI, 1996.

— (ed.), *Gainsborough Pictures*, Cassell, 1997.

Costello, John, *Love, Sex and War: Changing Values, 1939–45*, Pan/Collins, 1986.

Courtade, François, *Les Malédictions du cinéma français*, Alain Moreau, 1978.

Crisp, Colin, *The Classic French Cinema 1930–1960*, Bloomington, Indiana: Indiana University Press, 1993.

Critchley, T.A., *A History of the Police in England and Wales, 1900–1966*, Constable, 1967.

Crosby, Travis L., *The Impact of Civilian Evacuation in the Second World War*, Croom Helm, 1986.

Crossley, C. and T. Small (eds), *Studies in Anglo-French Cultural Relations: Imagining France*, Macmillan, 1988.

Curran, James and Vincent Porter (eds), *British Cinema History*, Weidenfeld & Nicolson, 1983.

Daniel, Joseph, *Guerre et cinéma: grandes illusions et petits soldats 1895–1971*, Armand Colin, 1972.

Dank, Milton, *The French Against the French: Collaboration and Resistance*, Cassell, 1978.

Daquin, Louis, *Le Cinéma, notre métier*, Les Éditeurs Français Réunis, 1960.

Dauzat, Albert, *Le Village et le paysan de France*, Gallimard, 1941.

— *La Vie rurale, des origines à nos jours*, Presses Universitaires, 1946.

Day-Lewis, Tamsin (ed.), *Last Letters Home*, Macmillan, 1995.

de Beauvoir, Simone, *The Second Sex*, translated by H.M.Parshley, Penguin, 1972, first published as *Le Deuxième Sexe* in 1949.

De Comes, Philippe and Michael Marmin (eds), *Le Cinéma français, 1930–1960*, Atlas, 1984.

Degand, Claude, *Le Cinéma… cette industrie*, Éditeurs Techniques et Économiques, 1972.

Delarue, Jacques, *Trafics et crimes sous l'occupation*, Fayard, 1968.

Desert, G. (ed.), *La Normandie de 1900 à nos jours*, Toulouse: Privat, 1978.

Diamond, Hanna, *Women and the Second World War in France, 1939–1948*, Longman, 1999.

Dick, Eddie (ed.), *From Limelight to Satellite: A Scottish Film Book*, BFI, 1990.

Dickinson, Margaret and Sarah Street, *Cinema and State: The Film Industry and the Government, 1927–84*, BFI, 1985.

Diville, W. and A. Guilcher, *Bretagne et Normandie*, P.U.F., 1951.

Dixon-Wheeler, Winston (ed.), *Re-viewing British Cinema 1900–1992: Essays and Interviews*, Albany, New York: State University of New York Press, 1994.

Donnison, D.V., *Housing Policy Since the War*, Harmondsworth: Penguin, 1960.

Dourdin Institute, *'42,995,000 Frenchmen Can't Be Wrong (Because 3,578 Must Be Right)': A Survey Conducted by the Dourdin Institute for the French National Cinema Center'*, translated by Jack Palmer White, 1954.

Duby, Georges, *Histoire de la France urbaine: Volume 5: La Ville aujourd'hui*, Seuil, 1985.

— *Histoire de la France rurale, Volume 4: De 1914 à nos jours*, Seuil, 1976.

Duby, Georges and Michelle Perrot (eds), *Histoire des femmes en occident, volume 5*, Plon, 1991.

Duchen, Claire, *Women's Rights and Women's Lives in France 1944–1968*, Routledge, 1994.

Duchen, Claire and Irene Bandhauer-Schöffman (eds), *When the War Was Over: Women, War and Peace in Europe, 1940–1956*, Leicester University Press, 2000.

Durand, Jacques, *Le Cinéma et son public*, Sirey, 1958.

Durand, Yves, *Prisonniers de guerre dans les stalags, les oflags et les kommandos*, Hatchett, 1987.

Dutton, David, *British Politics Since 1945: The Rise, Fall and Rebirth of Consensus*, Oxford: Blackwell, 1991.

Dyer, Richard and Ginette Vincendeau, *Popular European Cinemas*, Routledge, 1992.

Ehrlich, Evelyn, *Cinema of Paradox: French Filmmaking under the German Occupation*, Columbia University Press, 1985.

Ellis, John, *The Sharp End: The Fighting Man in World War Two*, Pimlico, 1993.

Ellwood, David W. and Rob Kroes (eds), *Hollywood in Europe: Experiences of a Cultural Hegemony, Amsterdam*, VU University Press, 1994.

Emsley, Clive, *The English Police: A Political and Social History*, Longman, 1991.

Etien, Robert, *La SNCF: histoire, organisation, perspectives*, Bordeaux: LycoFac, 1991.

Etzioni, Amitai, *The Spirit of Community: Rights, Responsibilities and the Communitarian Agenda*, Fontana Press, 1995.

Evans, Mary and David Morgan, *The Battle for Britain: Citizenship and Ideology in the Second World War*, Routledge, 1993.

Ezra, Elizabeth and Sue Harris (eds), *France in Focus: Film and National Identity*, Berg, 2000.

Faure, Christian, *Le Projet culturel de Vichy: Folklore et revolution nationale, 1940–44*, Presses Universitaires de Lyon, 1989.

Fauvet, J. and H. Mendras (eds), *Les Paysans et la politique dans la France contemporaine*, Armand Colin, 1958.

Feldman, David and Gareth Stedman-Jones (eds), *Metropolis, London: Histories and Representations Since 1800*, Routledge, 1989.

Ferguson, Marjorie, *Forever Feminine: Women's Magazines and the Cult of Femininity*, Heinemann, 1983.

Ferguson, Sheila and Hilde Fitzgerald, *The History of the Second World War: Studies in the Social Services: United Kingdom Civil Series*, HMSO, 1955.

Feyder, Jacques and Françoise Rosay, *Le Cinéma: notre métier*, Callier, 1946.

Fishman, Sarah, *We Will Wait: Wives of French Prisoners of War*, Yale: University Press, 1991.

Fishman, Sarah, Laura Lee-Downs, Ioannis Sinanoglou et al. (eds), *France at War: Vichy and the Historians*, Berg, 2000.

Forbes, Jill, *Les Enfants du paradis*, BFI, 1997.

Ford, Charles, *Histoire du cinéma français contemporaine, 1945–1977*, Éditions France-Empire, 1977.

— *Pierre Fresnay: gentilhomme de l'écran*, Éditions France-Empire, 1981.

Forster, Margaret, *Daphne du Maurier*, Chatto & Windus, 1993.

Fowler, Roy, *The Film in France*, Pendulum Publications, 1946.

Franck, Christiane (ed.), *La France de 1945: Resistances, Retours, Renaissances*, Caen: Presses Universitaires de Caen, 1996.

French, Philip and Michael Sissons (eds), *The Age of Austerity*, Hodder & Stoughton, 1963.

Fussell, Paul, *Wartime: Understanding and Behaviour in the Second World War*, Oxford: Oxford University Press, 1989.

Garçon, François, *De Blum à Pétain: cinéma et société française*, Les Éditions du Cerf, 1984.

Gaute, J.H.H. and Robin Odell, *The Murderer's Who's Who: 150 Years of Notorious Murder Cases*, Harrap, 1979.

Gélin, Daniel, *Deux ou trois vies qui sont les miennes*, Julliard, 1977.

Geraghty, Christine, *British Cinema in the Fifties: Gender, Genre and the 'New Look'*, Routledge, 2000.

Gildea, Robert, *France Since 1945*, Oxford: Oxford University Press, 1997.

Giraudoux, Jean, *'The France of Tomorrow'*: an address delivered on February 22nd 1940 at the American Club of Paris, Centre d'Informations Documentaires, 1940.

Gledhill, Christine and Gillian Swanson (eds), *Nationalising Femininity: Culture, Sexuality and British Cinema in the Second World War*, Manchester: Manchester University Press, 1996.

Goodman, Derick, *Villany Unlimited: The Truth about the French Underworld Today*, Elek Books, 1957.

Gorer, Geoffrey, *Exploring English Character*, Cresset Press, 1955.

Gough-Yates, Kevin, *Michael Powell in Collaboration with Emeric Pressburger*, BFI, 1971.

Gouthier, J., *Naissance d'un grand cité: Le Mans au milieu du XXe siècle*, Colin, 1953.

Grafton, Pete, *You, You and You, The People Out of Step with World War Two*, Pluto, 1981.

Greene, Naomi, *Landscapes of Loss: The National Past in Postwar French Cinema*, Princeton University Press, 1999.

Guérif, François, *Le Cinéma policier français*, Veyrier, 1981.

Guillon, J.M. and P. Laborie (eds), *Mémoire et histoire: la Résistance*, Toulouse: Éditions Privat, 1995.

Halls, W.D., *The Youth of Vichy France*, Oxford: Clarendon Press, 1981.

Harper, Sue, *Picturing the Past: The Rise and Fall of the British Costume Film*, BFI, 1994.

— *Mad, Bad and Dangerous to Know: Women in British Cinema*, Continuum, 2000.

Harrisson, Tom, *Living Through the Blitz*, Collins, 1976.

Hayward, Susan, *French National Cinema*, Routledge, 1993.

Hayward, Susan and Ginette Vincendeau (eds), *French Film: Texts and Contexts*, Routledge, 1990.

Hennessy, Peter, *Never Again: Britain 1945–1951*, Vintage, 1993.

Hewison, Robert, *Under Siege: Literary Life in London 1939–1945*, Methuen, 1988.

— *Culture and Consensus: England, Art and Politics since 1940*, Methuen, 1995.

Hewitt, Nicholas (ed.), *The Culture of Reconstruction: European Literature, Thought and Film, 1945–50*, Basingstoke: Macmillan, 1989.

Higonnet, M.R., J. Jenson, S. Michel and M.C. Weitz (eds), *Behind the Lines: Gender and the Two World Wars*, Yale: Yale University Press, 1987.

Higson, Andrew (ed.), *Dissolving Views: Key Articles on British Cinema*, Cassell, 1996.

— *Waving the Flag: Constructing a National Cinema in Britain*, Oxford: Clarendon Press, 1997.

Hill, John, *Sex, Class and Realism: British Cinema, 1956–1963*, BFI, 1986.

Hillary, Richard, *The Last Enemy*, Macmillan, 1942.

Hiller, Bevis and Mary Banham (eds), *A Tonic to the Nation: The Festival of Britain, 1951*, Thames & Hudson, 1976.

Hirschfeld, E. and P. Marsh (eds), *Collaboration and France: Politics and Culture during the Nazi Occupation, 1940–1944*, Oxford: Berg, 1989.

Hobsbawm, Eric, *The Age of Extremes: The Short Twentieth Century, 1914–1991*, Michael Joseph, 1994.

Hoffman, Stanley (ed.), *In Search of France*, Massachusetts: Harvard University Press, 1963.

— *Decline or Renewal?: France Since the 1930s*, New York: Viking, 1974.

Hoggart, Richard, *The Uses of Literacy*, Chatto & Windus, 1957.

Holden, C.H. and W.G. Holford, *City of London: A Record of Destruction and Survival*, Architectural Press, 1951.

228 Film and Community: Britain and France

Holman, Bob, *Evacuation: A Very British Revolution*, Oxford: Lion Publishing, 1995.

Hopkins, Harry, *The New Look: A Social History of the Forties and Fifties in Britain*, Secker & Warburg, 1963.

Hopkinson, Tom, *Picture Post, 1938–1950*, Allen Lane, 1970.

Houston, Penelope, *Went the Day Well?*, BFI, 1992.

Howorth J. and P.G. Cerny (eds), *Élites in France: Origins, Reproduction and Power*, Frances Pinter, 1978.

Hurd, Geoff (ed.), *National Fictions: World War Two in British Films and Television*, BFI, 1984.

Inglis, Ruth, *The Children's War: Evacuation 1939–1945*, Collins, 1989.

Jackson, Julian, *France: The Dark Years: 1940–1944*, Oxford: Oxford University Press, 2001.

Jeancolas, Jean-Pierre, *15 ans d'années trente: Le Cinéma français, 1929–1944*, Stock, 1983.

Johnson, B.S., *The Evacuees*, Gollancz, 1968.

Judt, Tony, *Past Imperfect: French Intellectuals 1944–1956*, Berkeley: University of California Press, 1992.

Kedward, H.R. (ed.), *Resistance in Vichy France: A Study of Ideals and Motivation in the Southern Zone, 1940–1942*, Oxford: Oxford University Press, 1978.

— (ed.), *Vichy France and the Resistance: Culture and Ideology*, Croom Helm, 1985.

— *Occupied France: Collaboration and Resistance, 1940–1944*, Oxford: Blackwell, 1985.

— *In Search of the Maquis*, Oxford: Oxford University Press, 1993.

Kedward, H.R. and Nancy Wood (eds), *The Liberation of France: Image and Event*, Oxford: Berg, 1995.

Kennedy, Paul, *The Rise and Fall of the Great Powers: Economic Change and Military Conflict from 1500 to 2000*, Fontana Press, 1989.

Kirkham, Pat and David Wood (eds), *War Culture: Social Change and Changing Experience in World War Two*, Lawrence & Wishart, 1995.

Klein, Holger (ed.), *The Second World War in Fiction*, Macmillan, 1984.

Knight, Vivienne, *Trevor Howard: A Gentleman and a Player*, Sphere Books Ltd., 1986.

Kobal, John, *People Will Talk*, Aurum Press, 1986.

Kramer, Rita, *Flames in the Field*, Michael Joseph, 1995.

Kuisel, Richard, *Seducing the French: The Dilemma of Americanisation*, Berkeley: University of California, 1993.

Lacourbe, Roland, *Henri-Georges Clouzot*, Anthologie du Cinéma, 1966.

Lambourne, Nicola, *War Damage in Western Europe: The Destruction of Historical Monuments During the Second World War*, Edinburgh University Press, 2001.

Landy, Marcia, *British Genres: Cinema and Society, 1930–1960*, Princeton: Princeton University Press, 1991.

Lant, Antonia, *Blackout: Reinventing Women for Wartime British Cinema*, Princeton: Princeton University Press, 1991.

Lapierre, Marcel, *Aux Portes de la nuit: La roman d'un film de Marcel Carné*, Nouvelle Édition, 1946.

Larkin, Maurice, *France Since the Popular Front: Government and People 1936–1986*, Oxford: Oxford University Press, 1988.

Le Boterf, Hervé, *La Vie parisienne sous l'occupation 1940–1944*, Éditions France-Empire, 1974.

Lebovics, Herman, *True France: The Wars Over Cultural Identity, 1900–1945*, New York: Cornell University Press, 1992.

Leglise, Paul, *Histoire de la politique du cinéma français: Volume 2: Le cinéma entre deux républiques 1940–1946*, L'Herminier, 1977.

Lehning, James, *Peasant and French: Cultural Contact in Rural France During the Nineteenth Century*, Cambridge: Cambridge University Press, 1995.

Lejeune, C.A., *Chestnuts in Her Lap, 1936–1946*, Phoenix House, 1947.

Leprohon, Pierre, *Julien Duvivier*, Éditions Debresse, 1957.

Lewin, Christophe, *Le Retour des Prisonniers de Guerre: Naissance et Développement de la Fédération Nationale de Prisonniers de Guerre*, Publications de la Sorbonne, 1986.

Lewis, Jane, *Women in Britain Since 1945*, Oxford: Blackwell, 1991.

Lewis, Peter, *A People's War*, Methuen, 1986.

Lewis, Roy and Angus Maude, *The English Middle Classes*, Bath: Chivers, 1973, first published in 1949.

Lochner, Louis (ed.), *The Goebbels Diaries (1942–1943)*, translated by Louis Lochner, New York: Doubleday & Co., 1948.

Longmate, Norman, *The G.I.'s: The Americans in Britain, 1939–1945*, Hutchinson, 1975.

Lottman, Herbert, *The People's Anger: Justice and Revenge in Post-Liberation France*, Hutchinson, 1986.

Loubier, Jean-Marc, *Louis Jouvet: Biographie*, Éditions Ramsay, 1986.

Lowe, Philip and Maryvonnne Bodiguel (eds), *Rural Studies in Britain and France*, Bellhaven Press, 1990.

Macdonald, Kevin, *Emeric Pressburger: The Life and Death of a Screenwriter*, Faber & Faber, 1994.

Mack, Joanna and Steve Humphries, *London at War: The Making of Modern London, 1939–1945*, Sidgwick & Jackson, 1985.

Mannheim, Herbert, *Group Problems in Crime and Punishment and other Studies in Criminology and Criminal Law*, Routledge, 1955.

Manvell, Roger (ed.), *The Cinema: 1951*, Harmondsworth: Penguin, 1951.

Marais, Jean, *Histoires de ma vie*, Éditions Aubin Michel, 1975.

Marceau, Jane, *Class and Status in France: Change and Social Immobility 1945–1975*, Oxford: Clarendon Press, 1977.

Marchetti, Stephane, *Affiches 1939–1945: Images d'une certaine France*, Lausanne: Edita, 1982.

Marrus, Michael and Robert Paxton, *Vichy France and the Jews*, New York: Basic Books, 1981.

Marsh, Jan, *Back to the Land: The Pastoral Impulse in England 1880–1914*, Quartet Books Ltd., 1982.

Marwick, Arthur, *The Nature of History*, Macmillan, 1970.

— *War and Social Change in the Twentieth Century: A Comparative Study of Britain, France, Germany, Russia and the United States*, Macmillan, 1974.

— *The Home Front*, Thames & Hudson, 1976.

— *Class, Image and Reality in Britain, France and the USA since 1930*, Collins, 1980.

Maspetiol, Roland, *L'Ordre éternel du champs: essai sur l'histoire, l'économie et les valeurs de la paysannerie*, Librairie de Médicis, 1946.

Mass Observation, *The War Factory*, Gollancz, 1943.

— *The Journey Home*, John Murray, 1944.

— *Nella Last's War*, Fallingwall Press, 1981.

Matard-Bonucci, Marie-Anne and Edouard Lynch (eds), *La Libération des camps et le Retour des déportés*, Brussels: Éditions Complexe, 1995.

Mayer, J.P., *Sociology of Film*, Faber & Faber, 1946.

— *British Cinemas and their Audiences*, Dennis Dobson, 1948.

McAleer, Joseph, *Popular Reading and Publishing in Britain (1914–1950)*, Oxford: Clarendon Press, 1992.

McFarlane, Brian (ed.), *Sixty Voices: Celebrities Recall the Golden Age of British Cinema*, BFI, 1992.

— *An Autobiography of British Cinema*, Methuen, 1997.

McLaine, Ian, *Ministry of Morale: Home Front Morale and the MOI in World War II*, Allen & Unwin, 1979.

McMillan, J.F., *Housewife or Harlot: The Place of Women in French Society, 1870–1940*, Brighton: Harvester, 1981.

— *Dreyfus to De Gaulle: Politics and Society in France, 1889–1969*, Edward Arnold, 1985.

McNab, Geoffrey, *J. Arthur Rank and the British Film Industry*, Routledge, 1993.

Mellor, David (ed.), *A Paradise Lost: The Neo-Romantic Imagination in Britain, 1935–1955*, Lund Humphries, 1987.

Mendras, Henri, *Études de sociologie rurale: Novis et Virgin*, Colin, 1953.

— *La Fin des paysans: innovation et changement dans l'agriculture*, S.E.D.E.I.S, 1984.

Mercillon, Henri, *Cinéma et monopoles – le cinéma aux états-unis: étude économique*, Colin, 1953.

Meyer, Jacques (ed.), *Vie et morts des français*, Tallendier, 1980.

Micaud, H., *The French Right and Nazi Germany, 1933–39: A Study of Public Opinion*, Durham, North Carolina: Duke University Press, 1943.

Michel, Henri, *The Shadow War: Resistance in Europe, 1939–1945*, Corgi Books, 1972.

— *Pétain et le régime de Vichy*, P.U.F., 1978.

Michalczyk, John J., *The French Literary Filmmakers*, Philadelphia: The Art Alliance Press, 1980.

Miles, Peter and Malcolm Smith, *Cinema, Literature and Society: Elite and Mass Culture in Interwar Britain*, Croom Helm, 1987.

Millar, Ronald, *A View From The Wings*, Weidenfeld & Nicolson, 1993.

Mills, John, *Up in the Clouds, Gentlemen Please*, Harmondsworth: Penguin, 1981.

Milward, Alan S., *The New Order and French Economy*, Aldershot: Gregg Revivals, 1993.

Minar, David W. and Scott Greer, *The Concept of Community: Readings with Interpretations*, Chicago: Aldine Publishing Co., 1969.

Morgan, Guy, *Red Roses Every Night: An Account of London Cinemas Under Fire*, Quality Press, 1948.

Morgan, Kenneth O., *Labour in Power, 1945–1951*, Oxford: Clarendon Press, 1984.

Morgan, Michèle, *Mes yeux ont vu*, France Loisirs, 1977.

Morley, Sheridan, *A Talent to Amuse: A Biography of Noel Coward*, Harmondsworth: Penguin, 1974.

Morris, Terence, *Crime and Criminal Justice Since 1945*, Oxford: Blackwell, 1989.

Morsley, Clifford, *News From the English Countryside (1851–1950)*, Harrap, 1983.

Morton, H.V., *I Saw Two Englands*, Methuen, 1942.

Moss, Louis, *The Government Social Survey: A History*, HMSO, 1991.

Moulin, Annie, *Peasantry and Society in France Since 1789*, Cambridge: Cambridge University Press, 1991.

Muel-Dreyfus, Francine, *Vichy et l'éternel féminin*, Éditions de Seuil, 1996.

Munton, Alan, *English Fiction of the Second World War*, Faber & Faber, 1989.

Murphy, Robert, *Realism and Tinsel: Cinema and Society 1939–49*, Routledge, 1989.

— (ed.), *The British Cinema Book*, BFI, 1997.

— *British Cinema and the Second World War*, Continuum 2000.

Murray, Keith A.H., *The History of the Second World War: Agriculture: United Kingdom Civil Series*, HMSO, 1955.

Myrdal, Alva and Viola Klein, *Women's Two Roles: Home and Work*, Routledge & Kegan Paul, 1956.

Naumann, Claude, *Jacques Becker*, Bibliothèque du film/Durante, 2001.

Neagle, Anna, *There's Always Tomorrow*, Everest Pictures, 1974.

Nettlebeck, Colin A., *War and Identity: The French and the Second World War*, Methuen, 1987.

— *Forever French: Exile in the United States, 1939–1945*, Oxford: Berg, 1991.

Newby, Howard, *Community Studies: An Introduction to the Sociology of the Local Community*, Allen & Unwin, 1971.

— *Country Life: A Social History of Rural England*, Weidenfeld & Nicolson, 1987.

Niven, David, *The Moon's a Balloon*, Coronet Books, Hodder & Stoughton, 1972.

Noakes, Lucy, *War and the British: Gender, Memory and National Identity*, I. B. Tauris, 1998.

Noble, Peter (ed.), *The British Film Yearbook 1947–1948*, Skelton Robinson, undated.

Nora, Pierre (ed.), *The Realms of Memory: Rethinking the French Past: Volume 1: Conflicts and Divisions*, New York: Columbia University Press, 1992.

Novick, Peter, *The Resistance v. Vichy: The Purge of Collaboration in Liberated France*, New York: Columbia University Press, 1968.

Nuffield College, *Britain's Town and Country Pattern: A Summary of the Barlow, Scott and Uthwatt Reports*, Faber & Faber, 1944.

Ollier, Nicole, *L'exode sur les routes de l'an 40*, Laffont, 1970.

Orwell, George, *The Lion and the Unicorn: Socialism and the English Genius*, Secker & Warburg, 1941.

— *The English People*, Collins, 1947.

Orwell, Sonia and Ian Angus (eds), *The Collected Essays, Journalism and Letters of George Orwell, Volume 2: My Country Right or Left*, Harmondsworth: Penguin, 1970.

Orwin, C.S., *Speed the Plough*, Harmondsworth: Penguin, 1941.

Ory, Pascal, *La France allemande, 1933–1945*, Gallimard: Julliard, 1977.

— *L'Aventure culturelle française, 1945–1989*, Flammarion, 1989.

Ousby, Ian, *Occupation: The Ordeal of France 1940–1944*, John Murray, 1997.

Paxton, Robert, *Vichy France: Old Guard and New Order 1940–1944*, Barrie & Jenkins, 1972.

Pedersen, Susan, *Family, Dependence and the Origins of the Welfare State: Britain and France, 1914–1945*, Cambridge: Cambridge University Press, 1994.

Perrault, Gilles, *Paris under the Occupation*, André Deutsch, 1989.

Pétain, Philippe, *La France nouvelle: principes de la communauté*, Fasquelle, 1941.

Pierre, Marcel, *Aux Portes de la nuit: La roman d'un film de Marcel Carné*, Nouvelle Édition, 1946.

Polonski, Jacques, *La Presse, la propagande et l'opinion publique sous l'occupation*, Éditions du Centre de Documentation Juive Contemporaine, 1946.

Porter, Roy, *London: A Social History*, Hamish Hamilton, 1994.

Pourrat, Henri, *Le Paysan français*, Clermont, 1941.

Powell, Dilys, *Films Since 1939*, Longmans-British Council, 1947.

Powell, Michael, *A Life in Movies: An Autobiography*, Methuen, 1987.

Presle, Micheline, *L'Arrière Mémoire: conversation avec Serge Toubiana*, Flammarion, 1994.

Prévert, Jacques, *Le Crime de Monsieur Lange, Les Portes de la nuit: Scénarios*, Gallimard, 1990.

Priestley, J.B., *English Journey*, Harmondsworth: Penguin, 1977, first published in 1934.

— *Postscripts*, William Heinemann, 1940.

— *Out of the People*, Collins/William Heinemann, 1941.

— *The Arts Under Socialism*, Turnstile Press, 1947.

— *All England Listened*, New York: Chilmark Press, 1967.

Pronay, Nicholas and Frances Thorpe, *British Official Films in the Second World War: A Descriptive Catalogue*, Clio Press, 1980.

Pronay, Nicholas and D.W. Spring (eds), *Propaganda: Politics and Film, 1918–1945*, Macmillan, 1982.

Quoist, Michel, *La Ville et l'homme: Rouen: étude sociologique d'un secteur prolitarien*, Les Éditions Ouvrières, 1952.

Raison-Jourde, F., *La Colonie auvergnate de Paris au XIX siècle*, Commission de travail historiques, 1976.

Rattigan, Neil, *This is England: British Film and the People's War, 1939–1945*, Associated University Presses/Farleigh Dickinson, 2001.

Rearick, Charles, *The French in Love and War: Popular Culture in France 1914–1945*, Yale: Yale University Press, 1997.

Redgrave, Michael, *In My Mind's Eye: An Autobiography, Coronet Books*, Hodder & Stoughton, 1983.

Reed-Danahay, Deborah, *Education and Identity in Rural France: The Politics of Schooling*, Cambridge: Cambridge University Press, 1996.

Régent, Roger, *Cinéma de France, de 'La Fille du pusiatier' aux 'Enfants du paradis'*, Éditions d'Aujourd'hui, 1975.

Reynolds, Siân (ed.), *State and Revolution: Essays on Power and Gender in Europe since 1789*, Wheatsheaf, 1986.

Richards, Jeffrey, *Films and British National Identity: From Dickens to Dad's Army*, Manchester: Manchester University Press, 1997.

— (ed.), *The Unknown 1930s: An Alternative History of the British Cinema, 1929–1939*, I. B. Tauris, 1997.

Rigby, Brian and Nicholas Hewitt (eds), *France and the Mass Media*, Macmillan, 1995.

Riley, Denise, *War in the Nursery: Theories of the Child and the Mother*, Virago, 1983.

Rioux, Jean-Pierre, *The Fourth Republic*, translated by Geoffrey Rogers, Cambridge: Cambridge University Press, 1987.

Rogers, Susan Carol, *Shaping Modern Times in Rural France: The Transformation and Reproduction of an Aveyronnais Community*, Princeton: Princeton University Press, 1991.

Ross, Kristen, *Fast Cars, Clean Bodies: Decolonisation and the Re-ordering of French Culture*, Massachussetts: The MIT Press, 1995.

Rousso, Henry, *The Vichy Syndrome: History and Memory in France Since 1944*, translated by Arthur Goldhammer, Cambridge, Massachusetts: Harvard University Press, 1994.

Sadoul, Georges, *French Film*, Falcon Press, 1953.

— *Gérard Philipe*, Pierre L'Herminier, 1979.

Samuel, Raphael (ed.), *Patriotism: The Making and un-making of British National Identity, Volume 3: National Fictions*, Routledge, 1989.

— *Theatres of Memory: Volume 1: Past and Present in Contemporary Culture*, Verso, 1994.

Sansom, William, *The Blitz: Westminster at War*, Oxford: Oxford University Press, 1990.

Sartre, Jean-Paul, *Situations III*, Gallimard, 1949.

Savage, Mike and Andrew Miles, *The Remaking of the British Working Class 1840–1940*, Routledge, 1994.

Scargill, Ian, *Urban France*, Croom Helm, 1983.

Scherer, Jacqueline, *Contemporary Community: Sociological Illusion or Reality?*, Tavistock, 1972.

Sheridan, Dorothy and Jeffrey Richards, *Mass Observation at the Movies*, Routledge & Kegan Paul, 1987.

Shinwell, Emanuel, *When the Men Come Home*, Victor Gollancz, 1944.

Short, John R., *The Post-war Experience: Housing in Britain*, Methuen, 1982.

Short, K.M. (ed.), *Film and Radio Propaganda in World War II*, Beckenham: Croom Helm, 1983.

Sibley, David, *Outsiders in Urban Societies*, Oxford: Basil Blackwell, 1981.

Siclier, Jacques, *La France de Pétain et son cinéma*, Henri Veyrier, 1981.

Sieglohr, Ulrike (ed.), *Heroines without Heroes: Reconstructing Female and National Identities in European Cinema, 1945–51*, Cassell, 2000.

Signoret, Simone, *Nostalgia Isn't What It Used To Be*, Harper & Row, 1978.

Sinclair, Andrew, *War Like a Wasp: The Lost Decade of the Forties*, Hamish Hamilton, 1989.

Smith, Harold L. (ed.), *War and Social Change British Society in the Second World War*, Manchester: Manchester University Press, 1986.

Sorlin, Pierre, *European Cinemas, European Societies*, Routledge, 1991.

Street, Sarah, *British National Cinema*, Routledge, 1997.

Sullerot, Evelyne, *La Presse féminine*, Armand Colin, 1963.

Summerfield, Penny, *Women Workers in the Second World War: Production and Patriarchy in Conflict*, Croom Helm, 1984.

Sweets, John F., *Choices in Vichy France: The French under Nazi Occupation*, Oxford: Oxford University Press, 1986.

Taylor, A.J.P., *English History, 1914–1945*, Oxford: Clarendon Press, 1964.

Taylor, D.J., *After the War: The Novel and England Since 1945*, Chatto & Windus, 1993.

Taylor, Philip M., *Britain and the Cinema in the Second World War*, Macmillan, 1988.

Thomas, R.T., *Britain and Vichy: The Dilemma of Anglo-French Relations, 1940–1942*, Macmillan, 1979.

Tims, Hilton, *Once A Wicked Lady: A Biography of Margaret Lockwood*, Virgin, 1989.

Titmuss, Richard, *The History of the Second World War: Problems of Social Policy: United Kingdom Civil Series*, HMSO, 1950.

Turk, E.B., *Child of Paradise: Marcel Carné*, Cambridge, Massachusetts: Harvard University Press, 1989.

Turner, Barry and Tony Rennell, *When Daddy Came Home: How Family Life Changed Forever in 1945*, Hutchinson, 1995.

Vernant, Jacques, *The Refugee in the Post War World*, George Allen & Unwin Ltd., 1953.

Vesey-Fitzgerald, Brian, *The British Countryside*, Odhams Press, 1946.

Veillon, Dominique, *La Mode sous l'occupation: débrouillarde et coquetterie dans la France en guerre, 1939–1945*, Éditions Payot, 1990.

Vey, Jean-Louis, *Jacques Becker ou la fausse évidence*, Aléas, 1995.

Vincendeau, Ginette and Keith Reader (eds), *La Vie est à nous: French Cinema of the Popular Front*, BFI, 1986.

Waller, Jane and Michael Vaughan Rees, *Women in Wartime: The Role of Women's Magazines, 1939–1945*, Macdonald Optima, 1987.

Walter, Gérard, *La Vie à Paris sous l'occupation 1940–1944*, Armand Colin, 1960.

— *Histoire du paysan français*, Flammarion, 1963.

Wapshott, Nicholas, *The Man Between: A Biography of Carol Reed*, Chatto & Windus, 1990.

Ward, Sadie, *War in the Countryside*, Cameron Books, 1988.

Warren, Henry C., *England is a Village*, Eyre & Spottiswoode, 1940.

Webster, Wendy, *Imagining Home: Gender, 'Race' and National Identity, 1945–64*, UCL, 1998.

Weight, Richard and Abigail Beach (eds), *The Right to Belong: Citizenship and National Identity in Britain, 1930–1960*, I. B. Tauris, 1998.

Welsby, Paul, *A History of the Church of England, 1945–1980*, Oxford: Oxford University Press, 1984.

Werth, Alexander, *The Last Days of Paris*, Hamish Hamilton, 1940.

White, Cynthia P., *Women's Magazines, 1693–1968*, Michael Joseph, 1970.

Wicks, Ben, *Welcome Home: True Stories of Soldiers Returning from World War Two*, Bloomsbury, 1991.

Wiener, Martin J., *English Culture and the Decline of the Industrial Spirit, 1850–1950*, Cambridge: Cambridge University Press, 1981.

Wieviorka, Annette, *Déportation et génocide: entre mémoire et l'oubli*, Plon, 1992.

Williams, Raymond, *The Country and the City*, Chatto & Windus, 1972.

— *Keywords: A Vocabulary of Culture and Society*, Croom Helm, 1976.

Wilson, Elizabeth, *Women and the Welfare State*, Tavistock, 1977.

Wolfenstein, Martha and Nathan Leites, *Movies: A Psychological Study*, Glencoe, Illinois: The Free Press, 1950.

Wormser-Migot, Olga, *Le Retour de deportés: Quand les Alliés ouvrient les portes*, Brussels: Éditions Complexe, 1985.

Worpole, Ken, *Dockers and Detectives*, Verso, 1983.

Wright, Gordon, *Rural Revolution in France: The Peasantry in the Twentieth Century*, Stanford: Stanford University Press, 1964.

— *Between the Guillotine and Liberty: Two Centuries of the Crime Problem in France*, Oxford: Oxford University Press, 1982.

Wright, Patrick, *On Living in an Old Country: The National Past in Contemporary Britain*, Verso, 1985.

Wylie, Laurence, *A Village in the Vaucluse*, Cambridge, Massachusetts: Harvard University Press, 1957.
Young, John W., *Britain, France and the Unity Of Europe, 1945–1951*, Leicester: Leicester University Press, 1984.
Young, Malcolm, *An Inside Job: Policing and Police Culture in Britain*, Clarendon Press, 1991.
Young, Michael and Peter Willmott, *Family and Kinship in East London*, Routledge & Kegan Paul, 1957.
Zeldin, Theodore, *France 1848–1945: Intellect and Pride*, Oxford: Oxford University Press, 1980.

Novels and plays
Ambrière, François, *Les Grandes vacances*, Éditions du Seuil, 1956.
Alington, Adrian, *These Our Strangers*, Chatto & Windus, 1942.
Boileau, Pierre and Thomas Narcejac, *Vertigo*, Bloomsbury Film Classics, 1997, translated by Geoffrey Sainsbury from *D'Entre les morts*, first published in 1956.
Bory, Jean-Louis, *Mon Village à l'heure allemande*, J'ai Lu, 1945.
Braine, John, *Room at the Top*, Penguin, 1958.
Camus, Albert, *The Outsider*, translated by Joseph Laredo, Harmondsworth: Penguin, 1982, first published in 1942.
Collins, Norman, *London Belongs to Me*, Collins, 1945.
de Maupassant, Guy, *Boule de suif and other stories*, translated by H.N.P. Sloman, Penguin, 1949.
Dickens, Monica, *One Pair of Feet*, Penguin, 1973, p.7, first published in 1942.
Dutourd, Jean, *Au Bon Beurre*, Gallimard, 1952.
Ertz, Susan, *Anger in the Sky*, Hodder & Stoughton, 1943.
Greenwood, Robert, *The Squad Goes Out*, J.M. Dent & Sons, 1943.
Gunn, Neil, *The Silver Darlings*, Faber & Faber, 1941.
Hamilton, Patrick, *The Slaves of Solitude*, Constable, 1972, first published in 1947.
Hanley, James, *No Directions*, Faber & Faber, 1943.
Kaye-Smith, Sheila, *Joanna Godden*, Cassell & Company, 1921.
La Bern, Arthur, *It Always Rains on Sunday*, Nicholson & Watson, 1945.
Millar, Ronald, *Frieda*, English Theatre Guild, 1947.
Panter-Downes, Mollie, *One Fine Day*, Virago, 1985, first published in 1947.
Priestley, J.B., *Let the People Sing*, Macmillan, 1939.
— *Daylight on Saturday*, William Heinemann, 1943.
— *They Came to a City: Four Plays*, William Heinemann, 1944.
— *Three Men in New Suits*, William Heinemann, 1945.
Radiguet, Raymond, *Le Diable au corps*, Gallimard, 1982, first published in 1923.
Reid, P.R., *The Colditz Story*, Hodder & Stoughton, 1952.
Sadler, Elisabeth, *Sleep and Cease Crying*, Big Ben Books, 1943.
Shearing, Joseph [Marjorie Bowen], *Blanche Fury or Fury's Ape*, William Heinemann, 1939.

Simenon, Georges, *Les Fiançailles de M. Hire*, Fayard, 1933.
— *Les Inconnus dans la maison*, Gallimard, 1941.
Storm, Lesley, *Great Day*, English Theatre Guild, 1945.
Struther, Jan, *Mrs. Miniver*, Virago, 1989, first published in 1939.
Temple, Joan, *No Room at the Inn*, World Film Publications, 1948.
Tey, Josephine, *The Franchise Affair*, Harmondsworth: Penguin, 1951, first
      published in 1948.
Thirkell, Angela, *Peace Breaks Out*, Hamish Hamilton, 1946.
— *Love Among the Ruins*, Hamish Hamilton, 1948.
— *The Old Bank House*, Hamish Hamilton, 1949.
Vercors, *La Silence de la mer*, Éditions de Minuit, 1944.
Véry, Pierre, *Goupi Mains-Rouges*, Éditions J'ai Lu, 1959, first published in 1937.
Waugh, Evelyn, *Put Out More Flags*, Chapman & Hall, 1942.
Williams, Eric, *The Wooden Horse*, Collins, 1949.
Willis, Ted, *Woman in a Dressing Gown and Other TV Plays*, Barrie & Rockliffe, 1959.

Articles
Abrams, Mark, 'The British Cinema Audience', *Hollywood Quarterly*, vol. 3, no 2,
      Winter 1947–48, pp.155–58.
Adler, Karen H., 'Reading National Identity: Gender and "Prostitution" During the
      Occupation', *Modern and Contemporary France* (1999), 7 (1), pp.47–47.
Anderson, Lindsay, 'A Possible Solution', *Sequence*, Spring 1948, pp.7–10.
Atak, Margaret, 'Le Corbeau and Le Ciel est à vous: Entre le spectacle esthétique
      et la connaissance,' *Contemporary French Civilisation* 23 (1999), pp.337–54.
Barr, Charles, 'Projecting Britain and the British Character: Ealing Studios, Part
      One', *Screen*, vol. 15, no 1, Spring 1974, pp.87–121.
Berthomé, Jean Pierre, 'Louis Daquin', *Film Dope*, no 9, April 1976, pp.1–9.
Bertin-Maghit, Jean-Pierre, '"La Bataille du rail": de l'authenticité à la chanson du
      geste', in *Revue d'histoire moderne et contemporaine*, vol. XXXIII, April–June
      1986, pp.280–300.
Betjeman, John 'Second Opinion: The Bored and the Exhausted', *Sight and
      Sound*, January 1950, p.13.
Bosseno, Christian, '84 ans de cinéma paysan', *Cinémaction*, no 16, 1981, pp.32–36.
Boud, John, 'Film among the Arts', *Sequence*, December 1946, pp.4–6.
Boussard, Isabel, 'État de l'agriculture française aux lendemains de l'occupation,
      1944–1968', *Revue d'histoire de la deuxième guerre mondiale*, no 116,
      October 1979, pp.69–93.
Brossat, Alain, 'Images des femmes tondues', *L'Histoire*, July–August 1994, pp.52–53.
Brown, Geoff, 'Which Way to *The Way Ahead*?: Britain's Years of Reconstruction',
      Sight and Sound, Autumn 1978, pp.242–47.
Browning, H.E. and A.A. Sorrell, 'Cinemas and Cinema-going in Great Britain',
      Journal of the Royal Statistical Society, vol. 117, part II, 1954, pp.133–65.
Brownlow, Kevin, 'Cinematic Theology', *New Statesman*, vol. 99, no 2549,
      25 January 1980, p.34.

Chevallier, Jacques, 'La Caméra aux champs', *Image et Son*, April 1959, pp.4–9.

Chevandier, Christian, 'La Résistance des cheminots: le primat de la fonctionnaire plus qu'une réelle spécificité', *Le Mouvement Social*, no 180, July–September 1997, pp.147–57.

Cobban, Alfred, 'France – A Peasant's Republic', *The Listener*, vol. XLI, 1949, pp.429–30.

Cochet, François, 'Français retour d'Allemagne', *L'Histoire*, no 179, July–August 1994, pp.70–75.

Crang, J.A., 'Welcome to Civvy Street: Demobilisation of the British Armed Forces After the Second World War', *The Historian*, no 46, Summer 1995, pp.19–21.

De la Roche, Catherine, 'The Mask of Realism', *Penguin Film Review*, no 7, September 1948.

Delisle, Esther, review of H.R. Kedward and Nancy Wood (eds), *The Liberation of France: Image and Event*, Oxford: Berg, 1995, H-Net French History Discussion Group, December 1998.

Documentary News Letter, 'The British Cinema at the Gallup', June–July 1947, p.99.

Doniol-Volcroze, Jacques, 'Déshabillage d'une petite bourgeoisie sentimentale', *Cahiers du cinema*, no 31, January 1954, pp.2–14.

Duchen, Claire, 'Occupation Housewife: the Domestic Ideal in 1950s France', *French Cultural Studies II* (1991), pp.1–11.

Ellis, John, 'Art, Culture and Quality: Terms for a Cinema in the Forties and the Seventies', *Screen*, vol. 19. no 3, Autumn 1978, pp.9–49.

Englund, Steven, '"Les Lieux de mémoire": Ghost of a Nation Past', *Journal of Modern History*, vol. 64, no 2, June 1992, pp.299–320.

Ferro, Marc, 'Société du XX siècle et histoire cinématographique', *Annales: Économies, Sociétés, Civilisations,* no 23, 1968, pp.581–87.

Fielding, Steven, 'What Did "The People" Want?: The Meaning of the 1945 General Election', *Historical Journal*, 35. 3, 1992, pp.623–39.

Finlay, Richard J., 'National Identity in Crisis: Politicians, Intellectuals and the End of Scotland, 1920–1939', *History*, vol. 79, no 256, June 1994, pp.242–59.

Fink, Janet and Catherine Holden, 'Representations of Spinsters and Single Mothers in the Mid-Victorian Novel, Inter-war Hollywood Melodrama and British Film of the 1950s and 1960s', *Gender and History*, vol. 11, no 2, July 1999.

Fishman, Sarah, 'Grand Delusions: The Unexpected Consequences of Vichy France's Prisoner of War Propaganda', *Journal of Contemporary History*, vol. 26, April 1991, pp.229–54.

— 'The Power of Myth: Five Recent Works on Vichy France', *Journal of Modern History*, no 3, September 1995, pp.666–73.

Fuller, Graham, 'A Canterbury Tale', *Film Comment*, March–April 1995, pp.33–36.

Grégoire, Ménie, 'La Presse feminine', *Esprit*, July–August 1959, pp.17–34.

Hackett, Hazel, 'The French Cinema Since the Liberation', *Sight and Sound*, Summer 1946, p.48.

Harman, Jympson, 'Truth and British Films', *Sight and Sound*, Spring 1946, pp.15–16.

Harrisson, Tom, 'The British Soldier: Changing Attitudes and Ideas', *British Journal of Psychology*: General Section, vol. XXXV, part II, January 1945, pp.34–39.

Hoffman, Stanley, 'The Effect of World War Two on French Society and Politics', *French Historical Studies*, vol. 11, no 1, Spring 1961, pp.28–63.

Hubert-Lacombe, Patricia, 'L'acceuil des films Américains en France pendant la Guerre Froide (1946–1953)', *Revue d'histoire moderne et contemporaine*, vol. XXXIII, April–June 1986, pp.301–13.

Huss, Marie-Monique, 'Pronatalism in the Inter-War Period in France', *Journal of Contemporary History*, vol. 25, no 1, 1990, pp.39–68.

Kavanagh, Dennis and Peter Morris, 'Is the Post-War Consensus a Myth?', Commentary Two, *Contemporary Record*, vol. 2, no 6, 1988, pp.14–15.

Koos, Cheryl A., '"On les aura!": The Gendered Politics of Abortion and the Alliance Nationale Contre la Dépopulation, 1938–1944', *Modern and Contemporary France* (1999), 9 (1), pp.21–22.

Koreman, Megan, 'A Hero's Homecoming: The Return of the Deportees to France, 1945', *Journal of Contemporary History*, vol. 32, no 1, January 1997, pp.9–22.

Kramer, S.P., 'La Crise économique de la Libération', *Revue d'histoire de la deuxième guerre mondiale*, no 111, July 1978, pp.25–51.

Lagrou, Pieter, 'Victims of Genocide and National Memory: Belgium, France and the Netherlands, 1945–1954', *Past and Present*, no 154, 1997, pp.181–222.

Lambert, Gavin, 'British Films 1947: Survey and Prospect', *Sequence*, Winter 1947, pp.9–14.

— 'French Cinema: The New Pessimism', *Sequence*, Summer 1948, pp.8–12.

Langlois, Suzanne, 'Images that Matter: The French Resistance in Film (1944–1946)', *French History*, December 1997, pp.461–490.

Laurent, F., 'Les Amoureux sont seuls au monde', *Image et Son*, 57–58, November/December 1952, pp.2–6.

Lean, David, 'Brief Encounter', *Penguin Film Review*, no 4, October 1947, p.31.

Lowenthal, David, 'British National Identity and the English Landscape', *Rural History*, 2.2, 1991, pp.205–30.

MacKenzie, S.P., 'The Treatment of POW's in World War Two', *Journal of Modern History*, no 66, September 1994, pp.487–520.

Mandler, Peter, 'Against "Englishness": English Culture and the Limits to Rural Nostalgia, 1850–1940', *Transactions of the Royal Historical Society*, 6th Series, vol. 7, 1997, pp.155–75.

Marie, Laurent, 'La Réception critique de L'Amour d'une femme', *1895*, October 1997, pp.83–99

Martin, Kingsley, 'Reflections on Air Raids', *Political Quarterly*, 12, 1941, pp.66–80.

Martin, Marcel, 'Résistance et collaboration dans les films français', *La Revue du cinéma*, 406, June 1985, pp.79–84.

Marwick, Arthur, 'The Second World War and British Experience: Print, Pictures and Sound', *Daedalus*, no 111, Fall 1982, pp.135–55.

Miller, Simon, 'Urban Dreams and Rural Reality: Land and Landscape in English Culture', *Rural History*, 6.1, 1995, pp.89–102.

Morgan, Claude, 'Le Démocratie et ceux qui en parlent', *Les Lettres françaises*, 16 December 1944, p.1.

Munholland, Kim, 'Wartime France: Remembering Vichy', *French Historical Studies*, vol. 18, no 2, 1994, pp.801–20.

Noble, Peter, 'Film Periodicals II: Great Britain', *Hollywood Quarterly*, vol. 3, no 2, Winter 1947–48, pp.20–26.

Oms, Marcel, 'Le Corbeau et ses quatre verités', *Cahiers de la Cinémathèque*, no 8, Winter 1973, pp.58–61.

— 'Le charme discret du cinéma du Vichy', *Cahiers de la Cinémathèque*, no 8, Winter 1973, pp.68–72.

— 'Le Film policier', *Cahiers de la Cinémathèque*, no 25, January 1978, pp.17–20.

Ory, Pascal, 'Présence paradoxicale de la petite bourgeoise dans l'oeuvre de Jean Grémillon', *Cahiers de la Cinémathèque*, no 50, February 1980, pp.57–61.

Pernot, Georges, 'D'ou vient, où va le mouvement familiale?', *Pour la vie*, 1, July 1945, pp.11–12.

Pimlott, Ben, 'Is the Post-War Consensus a Myth?', Commentary One, *Contemporary Record*, vol. 2, no 6, 1988. pp.12–14.

Pope, Rex, 'British Demobilization After the Second World War', *Journal of Contemporary History*, vol. 30, 1995, pp.65–81.

Porter, Vincent and Chaim Litewski, '*The Way Ahead*: Case History of a Propaganda Film', *Sight and Sound*, Spring 1981, pp.110–16.

Portes, Jacques, 'Les Origines de la légende noire des accords Blum-Byrnes sur le cinéma', *Revue d'histoire moderne et contemporaine*, vol. XXXIII, April–June 1986, pp.314–29.

Priestley, J.B., 'Britain's Silent Revolution', *Picture Post*, 27 June 1942, pp.21–22.

Ramsden, John, 'Refocusing 'The People's War': British War Films of the 1950s', *Journal of Contemporary History*, vol. 33, no 1, 1998, pp.56–57.

Richards, Jeffrey, 'Gainsborough: Maniac in the Cellar', *Monthly Film Bulletin*, September 1985, pp.291–93.

— '"The Real England": National Character in Wartime Films', *Encounter*, 65:1, 1985, pp.57–61.

Riley, Denise, 'The Free Mothers: Pro-natalism and Working Women in Industry at the End of the Last War in Britain', *History Workshop*, Issue 11, Spring 1981, pp.59–118.

Rioux, Jean-Pierre, 'La France a faim!', *L'Histoire*, no 179, July–August 1994, pp.38–42.

Rivette, Jacques and François Truffaut, 'Entretien avec Jacques Becker', *Cahiers du cinéma*, no 32, February 1954, pp.3–19.

Sadoul, Georges, 'Crisis over France', *Sight and Sound*, Summer 1948, p.95.

Schwartz, Paula, 'Partisanes and Gender Politics in Vichy France', *French Historical Studies*, vol. 16, no 1, Spring 1989, pp.126–51.

Seaton, Ray and Roy Martin, 'Gainsborough in the Forties', *Films and Filming*, June 1982, pp.13–20.

Spaak, Charles and Julien Duvivier, 'Panique', *L'Avant Scène*, no 390–391, March–April 1990, pp.67–165.

Sussex, Elizabeth, 'Cavalcanti in England', *Sight and Sound*, vol. 44, no 4, Autumn 1975, pp.205–11.

Thorne, Robert, 'The Setting of St. Paul's in the Twentieth Century', *London Journal*, 16 (2), 1991, pp.117–28.

Truffaut, François, 'Une Certaine Tendance du Cinéma français', *Cahiers du Cinéma*, no 31, January 1954, pp.15–29.

Védrès, Nicole, 'French Cinema Takes Stock', *Penguin Film Review*, no 3, 1947.

Vesselo, Arthur, 'Films of the Quarter', *Sight and Sound*, Autumn 1947, pp.120–21.

— 'Films of the Quarter', *Sight and Sound*, Winter 1947–48, pp.137–38.

Vincendeau, Ginette, 'Community, Nostalgia and the Spectacle of Masculinity', *Screen*, vol. 26, no 6, November–December 1985, pp.19–31.

Voldman, Danièle, 'La France en ruines', *L'Histoire*, July–August 1994, pp.98–105.

Wicking, Chris, 'Retrospective: A Canterbury Tale', *Monthly Film Bulletin*, November 1984, pp.355–56.

Weiss, J.H., 'An Innocent Eye?: The Career and Documentary Vision of Georges Rouquier', *Cinema Journal*, Spring 1981, pp.45–62.

Weitz, Margaret Collins, 'The Poster War: Propaganda on Paris Walls During the Occupation', *Contemporary French Civilisation*, 23, 1999, pp.309–36.

Wieviorka, Annette, 'Rendez-vous a l'hôtel Lutétia', *L'Histoire*, no 179, July–August 1994, pp.74–76.

Wieviorka, Olivier, 'Les Mécanismes d'épuration', *L'Histoire*, no 179, July–August 1994, pp.44–51.

Woodeson, Alison, '"Going Back to the Land": Rhetoric and Reality in Women's Land Army Memories', *Oral History*, vol. 21, no 2, Autumn 1993, pp.65–71.

Young, John W., 'Henry V, the Quai d'Orsay and the Well-Being of the Franco–British Alliance, 1947', *Historical Journal of Film, Radio and Television*, vol. 7, no 3, 1987, pp.320–21.

Unpublished PhD theses

Budrass, L., 'British Home Front Propaganda in World War II and the Bombing of Coventry', University of Warwick, 1986.

Dolan, Josie, 'National Heroines: Constructing Femininity and Representing the Past in Popular Film and Literature, 1930–1955', University of London, 1997.

Hutchings, Peter, 'The British Horror Movie: An Investigation of British Horror Production', University of East Anglia, 1989.

Langlois, Suzanne, 'La Résistance dans le cinéma français de fiction (1944–1994)', McGill University, 1996.

Parkin, Diana Jane, 'The Contested Nature of Identity: Nation, Class and Gender in Second World War Britain', London School of Economics, 1988.

Pollard, Miranda, 'Femme, Famille, France: Vichy and the Politics of Gender', University of Dublin, 1989.

Rattigan, Neil, 'Papering the Cracks: Representations of Class in British War Films, 1939–1945', Northwestern University, 1991.

Television Documentaries

'The Home Front', episode six of 'The World At War', Thames Television 1974, produced by Jeremy Isaacs.

'Forbidden Britain: Affairs', BBC2 1994, produced by Steve Humphries.

'Open Space: Not Forgotten', Channel 4 1994, produced by Hazel Chandler.

'Myths and Memories: The French Resistance', BBC2 1995, produced by Clare Hughes.

'Hooked', Channel 4 1998, produced by Steve Humphries.

'What Granny Did in the War', 'Hidden Love', Channel 4 1999, produced by Leanne Klein.

Radio Programmes

'The Evacuation', BBC Radio 4, 1999, produced by David Prest.

Index